BREAKING
THE
BARRIERS

Beatriz Chu Clewell
Bernice Taylor Anderson
Margaret E. Thorpe

BREAKING
THE
BARRIERS

Helping Female and Minority
Students Succeed in
Mathematics and Science

Jossey-Bass Publishers · San Francisco

For sales outside the United States, contact Maxwell Macmillan International Publishing Group, 866 Third Avenue, New York, New York 10022.

Manufactured in the United States of America

The paper used in this book is acid-free and meets the State of California requirements for recycled paper (50 percent recycled waste, including 10 percent postconsumer waste), which are the strictest guidelines for recycled paper currently in use in the United States.

10% POST CONSUMER WASTE

Library of Congress Cataloging-in-Publication Data

Clewell, Beatriz C.
   Breaking the barriers : helping female and minority students succeed in mathematics and science / Beatriz Chu Clewell, Bernice Taylor Anderson, Margaret E. Thorpe.
     p. cm. — (The Jossey-Bass education series)
   Includes bibliographical references and index.
   ISBN 1-55542-482-1
    1. Mathematics—Study and teaching (Secondary)—United States.
   2. Science—Study and teaching (Secondary)—United States.
   3. Minority students—Education (Secondary)—United States.
   I. Anderson, Bernice. II. Thorpe, Margaret E. III. Title.
   IV. Series.
   QA13.C538   1992
   510'.71'273—dc20   92-21619
                                 CIP

FIRST EDITION
HB Printing   10 9 8 7 6 5 4 3 2 1   *Code 9282*

*The Jossey-Bass
Education Series*

Contents

Preface

The ability of any nation to compete successfully in a global market today depends on the scientific and mathematical literacy of its citizens. In the case of the United States, this literacy has been called into question by the poor showing of U.S. students in mathematics and science assessments in both national and international studies (Dossey, Mullis, Lindquist, and Chambers, 1988; Jones and others, 1992; Lapointe, Askew, and Mead, 1992; Lapointe, Mead, and Askew, 1992; Mullis, Dossey, Owen, and Phillips, 1991; Mullis and Jenkins, 1988). To compound the problem, there has been a decline in the size of the talent pool that feeds mathematics- and science-related positions in industry, education, and government (National Academy of Sciences, 1987; National Research Council, 1989, 1991; Task Force on Women, Minorities, and the Handicapped in Science and Technology, 1988; U.S. Congress, Office of Technology Assessment, 1988a, 1988b). Two recent reports underscore the magnitude of the problem that this book addresses. *The National Education Goals Report* (National Education Goals Panel, 1991) indicates that the United States will be alarmingly short of reaching the president's goal of making the nation's students number one in the world in science and mathematics achievement by the year 2000. A new education report, based on a study conducted by the College Entrance Examination Board and the Western Interstate Commission for Higher Education

(1991), was released a few weeks before the goals report. It predicts that by 1995, one-third of U.S. public school students will be members of minority groups, which have traditionally been underrepresented among math and science professionals.

For the United States to maintain a preeminent position in the world economy, the mathematical and scientific skills of its populace must be upgraded, most likely through educational reform. A concomitant goal should be bringing into parity in math and science achievement the fastest-growing segment of the population (one that has traditionally underachieved in those areas): Black, Hispanic, and Native American citizens. Women, who make up roughly half of the nation's population, are also underachievers. Intervention programs in mathematics and science for minorities and females provide some effective remedies to enhance achievement and interest of these students in the subjects.

Purpose of the Book

Breaking the Barriers grew out of a need to document the knowledge about intervention programs that we acquired as a result of a project funded by the Ford Foundation. The foundation was ahead of its time in focusing on middle school as a point in the educational process where changes in mathematics and science instruction were crucial; previous, intervention in these subjects had focused on the high school and college years. The foundation commissioned a project to, first, document the range and activities of intervention programs in mathematics, science, and computer science for minority and female students in grades 4 through 8 and, second, identify characteristics and practices of effective programs. The first phase of the project resulted in the publication of a directory that describes 163 intervention programs nationwide, identifies gaps in service delivery, and recommends changes in policy (Clewell, Thorpe, and Anderson, 1987). In this book, we emphasize the findings of the second phase of the project—case studies of effective programs.

Although intervention programs have existed for thirty years, there has not previously been a concerted attempt to bring together what is known about these programs—the range of effective strategies and approaches as well as the structural components of effective programs — into a single book. Nor has there been a previous effort to link the most effective strategies utilized by these programs to the theory and empirical research that underlie them or to provide guidelines for establishing programs. This book attempts to do these things — to provide an in-depth examination of the strategies, structure, and operation of intervention programs for minority and female students in grades 4 through 8.

Audience

What we wished to accomplish in writing this book was to produce a handbook on the development and delivery of more effective services to young minority and female students. It is our hope that it will help practitioners, educators, and policy makers to realize the wealth of experience and knowledge that resides in intervention programs and that this realization will lead to an increased emphasis on the institutionalization of effective practices developed by the programs. At a time when the instruction of mathematics and science in our nation's schools is in desperate need of revitalization, we cannot afford to ignore a most valuable resource — intervention programs in mathematics and science.

Because the practices outlined in the book are translatable to the regular classroom setting, our intended audience includes not only directors or would-be directors of intervention programs but also state education agency staff members, professional associations, school district administrators, teachers, math and science coordinators and other curriculum specialists, and foundation staff. We have even included a chapter (Chapter Nine) that discusses the institutionalization of innovative practices and factors that encourage this difficult process, because we feel that these practices, pioneered by intervention programs, can significantly enhance the quality of mathematics and science instruction.

Overview of the Contents

The book is divided into four parts. Parts One and Two focus on barriers to achievement and participation in mathematics and science as well as strategies to overcome these barriers. In Part One, Chapter One discusses the barriers to participation in mathematics and science and the need for intervention. Chapter Two explains why intervention efforts are needed at the middle school level and describes the changes that can help minority and female students attain proficiency in math and science. In Part Two, Chapters Three and Four describe intervention approaches and strategies, link those approaches to their bases in research and theory, and provide concrete examples of their use in middle school intervention programs.

Parts Three and Four discuss the delivery systems for the strategies and approaches described in Parts One and Two, concentrating on the programmatic aspects of model intervention programs — their structure and implementation. In Part Three, Chapter Five develops a conceptual framework for analyzing programs and describes in detail the key components of an effective program and how they interact, and Chapter Six discusses program outcomes and contextual elements. The three chapters in Part Four present a guide to implementing a program and discuss issues of institutionalization. Chapters Seven and Eight describe the steps that go into planning, developing, and implementing a program; Chapter Nine suggests methods of disseminating program findings and strategies, discusses the problems of institutionalizing innovative practices, and identifies factors that encourage successful institutionalization.

The appendixes following Part Four present case studies of ten effective programs; a directory of successful intervention programs, including useful materials available from them; and a bibliography of research on personal, educational, and social influences on math and science learning.

Acknowledgments

We wish to acknowledge the many individuals who contributed to this book. First, we would like to thank the staff and participants of the ten case-study programs featured in this work for their participation in our interviews and site visits and their reviews of our case studies. Thanks also go to the 163 programs that responded to our request for program information that we included in the study. The research and production of the report on which this book is based were funded by a grant from the Ford Foundation, although the book's contents do not necessarily reflect the foundation's views. A special acknowledgment is due to our program officer at the Ford Foundation, Barbara Scott Nelson, who recognized the need for this project and provided support and guidance.

Special appreciation goes to Lesley Iura, editor of the Education Series at Jossey-Bass, and Christie Hakim, her editorial assistant, for their encouragement, support, and insightful suggestions during the preparation of this book. We also extend our thanks to Frank Welsch, project editor, who served as our liaison as the manuscript was edited and put into production. In addition to the staff at Jossey-Bass, we would like to thank the anonymous reviewers for their helpful comments. Their constructive criticism contributed to the improvement of our manuscript.

We appreciate the support received from the Educational Testing Service (ETS), especially Margaret Goertz, in this undertaking. We also extend our heartfelt thanks to our colleagues at ETS who were involved in the research, writing, proofreading, and typing that went into this publication: Thelma Benton, Carla Cooper, Rosalea Courtney, Joyce Gant, Jeffrey Marshall, and Mary Evelyn Runyon. We single out Barbara Bruschi for our very special gratitude for the care with which she edited and proofread our manuscript. (The opinions expressed in this book do not necessarily reflect official ETS position or policy.)

Angelica Braestrup, who made available a quiet hideaway (Copperhead Farm) ideal for writing, deserves a special mention.

Finally, we would like to thank our families for their encouragement and support throughout the duration of this project.

Princeton, New Jersey   Beatriz Chu Clewell
August 1992   Bernice Taylor Anderson
     Margaret E. Thorpe

The Authors

Beatriz Chu Clewell is a senior research scientist in the Division of Education Policy Research at Educational Testing Service. She received her B.A. degree (1970) in English literature and her Ph.D. degree (1980) in educational policy, planning, and analysis, both from Florida State University. Clewell's main research activities have focused on factors that encourage or impede equal access to educational opportunity for minorities and women. She has conducted research on institutional policies and practices that are successful in recruiting and retaining minority students in undergraduate and graduate education. Another area of interest has been intervention programs in science and mathematics and their role in achieving parity for underrepresented minorities and women. She has directed studies of intervention programs at both the middle school and the undergraduate levels. In 1992, she was selected as a Distinguished Scholar by the American Educational Research Association Standing Committee on the Role and Status of Minorities in Educational Research and Development. Clewell's publications include *Women of Color in Mathematics, Science, and Engineering: A Review of the Literature* (1991, with B. T. Anderson), *Building the Nation's Work Force from the Inside Out: Educating Minorities for the Twenty-first Century* (1991, with S. V. Brown), and *Intervention Programs in Math, Science, and Computer Science for Minority and Female Students in Grades Four Through Eight* (1987, with M. E. Thorpe and B. T. Anderson).

Bernice Taylor Anderson is a research scientist in the Division of Education Policy Research at Educational Testing Service. She received her B.A. degree (1974) from Norfolk State University in early childhood and elementary education, her M.A. degree (1976) from Ohio State University in early and middle childhood education, and her Ed.D. degree (1984) from Rutgers University in science and humanities education, with an early childhood education concentration. Anderson's research activities have focused largely on minority-related research issues. She has been involved in studies examining precollege academic performance of minority students in reading, mathematics, and science. Research activities at the postsecondary level have addressed the underrepresentation of Black Americans in teacher education, engineering education, and medical education. She has worked on several of Clewell's studies of intervention programs. Anderson's publications include *Women of Color in Mathematics, Science, and Engineering: A Review of the Literature* (1991, with B. C. Clewell) and *Intervention Programs in Math, Science, and Computer Science for Minority and Female Students in Grades Four Through Eight* (1987, with B. C. Clewell and M. E. Thorpe).

Margaret E. Thorpe is a special education consultant for the New Jersey State Department of Education, Division of Special Education. She trains and provides technical assistance to parents and educators of students with disabilities. She received her B.A. degree (1968) in history, her M.Ed. degree (1973) in special education–early childhood, and her Ed.D. degree (1987) in special education–educational psychology, all from Rutgers University. She worked in the Division for Education Policy Research at Educational Testing Service from 1980 to 1988. Her research activities have included field-based studies of the integration of students with severe disabilities into public schools and the use of technology to promote science learning among high school students. She has also participated in studies of programs and practices affecting mathematics and science learning of middle school minority and female students. Her interests include effective instructional and learning strategies for students with diverse learning styles and abilities. She is coauthor of *Intervention Programs in Math, Science, and Computer Science for Minority and Female Students in Grades Four Through Eight* (1987, with B. C. Clewell and B. T. Anderson).

PART ONE

Promoting Participation
in Mathematics and Science

Recently, there has been increasing concern about the human resource needs of the United States to compete in a global market that relies heavily on technological innovation. There has been a decline in the pool of people equipped to assume mathematics and science positions in industry and education (National Academy of Sciences, 1987; National Research Council, 1991; U.S. Congress, Office of Technology Assessment, 1988a, 1988b; Vetter, 1990). Recent reports have pointed out that the pool of White males trained in these areas is insufficient to provide the number of scientists, engineers, and technicians needed in our society and that there is an urgent need to increase the number of women and minorities in science and engineering (National Science Foundation, 1992; U.S. Congress, Office of Technology Assessment, 1988a, 1988b; Vetter, 1990). This finding appears to be particularly relevant because of the significant increase in the proportion of minority students in the school-age population and the fact that more females are entering the work force.

Part One explores the barriers that minority and female students experience in mathematics and science participation during the middle school years. Chapter One discusses the four barriers to participation in mathematics and science and

1

describes intervention programs in general. Chapter Two explains the need for intervention efforts at the middle school level and describes intervention approaches. This chapter also connects program suggestions to the overall needs of middle school students.

1

Identifying Barriers to Female and Minority Participation

The underrepresentation of women and minorities – specifically, Black, Hispanic, and Native American citizens – in mathematics, science, and engineering (MSE) fields poses a probem of national scope. Recent reports by the Office of Technology Assessment expressed great concern at the steady decline in science and engineering majors among college students in the United States (U.S. Congress, Office of Technology Assessment, 1988a, 1988b). There are several reasons for this decline. Many White males who in the past would have been likely to be science or engineering majors have chosen majors in business instead. Gains in participation made by women and minorities in the 1970s seemed to level off in the 1980s. Moreover, the college-age population is declining steadily, and a greater proportion of this population will be members of minority groups. This does not mean, however, that there has been an increase in the proportion of minorities who enroll in higher education. In fact, between 1977 and 1986, the proportion of both Black and Hispanic high school graduates between the ages of eighteen and twenty-four who were enrolled in college dropped, while the proportion increased somewhat for Whites (American Council on Education, 1988). These developments have focused renewed attention on efforts to increase the talent pool of potential scientists and engineers, with emphasis on the relatively untapped resource of groups that have heretofore had limited representation in MSE fields – minorities and women.

3

Data from the National Science Foundation (1990) show that in 1988 a disproportionately small number of women (16 percent) held positions in science and engineering (S/E), despite their numbers in the total U.S. work force (45 percent). In the same year, the more striking absence of minority group members in math and science careers was documented. Black professionals made up 2.6 percent of all employed scientists and engineers, although Blacks accounted for 10 percent of total U.S. employment. Hispanics made up 1.8 percent of the S/E work force, while constituting 7.2 percent of the U.S. labor force; and Native American representation in the S/E work force was about the same as in the overall U.S. work force — less than 1 percent. Asians, on the other hand, were overrepresented in science and engineering fields, accounting for 5 percent of the S/E work force, compared to their representation in the overall labor force of 2 percent.

The problem of underrepresentation of certain minority groups and females in MSE fields is a problem for us all. In light of recent findings of the Task Force on Women, Minorities, and the Handicapped in Science and Technology (1988), the failure to recruit underrepresented minorities and women to MSE careers is undermining the nation's ability to maintain its leadership in science and engineering. The task force, which was charged by Congress to develop a long-range plan for broadening participation in science and engineering, also came to the following conclusions:

- Federal agencies have not acknowledged or addressed the demographic changes that are eroding the science and engineering work force and that threaten to affect the nation's research and development efforts in the twenty-first century.
- Although effective local intervention programs are demonstrating that youngsters from underrepresented groups can become highly able scientists and engineers, such programs are too isolated and underfunded to meet national demand.
- U.S. leadership in science and engineering cannot be maintained unless the educational system produces a larger and more diverse group of world-class scientists and engineers.

Barriers to the Entry of
Women and Minorities into MSE Fields

The causes of the underrepresentation of women and minorities in MSE fields are varied and complex (Beane, 1985; Clewell and Anderson, 1991; Lockheed and others, 1985; Oakes, 1990; Olstad, Juarez, Davenport, and Haury, 1981; Stage, Kreinberg, Eccles, and Becker, 1985). Research into these causes has revealed that females and minorities face similar barriers to participation in these fields: (1) negative attitudes regarding mathematics and science; (2) lower performance levels than those of White males in mathematics and science courses and on standardized tests of these subjects; (3) limited exposure to extracurricular mathematics and science activities and failure to participate in advanced mathematics and science courses in high school; and (4) lack of information about and/or interest in mathematics- or science-related careers (Clewell, 1987; Clewell, Anderson, and Thorpe, 1988).

Negative Attitudes and Perceptions

Research on minority and female attitudes toward mathematics and science suggests that both groups tend to have favorable attitudes but that positive attitudes begin to decline as they reach the junior high school years (Fennema and Sherman, 1978; James and Smith, 1985; Schreiber, 1984). Factors affecting females' and minorities' attitudes include a poor self-concept as a "doer" of math or science; their negative perception of the utility of these subjects in "real life"; the stereotyping of math and science as White male activities; and the influence of significant others, such as parents, teachers, and peers, in discouraging participation in these subjects (Beane, 1985, 1990; Hall, 1981; Kelley, 1981; Matthews, 1984; Oakes, 1990). Young females report that science fails to instill feelings of confidence, success, or curiosity (Kahle and Lakes, 1983). Females often internalize societal messages that mathematics and science are inappropriate, "unfeminine" activities (Armstrong, 1980; Bossert, 1981; Fox, 1976). They also experience a strong conflict between interest in math and science and popularity, especially with males (Schreiber, 1984).

Poor Academic Performance or Achievement

As early as age nine, minority students perform at lower levels
in mathematics and science than do White students (Dossey,
Mullis, Lindquist, and Chambers, 1988; Mullis and Jenkins,
1988), and there is some evidence that Black and Hispanic students begin performing at lower levels in math from the end
of the second grade (Gross, 1988). In mathematics, females perform as well as males in the elementary and junior high or middle
school grades, but large differences emerge by high school, with
males significantly outperforming females (Duran, 1987; Gross,
1988). The same pattern applies to science performance, with
the greatest differences in the physical sciences (Mullis and
Jenkins, 1988). Factors affecting differential performance of
minorities and females include their lack of confidence in their
math or science ability, the stereotyping of mathematics and
science as White male domains, linguistic and cognitive factors,
failure to take advanced-level mathematics and science courses
in high school, and attitudinal factors, such as their own negative attitudes as well as the negative influences of parents, teachers, and peers toward their participation in these subjects. Too
often minority students receive less of everything that is needed
to succeed in mathematics and science: their teachers are less
well trained, their schools and classes lack proper equipment,
and their courses lack rigor and relevance (Malcom, 1990).

Maladaptive motivational patterns (low expectations,
challenge avoidance) have been linked to achievement discrepan-
cies. Females exhibit little confidence in their mathematics and
science abilities (Armstrong and Kahl, 1981; Fox, Brody, and
Tobin, 1985). They are more likely than males to attribute their
difficulty in solving problems to their own lack of ability, while
males attribute failure to situational and external factors (Dweck,
1986). Additionally, sex stereotypes and the perception of science
as a male domain are related to willingness to learn science (Kelly
and Smail, 1986). A lack of parental expectations and encouragement for females to excel in these subjects contributes to differential performance (Kelley, 1981). Parents tend to believe and
communicate the message that males do better in mathematics
and to feel that mathematics is harder for adolescent females

than for adolescent males (Parsons, Adler, and Kaczala, 1982).

Female and minority students tend to be influenced by what they believe the teacher thinks of them and their ability in mathematics and science. There is evidence that teachers expect gender difference in achievement (Becker, 1981). Teachers treat females and males differently in math and science classes: males receive more teacher praise and criticism concerning their performance and are expected by teachers to perform better and to excel in competitive activities (Eccles-Parsons, 1984; Wilkinson and Marrett, 1985).

It has also been suggested that females lag behind males in the development of cognitive skills necessary to perform well in mathematics. For example, females may develop logical thinking abilities later than males, or they may lag behind males in Piagetian tasks and stages of development relevant to math learning (Graybill, 1975). Differences in spatial abilities favoring males have also been noted (Treagust, 1980). However, some argue that the focus should be on how the different experiences of males and females affect their cognitive development and acquisition of certain cognitive skills rather than differences in their cognitive skills per se (Coles and Griffen, 1987).

Mathematics and science are perceived as higher-order disciplines, and teachers often perceive minority students as low achievers and send subtle messages that these disciplines are White male domains (Beane, 1985). Furthermore, minority students, especially high achievers, often feel that they must prove themselves to the teacher each time they enter a new math class (Gross, 1988). Other minority students come to math and science classes feeling inadequate. They lack confidence in using reasoning skills to solve problems, have low expectations and aspirations for academic achievement, and have poorly developed mathematical and verbal skills. Because of these factors, minority students generally do not develop skills in the areas of persistence, logical thinking, and self-reliance in problem solving.

Lack of sufficient mathematics skills and background has been described as a "critical filter" that contributes to differences in career attainment of minority students (Beane, 1985; Turner, 1983). Minority students are often excluded from technical careers because of poor mathematics preparation. Females are often filtered out of three-fourths of career opportunities before they even get to college because they have inadequate backgrounds in mathematics (Iker, 1980).

Instructional strategies and materials in math and science classes tend not to complement the learning styles of female and minority students (Beane, 1985; Belenky, Clinchy, Goldberger, and Tarule, 1986; Gilligan, 1982). Females tend to enhance objective knowledge by using intuition and self-understanding to give such knowledge personal relevance, whereas the traditional male model establishes "truth" by objective, dispassionate methods. For Black students, learning is more affective and cognitively united than the prevailing White European tradition of universal facts and knowledge (Hale-Benson, 1984). Different cultures interpret and generalize about the physical world in many different ways; textbooks do not take this into consideration and therefore tend to be inadequate and unsatisfactory for students who do not come from White European backgrounds (Gore, 1980).

Minority students are less exposed to higher-order activities than their White peers. Simple drill-and-practice sessions do not allow them to transfer knowledge to a higher level of learning (Coles and Griffen, 1987). This failing is then attributed to their innate lack of ability to perform higher skills rather than to limited training. Failure to adjust approaches for teaching math and science to accommodate minority learners who are field-dependent (tend to process information in a global fashion) and who have an external locus-of-control orientation (tend to feel that success or failure is related to external situations and factors) has an adverse impact on minority performance in these subjects. Additionally, disproportionate numbers of minority students are enrolled in general and remedial classes (Malcom and others, 1984). This practice further limits minority students' exposure to activities involving higher-order thinking skills and to an array of topics in mathematics and science that standardized tests and assessments usually include. This disparity often results in poor test performance in mathematics and science.

Insufficient Course and Extracurricular Preparation

Failure to participate in higher-level math and science courses in high school is another barrier to female and minority participation in MSE fields. Decisions not to elect advanced courses are made when female and minority students are in middle or junior high school. Traditionally, these groups (with the exception of Asian Americans) have enrolled in fewer optional or advanced courses than White male students (Anderson, 1989; Davis, 1989; Fennema, 1984; Jones, 1984; Marrett, 1981; Mullis and Jenkins, 1988; Peng, 1982). Minority students are more apt to be found in introductory and lower-level math courses than in advanced courses. Differential patterns of course taking have been related to gender and ethnic differences in mathematics and science achievement. Factors affecting minorities' and females' failure to take higher-level courses are similar to those affecting their achievement and attitudes.

Several beliefs of female and minority students have been cited as reasons for their avoidance of advanced mathematics and science courses (Armstrong, 1980; Oakes, 1990; Parsons, 1983). They do not perceive these subjects as helpful to their future educational and career plans. They view these subjects as difficult and the amount of effort necessary to do well in them as just not worthwhile. Additionally, females think that taking these courses might hamper their social relationships with males and/or make them appear masculine. Math anxiety is another factor that contributes to differences in enrollment in math courses. Females are more likely than males to suffer from a debilitating mathematics anxiety (Aiken, 1970; Tobias, 1978).

While science is part of the uniform curriculum for all middle schools, there are substantial differences among schools in the amount and quality of science instruction that they offer. In science classes, females have fewer opportunities to use scientific apparatus and fewer hands-on activities than their male peers (Kahle and Lakes, 1983). They experience fewer opportunities in problem-solving activities and engage less often in performing experiments. They report having more experiences with plants and animals than males but substantially fewer experiences with mechanical and electrical activities. Females also take fewer mathematics courses than males. Counselors often do not encourage females to enroll in advanced mathematics and science courses, believing that these courses are too difficult for females and/or unnecessary for their future (Casserly, 1975; Haven, 1972; Luchins, 1976).

The underrepresentation of minority students in higher-level high school mathematics courses is in part the result of the cumulative effect of their lower performance that begins in elementary school (Gross, 1988; Marrett, 1986). By the end of elementary school, as critical decisions are being made concerning class placement for high school mathematics, as many as one-third to one-half of minority students have fallen far behind in mathematics, resulting in a disproportionate number of minority students in remedial or general math and science courses. A lack of success in previous math and science classes and negative experiences with teachers account for some avoidance of future course work in these subject areas by minority students.

Several societal factors contribute to the avoidance of math and science courses. Parents tend to view mathematics as less important for their daughters than for their sons. Sons are more likely to receive encouragement and support for taking math courses and participating in related extracurricular activities and programs. Parents are more likely to provide boys with mathematical or scientific games and toys. Males more frequently have early extracurricular experiences that develop mechanical inquisitiveness and skills. Females' play experiences tend to be stationary, stimulating little interest in understanding natural laws that govern the physical world; females have few play experiences that build spatial and physical concepts (Hensel, 1989).

The amount of information and encouragement that minority parents can give their children is limited since they are often unaware of course offerings and requirements for college and/or science-related careers. The literature also suggests that a shortage of role models has a major impact on both minority and female students' math and science course-taking patterns (Clewell and Anderson, 1987; Rendon, 1983).

A study of A Better Chance alumni revealed that the best predictors of enrollment in advanced high school mathematics and science courses for minority students were self-perception of ability in the subject matter, student perception of high school mathematics curriculum, the identification of a high school mathematics or science teacher as the most influential person in the student's school experience, and the academic atmosphere of the high school (Johnson and Prom-Jackson, 1983).

Limited Knowledge of Mathematics and Science Professions

Female and minority students tend to have limited knowledge of the array of career options in mathematics and science fields (Chipman and Thomas, 1984; Johnson, 1981; Kahle and Lakes, 1983; Lantz and Smith, 1981; Matthews, 1981, 1984). Minority students do not have clear options in mind concerning science and technical fields, and few can identify with the process of becoming a scientist. Both female and minority students are often unaware of the relevance of mathematics to many professions. Females express less interest in learning about science-related careers than their male peers, have lower aspirations for math-based and science-related fields, and are less confident that there are science jobs that they can learn to do. They are strongly influenced by the belief that it is "unfeminine" to study math or science; consequently, few of them plan to or actually pursue these traditional male-oriented fields.

Academic and career counseling has often failed to make female and minority students aware of the vast range of occupations in which math is either necessary or highly useful (Fox, 1976; Iker, 1980; Johnson, 1981; McBay, 1978). These students are not given adequate information about either traditional or emerging scientific careers. Additionally, although math and science textbooks have improved somewhat, female and minority adults still tend to be unequally represented in textbook illustrations of people in science-related occupations (Garcia, Harrison, and Torres, 1990; Powell and Garcia, 1985).

While most parents encourage academic performance in general, they tend to discourage their daughters from entering quantitative fields of study in college. Social- and service-oriented careers have traditionally been viewed as more appropriate for women than for men. Females are socialized very early to be more affective and service-oriented and less analytical and quantitative in their career interests (Ethington and Wolfle, 1987; Klein and Bailey, 1975). Minority students are socialized into traditional, low-paying occupations (Steel, 1978; Thomas, 1989; Young, 1983). They are not generally encouraged to study science and are frequently discouraged from studying it. Race-role stereotyping of occupations affects the number of options that minority students perceive as acceptable and attainable.

Female and minority students are not exposed to enough powerful role models in MSE disciplines to form realistic images of scientists (Fort and Varney, 1989; Pearson, 1985). Females tend to characterize scientists with "masculine" traits that conflict with behaviors that are encouraged for young females (Jones and Wheatley, 1988; Rossi, 1965b). Many minority students view scientists as aloof, antisocial, and inflexible. Such perceptions may present cultural conflicts, since these traits are not highly valued culturally (Tibord, 1973).

In attempting to address the barriers that impede minority and female participation in MSE fields, it is important to understand the process through which a student becomes a scientist or an engineer in order to ascertain the points at which certain types of intervention are most helpful. In tracing the progression of different groups through the math and science channel, Berryman (1983) considered the process that a student must undergo to remain in the science talent pool through the undergraduate years. In order to participate in an MSE career, a student must develop an interest in mathematics or science, acquire the necessary skills to do well in the courses, take a sufficient number of courses in high school, and persist in an MSE major through college. Berryman (1983) and Lee (1987) also found that the talent pool seems to reach its maximum size before high school, although some migration into the pool still occurs through grade 12 and perhaps beyond.

The work of Berryman and others on the math and science channel, together with research on the barriers to participation faced by minorities and women, has provided the basis for efforts to increase the presence of underrepresented groups in MSE fields. A large part of these efforts has occurred through intervention programs (Clewell, 1989; Matyas and Malcom, 1991).

Intervention Programs in Science and Mathematics

Intervention programs to increase minority and female particpation in MSE careers are a fairly recent phenomenon. They emerged from the civil rights movements of the 1960s and 1970s and had their origin in the realization that women and certain minority groups were severely underrepresented in MSE careers. At first, the programs were mainly local initiatives based on locally identified needs. Resources, too, were derived locally. Once these programs had been in existence for some years, however, they began to attract national attention and, as a result, federal and foundation funding (Malcom and others, 1984).

Since intervention programs arose out of the recognition that formal education had failed to address the problem of low minority and female representation in MSE careers, it is logical that the programs should utilize approaches somewhat different from those of the traditional educational system. As a result, intervention programs have a number of characteristics that set them apart (Clewell, 1987):

- They operate separately from the school system (although they may be in-school programs offered during the school day).
- They often involve a disadvantaged group or groups, such as minorities, women, and/or disabled people, and aim at counteracting some educational inequity suffered by one or more of these groups.
- They use innovative instructional techniques, materials, and curricula.
- They often focus on addressing one problem area, such as math or science, rather than the whole range of educational problems.
- They engage in activities that address many aspects of the problem, not just those that are achievement focused.
- They employ multiple strategies to obtain their objectives.
- They are sensitive to the needs of the groups that they intend to serve and develop their intervention approaches around those needs.

The efficacy of intervention programs has been widely acknowledged. In 1983, the National Science Board Commission on Precollege Education in Mathematics, Science, and Technology stated that "[f]ormal education must be supplemented by a wide range of activities that can reinforce the lessons of the classroom and lend meaning and relevance to the rigor and discipline of formal study" (National Science Board, 1983, p. 59). The Office of Technology Assessment has stated that "[i]ntervention programs effectively encourage women and minorities to consider science and engineering careers" (U.S. Congress, Office of Technology Assessment, 1988a, p. 40). In addition to motivating students and providing an opportunity for them to engage in informal or experiential learning, intervention programs for minority and female students focus on addressing factors that impede these groups' full participation in MSE careers (Clewell, 1989).

2

Breaking the Barriers:
The Critical Middle School Years

Losses of aspiring or potential science and engineering students occur at each juncture in the educational process — elementary school, high school, and college (U.S. Congress, Office of Technology Assessment, 1988b). The greatest influence on the size and quality of the science and engineering work force is the precollege experience. Although the first intervention programs targeted students in high school or college, there has been a growing awareness that the factors impeding minority and female access to MSE careers are present long before high school. The research of Berryman (1983) and others suggests that intervention to increase the science talent pool is best undertaken before the ninth grade, while strategies to decrease attrition from the pool should be targeted at any point in the process.

What events occur at the middle school phase of the mathematics and science process that make it a crucial point for intervention? First of all, the middle school years (defined here as grades 4 through 8) determine whether a student will participate in the academic track, a prerequisite for access to advanced mathematics and science courses (which, in turn, predict higher performance levels in these subjects). Second, these years have been pinpointed as the period during which female and minority interest and achievement in mathematics and science decline. Third, the middle school years — the preadolescent period — are a time of great developmental change in the psychomotor, affective, social, and cognitive domains, dictating special educational needs (Dorman, 1981; Hill, 1980; Lipsitz, 1977). Fourth, as students enter eighth grade, they must consider academic options and make decisions about course selections that will affect their future career choices.

The realization on the part of researchers, practitioners, and funding sources that intervention aimed at increasing the pool of potential MSE majors among minority and female students must begin before high school has resulted in an increase in the number of intervention programs targeting middle school students. A recent study funded by the Ford Foundation describes the nature and scope of these intervention programs, identifies gaps in service delivery, and makes policy recommendations based on its findings (Clewell, Thorpe, and Anderson, 1987). The Ford study identifies and describes 163 mathematics, science, and computer science intervention programs for middle school students in the United States, including Puerto Rico. Of these, 33 percent target minorities, 13 percent females, and 54 percent both minorities and females. Activities and services provided by the programs include exposure of participants to role models, direct instruction, counseling, field trips, guest speakers, hands-on experiences, special projects, contests and science fairs, study groups, tutoring, test preparation, and job shadowing. In terms of geographical distribution, the West has the highest number of programs — 30 percent of the total. This region is followed by the Northeast, with 28 percent; the central states, with 24 percent; and the Southeast, with 18 percent.

In addition, the study found that there are many more intervention programs in mathematics and science serving middle school minority and female students than a review of the literature and anecdotal information led us to expect. In spite of this finding, there are gaps in service delivery. The number of programs focusing on middle school girls and minority students appears low in relation to the population of minority and female students within this age range (U.S. Department of Commerce, 1986). On a positive note, of the intervention programs that we identified that target minority students, many are incorporating strategies related to academic achievement. Some programs are also offering services that address motivational factors related to participation and achievement, including exposure to careers and opportunities to interact with role models or mentors.

For female students, a somewhat different picture emerges. Programs identified as female-focused are emphasizing attitudinal more than instructional activities. The preponderance of programs for both minorities and females focus at or above grade 6. Many of these programs also extend into the high school years. Only one-third serve students in the fourth or fifth grade. While many programs provide counseling or academic guidance critical to future academic and career planning, very few programs offer test preparation activities.

There is a dearth of intervention programs targeting middle school students in the Southeast. Since this area contains a large Black population, it is possible that Black middle school students in the Southeast are being underserved. The same situation exists for Native Americans. Several of the states with a high concentration of Native Americans seem to have no intervention programs for middle school students.

What implications do these findings have for policy? The following are specific recommendations generated by our look into the state of intervention in mathematics and science for females and minorities in middle school:

- Increase the number of female-focused and minority-focused programs serving middle school students.
- Increase the number of female-focused programs that offer activities to enhance the achievement and participation of girls in math and science.
- Increase the number of minority-focused programs offering role models, career awareness, and counseling activities.
- Add test preparation to programs offering awareness and motivational activities and substantive achievement activities. (Test preparation should not, however, be considered a substitute for substantive intervention.)
- Serve greater numbers of Native Americans, especially in states where there is a high concentration of members of this group.

- Establish more programs in the Southeast, especially in those states where there are none.
- Expand the services of existing female- and minority-focused programs to fourth- and fifth-graders.

To be effective, intervention approaches must be grounded in an understanding of the growth and developmental needs of students in grades 4 through 8, as well as a sound knowledge of educational experiences and instructional strategies that promote learning and enjoyment of mathematics and science. The rest of this chapter addresses these issues and presents a framework that attempts to coordinate these components. A comprehensive approach to breaking the barriers will result in programs that have great potential for motivating, enriching, and possibly sustaining middle school students' interest and participation in math and science.

The Needs of Middle School Students

An understanding of the general developmental needs of middle school students, regardless of sex and race, can help establish guidelines for determining teaching strategies, including planning teacher-student activities, selecting materials, and organizing learning situations, and thus help make the teaching and learning processes profitable and rewarding experiences for both educators and students. Combining and synthesizing the work of social and behavioral scientists and clinicians, Hill (1980) offers a useful framework within which to consider what is known about adolescent development and how it affects adolescents' positions in the family, the peer group, and the school. Lipsitz (1977) reviewed the biological, socioemotional, and cognitive research on young adolescents as well as the social institutions that serve them, including the school. On the basis of the work of these two researchers, the Center for Early Adolescence (Dorman, 1981) compiled the following list of physical, social, emotional, and cognitive needs of young adolescents:

- Diversity
- Self-exploration and self-definition

- Meaningful participation in their school communities
- Social interaction with peers and adults
- Physical activity
- A sense of competence and achievement
- Structure and clear limits

The following discussion briefly addresses these needs of students in grades 4 through 8 and notes implications for intervention efforts.

Diversity

The preadolescent years represent a period of rapid physical, sexual, psychological, cognitive, and social change to which the young person must adjust (Mussen, Conger, and Kagan, 1979). Students grow at varying rates and undergo changes at different ages. Students exhibit a wide variety of interests and social concerns, and individual differences are pronounced. In any one class of preadolescents, a range of maturity levels can be observed. To accommodate the wide range of abilities, interests, and skills of preadolescents, intervention programs should allow for variety in the curriculum and activities, varied instructional and resource materials, and flexibility in the schedule and use of available space.

Self-Exploration and Self-Definition

An important part of socioemotional development is the establishment of a sense of identity, which involves perceiving oneself as a distinct, consistent person in one's own right (Mussen, Conger, and Kagan, 1979). During this period, students must begin to develop their self-esteem through their own efforts and abilities. An intervention program should provide the kind of support that facilitates the development of independence, self-esteem, and self-reliance; be success-oriented; offer basic subjects, exploratory courses, activities on content and skills acquisition, and enrichment experiences to help students integrate their developing capabilities, interests, and relationships into a sense of who they are; encourage students to pursue answers to their own questions, in addition to their teachers' questions; offer guidance activities focused on self-exploration that are prevention-oriented, not problem- or crisis-oriented; and offer career guidance by exploring students' occupational and personal interests, not by making occupational decisions for them.

Meaningful Participation in School and Community

School and community are important forces in the socialization process. Schools need to provide a climate that makes learning a rewarding and relevant experience, one that makes the most of students' talents and interests. The socialization process is further strengthened when school activities are expanded to incorporate meaningful community experiences in and outside the classroom. Students' interests need to be considered and used as a basis for classroom and schoolwide activities (Bloom, 1971). Schools can provide the structure and the means for young adolescents to have a real voice in operating their schools and to make meaningful contributions beyond the classroom through student-initiated study and activities, student councils, and student committees. An intervention program should provide opportunities for young adolescents to identify and carry out projects that will both improve the school environment and allow them to contribute their knowledge, competencies, and skills to the communities.

Social Interaction with Peers and Adults

During the middle school years, the peer group becomes powerful and begins to replace parents as the major source of behavioral standards and recognition of achievement. It provides young people with an opportunity to learn to interact with age mates, to deal with hostility and dominance, to relate to a leader, to lead others, and to deal with social problems (Biehler, 1971). Positive adult relationships also provide an opportunity for young adolescents to learn social skills, control their behavior, and share their problems and feelings.

    An intervention program must take into account young

adolescents' need to be accepted by peers and respected by adults other than their parents. It should provide a supportive environment that protects young adolescents from the negative aspects of peer pressure and provide many opportunities (for example, small-group learning activities or cooperative learning) for positive peer interactions. Positive social interactions between adults and students are facilitated by adviser-student relationships, staff participation in student activities, and informal contact between students and staff outside the classroom.

Physical Activity

The challenging and sometimes difficult period of early adolescence is marked by spurts in the energy level. During this period, most students experience a period of very rapid physical growth, which often has an unsettling effect on the preadolescents' emotions and a spiraling effect on their physical and mental endurance. A responsive program will provide structured outlets for this physical energy. Breaks are needed to allow students to release tension. Since attention spans vary, activities should not be too long. Students should be allowed to move around in the classroom and to relax or work in unorthodox sitting positions, so long as such activity does not interfere with learning. To sustain interest during this period of much energy, a program should provide students with a variety of activities in a variety of educational settings.

Competence and Achievement

Improvement in cognitive processes is remarkable during this period of development. Attention spans continue to increase with all activities, with the most striking gains being in problem solving. According to Piaget (1956), students in this age range begin to shift from concrete to formal operations. Although concrete operations are logical and systematic, thinking at this stage is still tied to direct experiences. As students begin to shift to formal operations, they think more abstractly, formulate and test hypotheses, and consider what might be rather than merely what is.

In their efforts to facilitate the acquisition of these higher-level cognitive processes, intervention program developers must first realize that students differ widely in the attainment of higher-order thinking skills and that students initially need the opportunity to explore new concepts in concrete forms prior to dealing with more abstract, representational forms. Middle school students need hands-on experiences or activity-based instruction. In addition, a program to promote competence and achievement-oriented behavior among students should have positive academic expectations for all students, provide rewards and praise generously but honestly, and offer opportunities for students to increase their independence and responsibility to evaluate their own performance. If it does this, students will know what they are doing, why they are doing it, and whether they are doing it well.

Structure and Clear Limits

Young adolescents continue to need rules and schedules for the use of space and materials and standards for acceptable and unacceptable classroom and school behavior. Structure and clear limits can provide the security that young adolescents need to learn and grow during a time of rapid and pervasive change. Clearly stated limits should be accepted by students, teachers, and staff for the promotion of optimal learning in a setting of trust and responsibility.

Effective Strategies and Techniques
at the Middle School Level

Most intervention programs at the middle school level employ multiple strategies for increasing female and minority students' interest and performance in mathematics and science. While no single method has emerged as most effective, a variety of instructional methods do work. Effective strategies include:

      Hands-on activities
      Sufficient time-on-task

    Adequate precollegiate training
    Contacts with role models in scientific and technical careers
    Laboratory work
    Cooperative learning
    Manipulative instructional materials
    Nonthreatening competition
    Independent projects
    Test preparation
    Support from parents, teachers, and peers
    Positive academic and personal counseling

(A detailed discussion of specific techniques is presented in Chapters Three and Four.)

Strategies should be related to both the developmental needs of students and intervention goals to enhance minority and female representation in math and science. A framework for linking intervention goals, strategies, and student needs is presented in Table 2.1.

Intervention Approaches at the Middle School Level

There is general agreement that intervention programs are crucial to increasing the minority and female scientific pool. However, the focus of intervention at the middle school level remains an issue involving a balance between career awareness approaches and skill-building and enrichment approaches. Although there is a tendency to suggest working on interest first, then skills, it is important to remember that the two processes occur simultaneously and not in isolation from one another.

Career Awareness Approaches

Fostering positive attitudes toward mathematics and science and increasing students' interest in science and technology careers are critical to addressing the inequities in the participation of females and minorities in these areas. For interventions at the middle school level, the following recommendations are crucial for enhancing attitudes and increasing interest (Clewell, 1987):

Table 2.1. Intervention Approaches at the Middle School Level to Improve the Perceptions, Performance, and Participation of Minority and Female Students in Mathematics and Science.

Intervention Goals	Strategies and Techniques	Needs of Middle School Students						
		Diversity	Self-Exploration/ Self-Definition	Hands-on Experience/ Meaningful Participation	Positive Social Interaction with Peers and Adults	Physical Activity	Competence and Achievement	Structure and Clear Limits
Math and science perceptions and career awareness								
Improve attitudes toward math and science	Increase the encouragement received from significant others		●		●			
	Socialize students to the demands and rewards of rigorous scientific work	●	●		●		●	
Increase career awareness	Acquaint students with varied math and science careers available and the preparation needed for them	●	●	●	●		●	●
	Arrange contacts with role models in scientific and technical careers (field trips, internships, demonstrations)		●			●	●	
Increase confidence in doing math and science	Structure activities so that everyone can experience some success	●	●	●	●		●	
	Recognize and provide awards for outstanding student achievement in math and science		●		●		●	

Performance in math and science and
participation in advanced math and science courses

Increase math and science knowledge
- Provide substantial time-on-task and homework at all levels
- Be sensitive to individual differences in selecting cues, processing information, and analyzing data

Increase use of math and science
- Provide early hands-on experiences; "do" science in order to convey its utility
- Participate in math competitions, science fairs, and so on
- Enhance instruction through cooperative learning or small-group methods
- Provide tutoring

Improve test performance in math and science
- Emphasize the mastery of scientific process and abstract thinking as well as the assimilation of facts
- Provide test-taking workshops

Increase enrollment in math and science classes
- Counsel students to enroll in advanced-level math and science courses or help middle school students choose a direction for their high school studies and eventual math and science careers
- Establish high standards for minority and female participation in the sciences

Increase out-of-school math and science activities
- Encourage participation in math and science clubs, hobbies, and community programs

- Intervention efforts to affect the attitudes of minority students should begin before the seventh grade. Career awareness programs for females should begin in the early elementary school years, followed by more intensive programs in the middle and high school years.
- Intervention efforts to affect the attitudes of minority students should ensure that the participants have access to skill enhancement.
- Intervention should emphasize that females and minorities can excel in mathematics and science.
- Minority and female students should be exposed to more mathematics and science experiences, activities, and hobbies at an early age, both in and out of school.
- Efforts should include combating the perception of math and science as a White male domain and stressing the usefulness of math, science, and technology in the present and the future.
- Intervention efforts for minority and female students should include role modeling and career information. Many opportunities to interact with people from industry, universities, and professional societies should be provided.
- Intervention approaches should focus on providing social support and acceptance of competitiveness of young females and reducing the degree to which characteristics of self are sex typed in order to combat females' negative attitudes about becoming scientists.
- Parents should be made aware of their role in encouraging their minority and female children to participate in mathematics, science, and technology.
- Teachers should be made aware of the importance of increasing minority and female students' self-concept and belief in their ability to succeed in quantitative and problem-solving activities.
- Guidance counselors should be educated about the importance of encouraging minority and female students to participate in mathematics and science.
- Intervention should provide means of utilizing the positive influence of peers on values, attitudes, and aspirations in

helping minority and female students to maintain an interest in mathematics and science.

Skill-Building Approaches

It is critical during the elementary and junior high school years that minorities and females perform well in mathematics and science as well as plan to take high school science and mathematics courses. Minority and female students need a strong background in mathematics and science not only because college majors require it but also because there is a growing need for a more scientifically literate populace. Recommendations for improving performance of minorities and females in middle school mathematics and science and increasing the chances that they will opt to elect high school math and science courses are listed below (Clewell, 1987; Clewell and Anderson, 1987):

- Math and science skills should be strengthened with the goal of preparing and motivating students to take advanced-level courses in high school.
- Instruction should be activity-based, proceed from concrete to abstract, and encourage active involvement with a variety of manipulative materials at all ages.
- Students should seek solutions to problems through hands-on experiences, and teachers should relate problems to the students' interest and experience.
- Teachers should expect high achievement from every student and show confidence in each student's ability to learn. It is also important to give feedback and reinforcement as soon as possible, providing ongoing evaluation and routinely making growth apparent to the student. Teachers should help students to realize that they can succeed in mathematics and science.
- Test preparation should be a part of intervention activities. Students should be tested in the language of instruction.
- Teachers need to adapt their teaching methods to accommodate varying stages of cognitive development. Instruc-

tional approaches should also accommodate students' different cognitive styles and locus-of-control orientations.

- Teachers should be aware of how their expectations, attitudes, behavior, and interactions with students affect students' achievement.
- Minority and female students need early exposure to science and active participation in science projects.
- Females should be exposed to male-oriented science activities that allow exploration of mechanical apparatus, computation, and the development of science-related skills.
- Interaction among students enhances achievement. Grouping students according to ability is less effective than working with a mixed-ability group as long as differences are not too great. Peer tutoring can be a useful tool that benefits both tutors and the tutored.
- Intervention concerning the selection of math and science courses in high school should begin in the fifth and sixth grades.
- Parents should be provided with information and training to help them support their children academically and influence their career and high school study plans.
- Intervention efforts should encourage minority and female students to enroll in hard-core science and mathematics courses.

PART TWO

Effective Intervention Strategies

Although we know much about the causes of underrepresentation, we know less about effective intervention to overcome barriers that prevent minorities and females from participating in mathematics and science fields at an equal rate with White males. Specifically, there seems to be a gap between theoretical and empirical research and intervention practice. The two chapters in Part Two attempt to bridge this gap by identifying effective strategies for intervention approaches, linking these strategies to their bases in research and theory, and describing how these strategies have been implemented in middle school intervention programs in math and science for young females and minorities.

Chapter Three focuses on career awareness programs. It describes strategies that have proved effective in promoting positive attitudes, including role modeling, out-of-school activities, and provision of a supportive environment; provides examples of their use in actual programs; and cites research evidence of their effectiveness.

Chapter Four deals with strategies for skill building and enrichment programs. The chapter describes research and practice regarding strategies aimed at improving achievement and performance in mathematics and science, including instructional approaches (such as cooperative learning, activity-based instruction, and the discovery method), tutoring approaches, and test preparation.

3

Changing Student Attitudes Toward Mathematics and Science

During the middle school years, students are forming and changing their attitudes about themselves, their families, their friends, and their world. They are developing conceptions about who they are, their likes and dislikes, what is important to them, and what they may become. Throughout this period of transformation, they begin to develop a system of preferences and beliefs, including those related to mathematics and science, that affect their present and future choices and actions. Students' attitudes concerning mathematics and science encompass a number of dimensions, including:

> *Expressed liking:* enjoyment or pleasure associated with engaging in mathematics or science studies or activities
> *Perceived value or utility:* belief that mathematics and science are useful or important to their present and future lives
> *Appropriateness:* perception that mathematics or science is consistent with their identity or role as a member of a gender or ethnic group
> *Self-concept of achievement:* belief in their ability to perform or succeed in mathematics or science

The middle school years provide opportunities for students to begin picturing themselves in the world of work and thinking about what they may wish to do with their knowledge and skills during their lifetime. It is a very appropriate time to increase students' knowledge of career options in math and science, to show the attractiveness of such careers, and to emphasize them as appropriate and realistic career directions for female and minority students. Thus, when strategies to foster the participation and performance of young minority and female students in mathematics and science are considered, attention must be given to enhancing students' attitudes about these subject areas and expanding their knowledge about career options in mathematics- and science-related fields.

Middle school intervention programs that focus on encouraging positive attitudes toward mathematics and science and on increasing students' awareness of career choices and work opportunities in these fields have used a number of approaches, including role models and mentors, career awareness activities, exposure to extracurricular science and mathematics activities, and provision of a supportive environment. Intervention programs tend to use these approaches in a variety of ways. Different strategies for implementing these approaches and the benefits that they provide are described in Exhibit 3.1.

Role Models and Mentors

Adults and peers serve as role models and may exert a powerful socializing influence that can serve as a positive force for promoting favorable attitudes. Therefore, providing students with opportunities to have contact with models who have favorable attitudes and experiences in science and mathematics may be an effective way to encourage students' participation and achievement in these areas.

Research and Theory

Social learning, developmental, and instructional theories view role models as an important vehicle for learning (Bandura, 1977; Gagné, 1977; Hill, 1980). Through observation and imitation, people learn new attitudes and behaviors. Studies have reported

Exhibit 3.1. Approaches for Encouraging Positive Attitudes.

Role Models

Strategies	Benefits
Media and/or materials	Provide high-interest format; can be easily incorporated into school curricula
Creative arts	Tap students' affective as well as cognitive abilities to learn about and "model" new roles
Researching lives of famous scientists	Promotes interest in math and science fields by appealing to middle school students' interest in the nature and quality of individuals' personal lives
Contact with professionals	Provides opportunity for dialogue about personal and social as well as academic and technical issues regarding career options
Mentoring	Provides continued support and guidance in personal, academic, and career decisions through sustained one-to-one contact with an adult or peer mentor and learning about personal lives and career paths of successful professionals in math and science careers

Career Awareness

Strategies	Benefits
Media and/or materials	Provide information on a variety of career options and shows members of target group an array of scientific careers
Contact with professionals	Gives students opportunities to discuss the realities of preparing for and pursuing math and science careers, including professional and personal demands and rewards
Counseling	Provides information on academic and/or training requirements, sources of financial assistance, and college or vocational program selection and placement
Visits to industry	Allow students to observe professionals performing their roles in real work settings
Job internships	Allow students to learn by assisting professionals in their work

Extracurricular Activities

Strategies	Benefits
Exhibits	Expose students to a variety of science phenomena
Trips	Translate concepts into real-life experiences

Exhibit 3.1. Approaches for Encouraging Positive Attitudes, cont'd.

| Special projects and programs | Provide extended experience with a variety of high-interest activities and/or give students an opportunity to pursue their own interests, at their own pace, with assistance and guidance as requested. |

Provision of a Supportive Environment

Strategies	*Benefits*
Parental involvement	Makes parents aware of the barriers and how to combat them; provides parents with career information needed to support their children's curriculum choices and career interests
Teacher and counselor training	Raises educators' awareness of the math and science educational process, identifying retention problems and their causes; helps educators to develop and/or refine skills to enable females and minorities to remain in the math and science talent pool
Peer support	Dispels sex- and race-role stereotyping of subjects and careers; helps students to develop positive relationships with peers with similar interests.

associations between encouragement and expectations from significant others and young girls' attitudes, performance, or enrollment in mathematics. Research studies have also reported an association between role models and students' attitudes and career choices. One such study reported that exposing students to women scientists positively influenced both male and female students' attitudes toward scientists in general and toward female scientists in particular. Other investigations have underscored the effectiveness of peer models in reducing role stereotypes. In a study that asked college students and professionals to reflect on why they had chosen their professions, both females and minorities indicated that role models were important factors in their decisions to pursue science and math. Mentoring has also been found to be highly effective in providing the encouragement and support needed for students to persist in science or math. Studies that support the positive influence of role models on students' attitudes and career choices include Armstrong

(1980), Fennema and Sherman (1978), Parsons, Adler, and Kaczala (1982), Smith and Erb (1986), Scott and Feldman-Summers (1979), Ashby and Wittmaier (1978), Casserly (1975), and Thomas (1986).

Program Examples

Intervention programs have recognized the importance of providing role models to students. Role models serve students as a source of identification and motivation to pursue mathematics and science studies and to consider a career in related fields. For young minority and female students, role models deliver an important message that being a scientist or mathematician is appropriate and possible. Intervention programs tend to use role models in a variety of ways.

Recognizing the impact of models in shaping attitudes and behavior, a number of intervention programs have used media and materials to challenge and expand female and minority students' views of appropriate roles and career options. Operation SMART (Science, Math, and Relevant Technology) of Girls Incorporated (formerly Girls Clubs of America) uses print, television, and film to counteract negative stereotypes and to promote positive images of women and minorities. These media serve as a prompt for discussions to evaluate the portrayal of women and minorities in traditional and nontraditional roles. Such activities help young students become aware of how the media may perpetuate some negative stereotypes through the absence or unfavorable representation of women or minorities. Students also learn that media may, in fact, promote positive messages by identifying instances in which women or minorities are favorably portrayed. Through these activities, students learn to critically evaluate media's unspoken messages and to recognize the impact of these images on attitudes and behavior.

Some programs have developed their own media, oriented specifically to young audiences, that depict minorities and women in successful positions in mathematics- and science-related areas. The Detroit Area Pre-College Engineering Program (DAPCEP) has developed videotapes using middle school students as moderators to interview women and minorities about their personal lives and professional careers in mathematics and science. These tapes are particularly effective because they raise questions of interest to student viewers. (Further examples of media and materials are provided in the discussion of career awareness strategies below.)

A few programs use the creative arts as a modeling strategy In the Saturday Science Academy at Clark Atlanta University in Georgia, students develop original skits in which they portray scientific behavior and attitudes. Operation SMART provides students with opportunities to use their creative energies in activities such as developing collages illustrating women in technical roles. These activities provide students with a means to express their own conceptions as well as to clarify and extend their understanding of professional careers.

In some programs, students learn about famous minority and/or female mathematicians or scientists through reading and discussions. Programs such as DAPCEP encourage young minority students to research the lives of famous people in mathematics- or science-related fields and then to report their findings to others. By directing their own studies into the personal lives as well as the professional accomplishments of such people, students have an opportunity to develop a further understanding of their humanity and life experiences. For some students, this approach provides a means of personal identification with the early life experiences of these famous people and possibly a means of expanding their views of their own potential. A similar approach is taken by Go Power for Girls, a program implemented in the Ames, Iowa, community schools. To spark the interest of young girls in mathematics and science, this program recommends that they read biographical material about scientists. This strategy builds on the girls' interest in people, showing science as a social activity and scientists in terms of their relationships with others (Smail, 1984).

A number of intervention programs use presentations and discussion and, at times, demonstration formats to inform students about career options and give them an opportunity to interact formally and informally with role models. There is considerable variation in the format, organization, and duration of these activities. In some programs, students have an opportunity for direct contact with professionals who visit schools to describe their careers, their academic preparation, and the impact of their profession on their personal lives. One such program is the Community Ambassador Program, sponsored by Westinghouse Electric Corporation. This program is in effect at the headquarters location in Pittsburgh, Pennsylvania, and several other sites. Community ambassadors are math and science professionals who speak at schools, minority organizations, career conferences, universities, and parents' groups to encourage youth to pursue high-technology careers. They discuss with students, parents, and educators the types of high-technology careers available in the future and the steps necessary to achieve such careers. They speak from their own personal experience and act as role models for youth who might not otherwise consider high-technology careers as an option. They use the Westinghouse "A New World" brochure to show the creativity and challenge of technical careers. In the Visiting Technical Women's Program, which operates within the Department of Mathematics at the University of Michigan, women scientists visit schools to talk to students in large or small groups about their careers and lives as women in science.

Other programs, such as the Xerox Science Consultant Program for the Rochester City School District in New York, are developed as an integral part of the school program. Their mission is to foster interest in science by working with teachers to enrich the existing curriculum. The Xerox Science Consultant program selects and trains volunteers to work as a team with elementary school teachers in urban schools. Volunteer professionals receive training in how to talk to young students and how to plan with teachers to integrate their activities with classroom curricula and management strategies. In bimonthly classroom visits, they present lessons that they have prepared themselves or selected from materials developed by the program, emphasizing hands-on activities or demonstrations. Ongoing contact with a practicing scientist fosters students' continued interest in science activities.

An example of programs offered outside school is the Multiply Your Options (MYO) conference organized by the Project to Increase Mastery of Math and Science at Wesleyan University in Connecticut. This model is a series of one-day conferences (approximately six per year throughout the state) to provide female students in grades 6 through 10 with information on careers in mathematics, science, and technology and with opportunities to speak with successful women about personal as well as professional issues. In addition to demonstrations and hands-on math and science activities to spur interest in these areas, there are also workshops and panel discussions geared to the social and personal concerns of young girls. In these sessions, female professionals share experiences about their present lives: how they balance their personal and professional roles, what the social environment of their workplace is like, and the personal, economic, and intellectual demands and rewards of their professions. They emphasize the importance of persisting in math and science courses and provide examples of the steps that they took to arrive at their present positions. Another out-of-school program is the Engineering Summer Institutes offered by Arizona State University, in which students participate in a one-week orientation to engineering. As part of the program, they attend seminars and presentations conducted by undergraduate engineering students as well as professionals who share their secondary and college experiences with student participants. The participants are given an opportunity to ask questions and express their concerns and receive support and encouragement from the prospective engineers. Technical Career Counseling, a program sponsored by the Akron, Ohio, chapter of the National Technical Association, is described in Exhibit 3.2.

Mentors, who develop a sustained personal relationship with young minority and/or female students, not only serve as role models but also provide personal guidance, support, and direction for decisions and actions. Their role is to counsel young students to persist and succeed in math and science studies and career goals. Intervention programs have used both adults and peers as mentors. Project Interface, a church-operated project

Exhibit 3.2. Technical Career Counseling (TC²).

The Akron, Ohio, Chapter of the National Technical Association designed and directed an enhancement project in order to: (1) promote the exposure of minority students to science- and math-related careers, while providing a relationship between it and everyday operations; (2) provide professional role models for students; (3) to supplement in-school career counseling, and (4) to encourage parental involvement in student career planning. The theme for the ten week program in 1985 was Chemical/Chemistry Careers and Mechanical Engineering. The project director summarized the project's success by saying:

"We had an excellent group of thirty receptive seventh graders who chose to be involved in TC² by filling out a simple application of their intent; wherein they briefly stated why they cared to participate, and signed a Student Agreement Statement of their responsibility while in the program, which was co-signed by their parents. The resource persons representing minority and female technical professionals from local industry serve as role models for the students. Each has a base in the technical theme area which adds significantly to the technical credibility of TC²."

Source: "Technical Career Counseling (TC²)," 1985, p.1

in Oakland, California, provides junior high minority students with a peer tutoring program. Because Project Interface also serves students through college age, college students are enlisted to serve as mentors to their younger peers. Several times a week, students meet in tutoring and counseling sessions with their mentors. Shared backgrounds and age proximity allow the older students to maintain a high level of influence and credibility with their young protégés. The older students receive training and compensation for their services; in return, they are held accountable for their performance as tutors and role models. They meet weekly with project staff to review their protégés' progress and goals. They are rated on their attendance, preparation, and conduct during tutoring sessions; compensation for their services is related to their performance.

In addition to peer mentors, the Mathematics, Engineering, Science Achievement (MESA) program, operating through seventeen college campuses in California, provides several adult mentors in the form of program advisers, who typically are mathematics or science teachers who direct all project activities. The advisers develop close personal relationships with their students. In addition to arranging project activities (which may include club meetings, study groups, peer tutoring, community volunteer activities, and field visits), they monitor students' academic performance and provide them with academic and personal counseling to help them to persist and do their best.

Career Awareness

Females and minorities need to change their images of mathematicians and scientists. During adolescence, when students are building a more stable picture of themselves, consideration of an occupation is mainly a matter of finding an occupational role in which they can express themselves in a manner consistent with their concept of self. This suggests that as students develop a positive self-image and have confidence in their ability to do well in math and science, they are likely to consider science-related careers as a possible occupational choice. Addressing career development needs through career awareness activities at the middle school level will help to foster vocational maturity and career competence.

Research and Theory

Theories of vocational development emphasize that students' interest in an area influences their attraction to a career in given fields (Ginsberg, 1951; O'Hara and Tiedeman, 1959; Super, 1957; Borow, 1976; Holland, 1985). Several research findings suggest that career awareness should be a central part of intervention efforts. Female and minority students need to change their images of mathematicians and scientists. Females are strongly influenced by the belief that it is unfeminine to study math or science; consequently, few females pursue these traditionally male-dominated fields. Research also indicates that minority and female students have limited knowledge of the applications of science and mathematics to everyday life and the solution of world problems (Dossey, Mullis, Lindquist, and Chambers, 1988; Mullis and Jenkins, 1988). Finally, most young minority and female students have not received the counseling necessary to persist in mathematics or science studies or to consider careers in these areas (Beane, 1985; Casserly, 1979; Olstad, Juarez, Davenport, and Haury, 1981).

Program Examples

Career awareness activities for intervention programs during the middle school years include self-exploration and vocational planning activities that allow students to learn about career options and the personal and academic requirements for preparing for and succeeding in these positions. Career guidance during this period should take the form of exploring occupational and personal interests, not making vocational decisions. These activities span from learning about careers by reading or discussions with knowledgeable professionals to direct exposure through on-the-job internships.

There is strong evidence that seeing adults with whom they can identify in nontraditional occupations increases students' acceptance of these occupations and their willingness to prepare for them. Therefore, visuals can aid greatly in eliminating stereotypes as well as providing career information. Futures Unlimited, an intervention effort of the Consortium for Educational Equity of Rutgers University, New Brunswick, New Jersey, offers several mixed-media packages of posters, videotapes, and related instructional print materials designed to encourage members of neglected groups or young women at risk (urban minority females, non-college-bound disadvantaged females, math underachievers) to see the value of staying in school and electing the math and science preparation that they will need to have access to the higher-paying technical fields. These visuals are photographs of real people, making very good money doing real jobs for real employers.

Videotapes and films are often used at career days and career conferences for females as a way of presenting female role models in the math and science world. Multiplying Options and Subtracting Bias is a videotape and workshop intervention program developed by the School of Education at the University of Wisconsin, Madison, for junior and senior high school students. The program is designed to eliminate sexism from mathematics education. The four thirty-minute, full-color videotapes use a variety of formats—interviews, dramatic vignettes, and expert testimony—to address the problem of mathematics avoidance and suggest some possible solutions.

Some projects develop or collect materials that provide information on various nontraditional careers. For example, MESA maintains a library of career awareness materials for use by intervention programs. Many programs use guest speakers to persuade female and minority students to consider an array of career options in math and science. Involving women and minorities in scientific fields provides an opportunity for dialogue about the utility of math and science skills as well as validating the participation of females and minorities in areas often perceived as predominantly White male. Project BAM (Blacks and Mathematics), sponsored by the Mathematical Association of America, has a visiting lecturer program designed to increase awareness of the need for mathematics courses. Visitors are local Black professionals in mathematics-related careers, such as chemistry, engineering, banking, insurance, and computer science. These professionals give typical examples of how such disciplines as algebra, geometry, and trigonometry are actually used in their specific positions. The lecturer serves as a positive role model and a career informant.

Conferences are another means for giving students contact with mathematicians and scientists. Expanding Your Horizons is a conference program of Skyline Community College in San Bruno, California, designed to increase young women's interest in math and science. It provides students with an opportunity to meet and form personal contacts with women working in traditionally male occupations. A typical conference starts with 700 to 1,000 young women gathering on a college campus to work with professional women to learn about their careers, work, school experiences, and home life. This is followed by a question-and-answer period. Students then take part in small workshops to delve into science and math activities and computer programming. After lunch, they break up into groups for career discussions and more information from industry people, working professional women, and university science or math majors.

The Math Instruction and Science Studies Career Options Conference (MISS) was organized by California's Orange Unified School District to introduce young females to a variety of career options that utilize mathematics, science, and computer science. Parents, teachers, and counselors were also invited to attend and share in a variety of creative and informative workshops on math and science career options, such as "The Sky Is the Limit — Aviation Careers," "The Technical Aspect of Success — Engineering Careers," "Get with the Program — Careers in Computer Science," "Place Yourself in Orbit — Careers in Space Sciences," and "Making It a Practice — Family Physician Careers."

The Engineering Fair in Oklahoma City, Oklahoma, also provides opportunities for students to meet professionals with different types of engineering careers. Student-oriented science and physics displays and hands-on exhibits are staffed by practicing engineers, university educators, and undergraduate engineering students, who discuss their displays and distribute information about the wide range of engineering and technology careers.

The Hawaii Association for Women in Science has developed the Share-a-Day-with-a-Scientist (Share) and Scientists-in-the-School (SIS) programs to encourage young women to seek careers in science. The Share project provides a unique opportunity for students to explore the many options available in science on a one-to-one basis with an experienced scientist. Students who participate in this program spend a day with scientists, watching them at work, seeing their work setting, and learning how they prepared for their careers. In the SIS project, scientists from different disciplines visit schools to speak about their careers and how they prepared for them. Both of these programs strive to expand students' views of science as a career, provide role models, and encourage students to make early and adequate academic preparations.

Various counseling strategies are used to improve female and minority students' motivation and preparation to enter scientific and technical careers. Through printed information, interest-assessment exercises, and individual sessions or group discussions, career counselors strive to provide personal and academic support. The goals are to assist young female and minority students to become aware of the opportunities and options for pursuing careers that emphasize math and science and to understand the importance of enrolling in and completing a high school academic program in math and science. Career counselors are usually present at career days or career fairs.

Go Power for Girls provides gifted girls with information about external and internal barriers to success and counseling to help them reach their potential. External barriers addressed include sex-role stereotypes, educational experiences that suggest that academic successes are attributable to luck and failure to lack of ability, and differential teacher treatment in the academic environment. Internal barriers addressed include the fear of success, students' doubts about their abilities, and conflicts concerning the coordination of personal life, family, and career. Development of long- and short-term personal goals for nontraditional careers is an essential counseling strategy.

Female and minority students who attend the Engineering Summer Institutes are given an orientation to postsecondary education and advised about the need for adequate high school preparation in math and science for an array of engineering career options. They are given information about college admission requirements, the application process, housing, support services, and academic scholarships and other sources of financial assistance.

Project Interface provides students with general information about a variety of career opportunities. Most importantly, it provides information on courses needed to major in math- or science-related fields.

Another strategy to foster awareness of career opportunities for women and minorities in math and science is the industry tour. Industry tours provide an opportunity for students to interact with role models as well as exposing students to career options. Industry tours and presentations are part of the student activities of the Engineering Summer Institutes. The tours provide students with information about opportunities in engineering and the work environment. This strategy offers interaction on a one-to-one or small-group basis with practicing engineers in their actual work environments. The tours generally consist of a presentation from an engineer and/or executive staff member, a question-and-answer session, a guided tour, and lunch.

In an effort to provide students with firsthand knowledge of the wide variety of careers for which mathematics and science education is necessary, the Mathematics-Science Summer Enrichment program of the Washington, D.C., public schools took students on tours of businesses and industries, government agencies, and universities. Such a strategy is particularly useful in helping students not only to consider careers in these disciplines but also to understand the necessity of electing math and science courses during high school.

Internships increase students' motivation to pursue majors in math and science by giving them firsthand knowledge of the challenges and rewards of scientific careers (Davis and Humphreys, 1985). Internships help to socialize students to the world of work. Often they provide an opportunity for first work experience and may result in valuable contacts, letters of recommendation, and even paid employment in the future. These field experiences give students an opportunity to determine whether they really like a particular career area. Understanding that minority and female students typically have very limited criteria by which to judge careers and job environments, some intervention programs have a student internship program to give students both information and experience. The goals of such programs are to prepare students for the technical work environment, reinforce their academic skills, and aid their economic development. Students are placed with area companies for a short period of time during the summer.

The DAPCEP Summer Bridge program helps students to gain practical experience by giving them the opportunity to work in an engineering firm during the summer. MESA programs also select students for summer internships, including research with engineering professors, working as an engineering aide at an industrial corporation, and working as an engineering assistant at an air force base. Additionally, participation in some summer programs includes writing an interest essay. A prompt to guide the preparation of a career awareness essay may read as follows:

> You have applied for admission to a program that is for students who enjoy math and science or are interested in exploring technical careers. Please describe an experience that made you interested in exploring technical things. What was it about the experience that excited you or captured your attention? What did you most like about the experience and what did you learn about yourself?

Extracurricular Activities

As the term implies, extracurricular activities are activities that are in addition to and not traditionally a part of the regular school curriculum. Unlike participation in regular school programs, participation in these activities is voluntary and responsive to students' interests and enjoyment. These activities provide a context in which children learn and play simultaneously. In these special environments, students work at their own pace, learning to take risks, fail, revise, and then persist to find answers to their questions. These low-risk, high-interest situations promote confidence building and an understanding of the scientific problem-solving process. They also serve a social function by creating a supportive environment of adults and peers who share similar interests.

Research and Theory

There are many elements within children's play that require mathematics and science concepts and operations. Linking these play experiences to more formal learning activities offers potential for greater interest and achievement. Personality theorists (Atkinson, 1964; Rogers, 1969) and developmental theorists (Mead, 1934; Piaget, 1956) support informal or extracurricular experiences.

Researchers and advocates of hands-on learning experiences suggest that students are bored with the routine nature of activities in mathematics classes. Most classes follow a pattern of lecture and/or discussion, followed by seatwork, homework, and tests. Students rarely have the opportunity to conduct projects, go on field trips, hear guest speakers, or engage in laboratory activities (Carpenter and others, 1980; Kahle and Lakes, 1983). Researchers have also found that early exposure to science activities, childhood hobbies, and participation in mathematics and science clubs are related to interest and career choice (Clark, 1985; Thomas, 1986).

Program Examples

Extracurricular activities may include exhibits, trips or special projects, and extended programs such as after-school science clubs. The distinction between curricular and extracurricular and between in-school and out-of-school activities sometimes blurs as more schools begin to integrate these types of exploratory activities into their regular school programs. The unifying theme for these and the related extracurricular activities described earlier in the discussions of career awareness and role models is that these activities are designed to excite, build confidence, and promote students' interest in math or science through enrichment as well as to foster a sense of utility and possibility.

Girls' and minority students' interest in science can be sparked through the creation of their own exhibits or visits to programs offering science exhibits. Of particular interest are the exhibits where students can manipulate and experiment with phenomena. The Cranbrook Institute of Science in Bloomfield Hills, Michigan, offers a series of programs in conjunction with the Girl Scouts of America. Girls can earn scout badges by participating in the institute's activities. Sleepovers in the museum, with a focus on astronomy and hands-on science, are very popular, as are Saturday workshops on topics such as "Earthworks," "Space Encounters," and "Water Everywhere." In addition, students are given a chance to explore "Physics Fun" through fifty interactive exhibits in the physics hall.

Field trips provide experiential activities that take science and math out of the classroom and the textbook and apply them to real-life situations. The Idaho Science Camp, operated through the College of Engineering of the University of Idaho, uses field trips and other activities as part of its two-week summer program geared to encouraging minority students to pursue careers in science or engineering. On one of their field experiences, students visit a local dam to collect water, soil, and air samples, which they then analyze using computer graphic technology.

The Mentor in Engineering Program, operated by the New York Alliance for the Public Schools, arranges field trips for individual classes to local laboratories, operating facilities, and sites under construction. Small groups permit students to have hands-on experiences with equipment and personal interaction with engineers. The program sends participating engineers a list of helpful hints to prepare them for the students. To focus students' attention, it also encourages the engineers or teachers to devise a set of questions to which students must find answers during the trip, a sort of "intellectual treasure hunt" that the students enjoy (see Exhibit 3.3). The activities are most effective when teachers conduct both preparatory and follow-up activities to complement and build on these experiences. MESA students make several field trips to the Lawrence Hall of Science at the University of California, Berkeley, where they participate in hands-on labs in biology, chemistry, computer

Exhibit 3.3. Mentor in Engineering Program.

Classroom Visits:
Double periods (one and one-half hours) were set aside for classroom visits. In order to assure that presentations were meaningful for the students, we made certain that the teacher and the engineer spoke on the telephone prior to the visit to discuss the concepts the students were learning in their math class, the material the engineer planned to present and ways to relate the two. In addition, we sent each engineer a list of "Helpful Hints" and called to arrange practical details. These visits may include scientific demonstrations, display of special equipment, slide shows, etc.
To illustrate the variety of these visits:

- *RCA:* RCA engineers devised a special activity called "Lost on the Moon" in which students had to work singly and in small groups to rank items necessary for survival; the simulation provided a vivid demonstration of how engineers must work together to solve problems.
- *American Cyanamid:* American Cyanamid's visit to a junior high school sparked a lively discussion of the medical and ethical implications of various issues.
- *AT&T:* When AT&T engineers visited a junior high school, they gave a step-by-step description of how a call to Puerto Rico is placed. The next week when these students visited AT&T's operating facility, they were able to see the equipment and follow the process *first-hand*.

Field Trips:
Seven of the firms have hosted field trips to their laboratories, operating facilities or sites under construction. With the exception of the trip to the Javits Convention Center in February and the boat trip "finale" around the Statue of Liberty renovation in May, field trips were scheduled for one class at a time. This allowed students an opportunity for "hands-on" experience with equipment and more personal interaction with the engineers. Most trips also included lunch to provide time for the students to talk with the engineers in a more informal setting.

As with classroom visits, we sent engineers a list of "Helpful Hints"and helped the school arrange transportation, special clearance, etc. We also encouraged the engineers or teachers to devise a set of questions to which students must find answers during the trip (a kind of intellectual "treasure hunt" which the students enjoyed). During the visits, students may be assigned to individual engineers to "try out" their jobs by interviewing them or shadowing them at work. Students may be asked to evaluate the jobs they observe in terms of educational and skills requirements, job responsibilities or application of specific mathematical concepts. Among the trips this spring:

- *Javits Convention Center* (hosted by Syska & Hennessy): Students were thrilled with the opportunity to tour the center before construction was completed and before the general public was allowed in.

Exhibit 3.3. Mentor in Engineering Program, cont'd.

- *The Lincoln Tunnel* (hosted by the Port Authority of New York and New Jersey): Students were permitted to operate some of the machinery and had an opportunity to speak with a variety of employees about their jobs. (The teacher said this was the best field trip he had ever been on.)
- *IBM:* Each class was taken on a tour of a computer center where students saw a talking computer, a computer which produces graphics for architects and structural engineers, and a computer program of a figure break-dancing. They were also guided through the "Seeing the Light" exhibition which featured displays illustrating the laws of sound and light.

Source: Mentor in Engineering. Report of the New York Alliance for the Public Schools, October 1986, pp. 5–7.

science, astronomy, and robotics. Students are also taken to engineering facilities and museums.

Operation SMART is an after-school program that uses an inquiry model to teach young girls how to apply science processes to solve everyday problems. In addition to a variety of career awareness activities, the program has developed a series of modules approximately an hour to an hour and a half long with hands-on math and science activities involving all of the senses. The activities' objective is to help girls apply critical reasoning to understand everyday problems. The program encourages girls to pose questions, find their own answers, and learn from, not fear, their mistakes. One activity involves taking a walk around the neighborhood, examining how sidewalks and buildings are constructed, how sewers work, and the operation of equipment at a gas station. Another involves experimenting with body movement in a swimming pool, noting how speed is affected by different types of movement and body position.

The Saturday Science Academy of the Atlanta Resource Center for Science and Engineering is a ten-week Saturday morning program for elementary and middle school minority students. The project offers a comprehensive program of career awareness activities, as well as enrichment classes in mathematics, science, computer science, and creative expression. Activities are fast-paced and inquiry-oriented and require active student participation. The intent is to stimulate students' interest and confidence in mathematics and science activities.

As one of its activities, DAPCEP encourages minority students to participate in the metropolitan Detroit annual science fair. This activity is seen as a means to motivate students and create a climate of excellence. Students write research papers on topics of their choice, including references and bibliographies. They then conduct experiments on their chosen topics, record the data, and develop displays to illustrate their experiments. Topics have included the effects of pollutants on single-celled organisms, factors affecting plant growth, conductivity of solar energy, heat absorption, and cancers in plant life. As one of its many activities, MESA sponsors preengineering summer projects for students. Students may participate in a research and design competition in conjunction with an industry firm, such as the Jet Propulsion Laboratory in southern California, or they may participate with scientists from EARTHWATCH in a special expedition to collect scientific data (Mathematics, Engineering, Science Achievement Program, 1985). The Hughes (Arkansas) High School chapter of the mathematics honor society Mu Alpha Theta conducts an annual math contest for seventh- and eighth-graders. A description of the contest is presented in Exhibit 3.4.

Provision of a Supportive Environment

Minority and female students need a supportive environment — an atmosphere in which there is a strong individual and group sense of achievement and success. Such an environment is fostered when students are nurtured with positive feedback and experiences with significant others (parents, teachers, counselors, peers) that encourage them to develop self-worth, to set high but realistic expectations, and to strive for excellence.

Research and Theory

Developmental theories related to children's social development provide much support for the efficacy of positive climates and

Exhibit 3.4. Mu Alpha Theta Math Contest.

Our high school chapter of Mu Alpha Theta, math honor society for grades 11 and 12, has for one of its annual projects conducting a math contest open to all local 7th and 8th graders.

The contest is held in February on a school day, but after school, in a large study hall. We issue a morning announcement inviting students to sign up in the counselor's office or math teacher's room in order to enter. Two weeks ahead is sufficient time. There is no charge for entering. Participation is voluntary. Further advance publicity is placed in the school newspaper.

About thirty-five students usually enter. Our contest is in its tenth year. The keys to success of such contests, I believe, are:

(1)   Give plenty of awards. We give three trophies, duplicates in case of ties, nice certificates to the next ten places, certificates of merit to any one else who entered. Note: make your trophies up ahead of time and announce where they may be seen when you open the contest for sign-ups.
(2)   Give publicity to winners. Use morning announcements, the school paper, and the local paper. We engrave a plaque with three winners' names each year and it is kept on display in the library.
(3)   Hold the contest when the weather is still cold so that indoor activities will appeal to the student more than outdoor activities.

Source: Betty R. Allen, Hughes High School, Hughes, Ark., 1986.

interactions with peers and adults and the significant role of parents in helping children to develop socially as well as cognitively and physically (Biehler, 1971; Curtis and Bidwell, 1977; Dorman, 1981; Havighurst, 1965; Hill, 1980; Hurlock, 1972; Lipsitz, 1977; Myers, 1986; Mussen, Conger, and Kagan, 1979). Comer (1984) supports three levels of parental involvement: program governance, instruction, and social functions. Parents' paricipation in these areas sends critical messages to their children that the educational program is important and that students are expected to behave well socially and achieve well academically.

Expectancy theory and social group theory suggest that educators' behavior toward students is influenced by their expectations of students' ability. These judgments of ability are often affected by students' gender or ethnic group membership. Theory also suggests that educators can be positive forces in the socialization and educational processes by providing a climate that makes learning a rewarding and relevant experience, one that makes the most of students' talents and interests (Atkinson, 1964; Maslow, 1954; Rogers, 1969; Rosenthal and Jacobson, 1968).

The peer group becomes powerful during the middle school years and begins to replace parents and other adults as the major source of behavioral standards and recognition of achievement. Being accepted by peers and especially having one or more close friends make a great difference (Biehler, 1971). Both developmental theory (Piaget, 1956; Sullivan, 1953) and motivational theory (Lewin, [1935] 1959) support peer interactions as a powerful mechanism for influencing students' interests and learning.

Several studies have indicated that significant others can enhance or deter interest in science and mathematics careers as well as affecting female and minority students' attitudes toward these subject areas (Bean, 1976; Casserly, 1975; Clewell and Anderson, 1991; Fennema, 1976; Fox, 1976; Kahle, 1982; Parsons, Adler, and Kaczala, 1982; Parsons, Heller, and Kaczala, 1979; Schreiber, 1984; Thomas and Stewart, 1971). Females often receive little direct encouragement from their mothers, observe little in the way of positive attitudes toward math and science by female teachers, and are treated differently from males by teachers and counselors. Females tend to receive positive reinforcement of negative attitudes toward science from parents, peers, and teachers. Minority students, particularly minority females, are also affected by these factors.

On the other hand, there is evidence that encouragement and support from significant others have been powerful influences leading minority and female students to consider and pursue science-related careers. Several studies have delineated factors that stimulate interest in and promote positive attitudes toward math and science, including parental encouragement and involvement, encouragement from significant others to pursue mathematics and science majors, and reinforcement of an interest in math by parents, teachers, and counselors (Clark, 1985;

Prillwitz, 1983; Thomas, 1986). Other studies confirm that the attitudes of students, especially female students, toward science are strongly influenced by friends and other peers who partici- pate in science and math activities (Keeves, 1975; Shapiro, 1962; Malcom and others, 1984).

Program Examples

To help students' significant others to become aware of their roles and responsibilities in encouraging female and minority students' interest in math and science and consideration of career options in these fields, many programs conduct special train- ing and awareness activities for peers and adults who are in close contact with underrepresented groups.

One of the first steps in involving parents to combat the underrepresentation of women and minorities in math and science is to inform them of the problem. The Girls + Math + Science = Choices program, conducted by Michigan's Calhoun Intermedi- ate School District, responds to this need by providing parents with facts regarding the gender differences in these disciplines. Through a handout entitled "Getting the Facts Straight," par- ents learn that:

- Females can learn mathematics as easily as can males.
- Many occupations require at least four years of high school mathematics.
- Many women are unable to enter a number of occupations because they lack the necessary mathematical background.
- Females are more likely than are males to stop taking mathe- matics classes, because they receive little encouragement, they are not expected to continue, they believe that they will not need such training in the future, and they lack confidence in their ability to learn mathematics.

Parents need information on ways to foster math and science interest and persistence in their children. The Girls + Math + Science = Choices program tells parents that it is important to have open lines of communication with their children regarding subject interests and career options. Periodic parent-child discussions are an important way to provide continuous support and address issues and concerns by talking about feelings toward science and math, discussing the usefulness of a good mathematical background in today's world, stressing the fact that girls can learn math just as well as boys can and that math is just as important for girls as it is for boys, and encouraging children to seek help and support if they are having problems in these subjects.

Parents of female and minority children should also be involved in active participation in their children's math and science education. It is important for parents to take an interest in the content of math and science homework, not just its completion. Parents should provide and engage in activities with their children that involve taking things apart, building, and so on, and games that develop investigative skills. They should take their children on visits to science centers and industry tours so that they can see math and science in action. Operation SMART, for example, encourages parents of participants to attend field trips.

Go Power for Girls shares the following strategies with parents to help them provide a warm and supportive environment where their daughters' interests and choices are respected:

- Provide your daughter with games, equipment, supplies, and experiences that will create an interest in mathematics and science at an early age.
- Involve your daughter in special programs designed to stimulate interest in science and mathematics.
- Hold high expectations for your daughter and instill positive beliefs about her capabilities.
- Help your daughter to become able to rely on her own judgment and develop independence and the ability to make her own decisions.
- Discuss your daughter's personal and career goals with her often and let her know that you support her choices and interests.

- Provide books and other materials that will expose your daughter to successful women role models in nontraditional careers.

Parents should take an active role in exposing their children to role models. Some programs request that parents assist teachers in bringing role models into the classroom. Others involve parents in organizing math and science career days. Moreover, parents who are themselves involved in scientific and technical occupations are invaluable resources and should be encouraged to volunteer their talents as role models. Operation SMART uses parents as career role models; the Saturday Science Academy holds parental orientation sessions and uses parent volunteers to help to organize activities and assist students.

Parents need to insist that their children continue to take mathematics and science even when these courses become optional. Many programs provide printed information for parents regarding the selection of high school courses. Others provide sessions with counselors during which parents are informed of career options in mathematics and science, course-taking requirements, financial assistance, and opportunities and application processes for postsecondary training and education. Parents of females in the Girls + Math + Science = Choices program are told that they have both the right and the obligation to discuss the selection of high school courses and their relationship to future career options with their daughters. They are also told that although counselors are supposed to stress the importance of math for every student, it still remains the parents' responsibility to ensure that their daughters are protecting their futures by becoming mathematically literate.

Educators also need to be informed about barriers to participation in math and science and specific strategies that they can employ to cultivate and stimulate interest in math and science for female and minority students. Taking the Road Less Traveled, an intervention program implemented by the Program for Women in Science and Engineering, offers career conferences for young women (grades 6–12), their parents, and educators. Sessions for parents and educators provide information and techniques for supporting young females academically and helping them to realize their potential in math and science.

Girls + Math + Science = Choices provides a handbook for educators that addresses such issues as the misconception that females do not need to study math ("engineering is a man's field," or "you're too pretty to be a mathematician"); the fact that women tend to specialize in fields that have low status, pay low salaries, and have traditionally been dominated by females; and the fact that as students pass through junior high school, both females and males expect females to do less well in math, which indicates that decreased expectations precede the decline in math achievement. Workshop training offers to educators solutions such as the following:

- Form special-interest groups for females in science and mathematics.
- Expose both sexes to role models of women in various careers in math, science, and engineering.
- Arrange opportunities for females to "shadow" a female scientist, mathematician, or engineer for a day to see what her work entails.
- Discuss the inequitable performance and participation of females in these disciplines.
- Talk about peer pressure and sex-role stereotypes of these subjects.
- Discourage sexist remarks and attitudes in the classroom.

Specific career awareness activities for the classroom are also suggested in the educators' handbook. Examples include having students write to professional associations or people in the state to request brochures, pamphlets, and other written information about careers in science; follow-up activities to expand students' awareness of careers in science; comparing the photographs of men and women in career fields; designing a bulletin board on science careers; and writing want ads for science jobs.

Project SEED (Special Elementary Education for the Disadvantaged) in Berkeley, California, encourages teachers to build students' confidence in their ability to think critically and to learn mathematics successfully. Confidence-building techniques include using students' names and acknowledging that they understand a concept, designating students who have caught on to a concept as experts for the day, praising students who ask a good mathematical question, praising students who ask questions when they do not understand something, and avoiding putting students on the spot for being wrong. The program informs teachers of the need to create an atmosphere of positive support and respect for disadvantaged students and to have high expectations for those students.

The Mathematics, Science and Minorities, K–6 program, operated by the Mid-Atlantic Equity Center in Washington, D.C., also emphasized having higher expectations for minority students. To facilitate high student expectations, teachers were asked to provide challenges, encourage further thought through the use of higher-order questioning, allow sufficient wait time for student responses, discuss wrong answers, and give praise for correct responses. Techniques to promote student persistence include providing opportunities for and assisting in student goal setting, both short- and long-term; providing opportunities to celebrate success and learn from and cope with failure; encouraging risk taking; and providing opportunities to increase students' skills in taking responsibility for outcomes of their own behavior.

DAPCEP offers teacher workshops to provide opportunities for interaction with other teachers and to help teachers develop ideas and strategies to take back to their classrooms. The following excerpt from a DAPCEP newsletter (Whitner, 1991, p. 2) describes what teachers at one middle school have gained from these workshops and the ways in which students have benefited.

> A lot of creative energy flows at the DAPCEP teacher workshops. Good ideas and interaction between teachers charges everyone up, and everyone comes away with a positive attitude. The key to being a good teacher is: Can you motivate your students to find information on their own? We want our students to understand that the effort they put

into a science project will give them a gift that no one can take away. The effort is its own reward. There are lots of motivators. We take pictures of all science projects, not just to recognize winners, but also for the younger kids to see what is possible. The prospect of a trip to Toronto without parents is a great motivator. I keep my classroom open for DAPCEP students every Friday from 9 a.m. to 10 p.m. Kids can get individualized help and we often have pizza parties.

Project BASE (Blacks for Academic Success in Education), a project of the Duval County, Florida, public schools, attempts to develop or refine the following teacher competencies through teacher training to promote positive attitudes:

- Being consistent and empathetic in the treatment of students
- Practicing good human relations
- Exhibiting a positive overall approach
- Demonstrating enthusiasm for teaching
- Nurturing creativity and curiosity
- Helping students to develop positive attitudes toward themselves
- Encouraging confidence and self-respect in students
- Demonstrating proper listening skills
- Accepting varied student viewpoints and asking students to extend or elaborate on answers or ideas

Counselors should encourage minority and female students to keep their career aspirations high and provide many opportunities for career exploration. These groups need non-sexist career guidance that includes some assessment of vocational interests, personality, and values. Additionally, counselors should advocate participation in extracurricular math and science activities. It is important for counselors to be informed about community resources that are available to stimulate interests in math and science: nature camps, science centers, after-school programs at schools, and so on.

The most critical task for counselors is to convince junior

high students to take math and science during high school. These
students need to know that a great array of both professional
and nonprofessional careers require math skills and that three
years of high school math will give them more career options
than almost any other subject. Girls + Math + Science = Choices
offers the following suggestions for advising students on course
selection:

Students Say	*You Say*
But I don't like math.	Math is becoming more and more important in all areas of work.
But I don't do well in math.	Most people, even those who go into math-related careers, were not straight-A students in math.
I'm not going to need it anyway.	The average teenager in high school today will work for over twenty years, whether male or female. You'll lose out on higher pay if you don't have a math background.
It's boring.	One of the chief reasons students find math boring is that they lack confidence in their abilities. You seem to be able to do it; now you have to convince yourself that you can do it.

The Colorado Minority Engineering Association (CMEA),
housed at the University of Colorado, Denver, provides training for guidance counselors to inform them about the educational and career background of engineers, to provide exposure
to different plant facilities and the work environment of engineers, to share information about various engineering fields of

study, and to make them aware of the increased emphasis on automation and its application and the use of robotics, as well as the need for research engineers in product development. Counselors in the Mathematics, Science and Minorities, K–6 program schedule meetings with students and parents to discuss issues of career education and to help minority students improve their self-concept.

Peer pressure at the middle school level often has a negative effect on female and minority students' interest in science. As noted earlier, females are often confronted with messages that it is inappropriate for them to like these subjects; minority students also must battle the belief that these disciplines are White male domains. Students who like these subjects are often viewed as different from their age mates and excluded by them. The Massachusetts Pre-Engineering Program (MassPep) at the Wentworth Institute of Technology recognizes this problem and provides a positive environment for students to interact where achievement and the concept that learning can be fun are part of the normative structure. One strategy utilized in this program is assigning students to project teams. These teams help to develop and sustain students' interest in science and help them learn the procedures and behaviors needed to gain confidence in the subject areas. Peers work together under the leadership of a core group of undergraduate, graduate school, and industry volunteers. In addition to developing supportive peer relationships, the project activities offer students opportunities to use a variety of tools (computers as well as lab facilities and equipment) in completing their projects while providing exposure to career information and to people who have achieved success in math and science fields and are willing to reach back and help others.

4

Improving Academic Performance

In an effort to increase the participation of minority and female students in advanced mathematics and science studies and careers, a number of intervention programs have targeted student performance as a primary objective. National and international studies have clearly documented achievement gaps among our nation's middle and high school youth, particularly in higher-level skills. The achievement differences are most prominent among non-Asian minority students. While the achievement gap between males and females is less pronounced in the early middle school grades, differences begin to emerge in those grades in higher-level mathematics problem solving and in physical science.

This chapter describes strategies used by intervention programs to bolster the academic performance of minority and female students. We define *performance* in terms of both process and products. *Process* refers to the procedures or steps in tackling a problem or area of knowledge. Process takes place over time and can follow various routes. *Products,* or *outcomes,* refers to the end result of the process. Products are a means of measuring a student's knowledge or skill at one point in time. Products can take a number of forms, such as a completed project or a score on a test. Thus, *performance* refers to demonstration of knowledge, skills, or abilities in the process and content of mathematics and science (for both in-school and out-of-school activities).

Traditionally, intervention programs have emphasized test scores as a means of measuring the effectiveness of their performance-oriented approaches. Through the influence of cognitive science, such programs are now placing greater emphasis on process by developing students' awareness and skills in learning how to learn and permitting a wider range of products. Knowledge of the process helps to demystify these subject areas and thus promotes greater accessibility to students who previously considered them beyond their comprehension or ability. Emphasis on a greater variety of product forms permits students greater opportunity to demonstrate their knowledge or skills.

Intervention programs that focus on improved academic performance and achievement in mathematics and science are using a variety of approaches. In this chapter, we discuss group instructional approaches, tutoring, test preparation and study skills, teacher training, and parental involvement. The following list summarizes the different strategies and benefits associated with these approaches:

Instructional Approaches

Strategies	Benefits
Inquiry learning	Explores students' own questions and interests; is highly motivating; simulates real-world unstructured or teacher-constructed problem solving
Activity-based instruction	Promotes acquisition of knowledge and skills as well as understanding of procedures through action and direct manipulation of concrete objects — learning through hands-on experiences
Cooperative learning	Promotes exchange of ideas; provides support, monitoring, feedback, and so on; allows

	students to develop facilitative interpersonal task behaviors, such as considering the perspective of their peers, negotiation, and facilitating attainment of group goals
Direct instruction	Directs lesson content and pace; reinforces student understanding of important concepts and relationships as well as the process of learning; gives opportunity to provide feedback and correct student misconceptions

Tutoring

Strategies	Benefits
Peer tutoring	Provides academic assistance and promotes development of a social support network
Adult tutoring	Provides personal and career advice as well as instructional assistance

Study Skills and Test Preparation

Strategies	Benefits
Anxiety reduction	Reduces stress associated with fear of failure and increases students' confidence in their ability to do well
Skill review	Increases students' knowledge and application of concepts and enhances problem-solving abilities
Study skills and habits training	Improves students' acquisition and retention of material to be learned
Exam strategies	Improve time management

and provide tips on how to select the most appropriate option given the construction of the item

Teacher Training

Strategies	Benefits
Addressing gender differences and needs	Addresses differential treatment of and expectations for girls and provides ways to promote sex equity in math and science
Addressing cultural differences and needs	Focuses on differential performance of and expectations for minority students and provides strategies for increasing academic performance and participation of racial minorities in math and science

Parental Involvement

Strategies	Benefits
Parent orientations	Provide information about program activities and requirements; solicit parents' commitment to program
Parent volunteers	Assist staff in planning and conducting a variety of program functions
Parental instruction	Provides home instruction to reinforce and/or extend students' understanding of material being taught
Parents as support people	Encourage students' participation in the program and expect their children to be successful

Instructional Approaches

Instructional approaches to increase students' achievement differ from traditional instruction in a number of ways. First, these approaches are consistent with what we know about students' developmental needs, including their need for structure, challenge, action, social interaction with peers, and close personal interactions with role models or mentors. For example, we know that middle school children learn best not by passively listening to a teacher's lecture but by performing their own actions. Second, intervention programs recognize the link between achievement and motivation. They strive to bolster students' self-esteem and self-concept in mathematics and science through successful, meaningful experiences. Students learn through their own successes that they can do math and science and that math and science learning is fun. Third, programs teach students to focus on the process of problem solving, not solely on the products. By understanding how to solve problems and monitor their own thinking during the solution process, students are better able to undertake and succeed in novel situations. Most programs use multiple strategies for instruction to increase students' confidence and motivation as well as their thinking skills and academic achievement. Frequently used instructional strategies in middle school intervention programs include inquiry learning, activity-based instruction, cooperative learning, and direct instruction.

Research and Theory

Cognitive and developmental theories support inquiry learning by emphasizing the importance of students' own activity in learning (Piaget, 1952; Gagne, 1977). Piagetian theory proposes that cognitive schemata are developed and reformulated as children actively engage in their own problem-solving activities. Gagne (1977) also supports student exploration to assist students in developing their own ideas and to provide them with opportunities to test their assumptions. A number of theorists, including Piaget (1959), Dewey ([1916] 1986), and Gagne (1977), emphasize the importance of children's own actions and manipulation of objects in learning. Manipulating objects allows children to examine phenomena at their own pace. Activity-based instruction also allows children the opportunity to repeat actions as needed in order to understand and assimilate new information.

Support for cooperative approaches is derived from theories of child development (Piaget, 1956; Sullivan, 1953) and motivation (Lewin, [1935] 1959) that suggest that peer interactions are a powerful mechanism to influence students' interests and learning. Linguistic theories also support language and interaction to discuss and refine ideas through communication with others (Cocking and Mestre, 1988; DiVesta, 1974; Vygotsky, 1962; Whorf, [1956] 1989). Support for direct instruction is based on several learning principles of behaviorism, including (1) frequency of repetition to guarantee retention and (2) generalization and discrimination, which suggest the importance of practice in varied contexts (Hilgard and Bower, 1975). Skinner (1953) and Gagne (1977) advocate instruction that is structured and hierarchical. According to Gagne (1977), once the teacher has "properly structured" the learning environment, the desired learning will occur.

The practices used by intervention programs for minorities and females are supported by the research base on effective mathematics and science instruction for all students (Clewell, 1987). Instructional arrangements promote students' responsibility and involvement in their own learning through cooperative groups. Problem-focused and activity-based learning as well as direct instructional approaches have also been shown to promote learning among minority and female students.

There is some research evidence favoring inquiry learning over traditional approaches for middle school students generally and females in particular (Linn and Thier, 1975; Lawson and Wollman, 1976; Saunders and Shepardson, 1987). The majority of studies comparing the effect of inquiry learning with that of traditional approaches in promoting knowledge of subject matter or thinking skills have been done in science. While most studies have not examined effects for students of different ethnic backgrounds, there is also some evidence supporting the positive effects of hands-on inquiry activities for middle school Black and Hispanic students (Cohen and DeAvila, 1983).

Research on cooperative goal structures has shown that they result in improvement in achievement and attitudes of diverse student populations in a variety of subject areas (Johnson and Johnson, 1987). Slavin (1985) reports positive effects in mathematics from cooperative instructional arrangements for diverse student populations.

Research studies also lend support to the use of activity-based learning, including hands-on experiences and engagement with concrete objects (Lawson and Wollman, 1976; Linn and Thier, 1975; Saunders and Shepardson, 1987). There is some evidence that more structured, direct instructional approaches may be needed for students of lower ability (Ryman, 1977).

Program Examples

A number of intervention approaches have been based on inquiry learning, which actively engages students in the learning process through their own exploration of phenomena. This instructional approach differs from traditional practice, where the teacher's role is to provide knowledge and the students' role is passively to receive "given truths," in that it requires students to construct their own knowledge through thought and action. Students explore situations (most often through the use of objects), develop their own ideas about the nature of what they are studying, and test their assumptions to confirm or refute their hypotheses.

Inquiry learning approaches differ in the degree of structure or direction that teachers provide. At one end of the continuum is discovery learning, in which the teacher serves as a facilitator. Using this strategy, teachers create an environment for learning by providing students with material and general instructions for free exploration. Students select their own problems; teachers seek to encourage and expand the students' thinking through questioning directed at the students' own avenues of investigation. This approach can be highly motivating, because students are pursuing their own questions. It also simulates problem solving in real work environments, where problems may be unstructured and individuals must develop questions and approaches to generate solutions. At the other end of the continuum, teachers take a more active role to guide student inquiry. Teachers present a specific problem to be solved and guide students' exploration of selected concepts with directive questioning that prompts students to describe and explain certain phenomena. Guided inquiry is a useful strategy to bridge traditional and free-inquiry approaches. Teacher-selected problems provide the initial direction or focus; students generate their own questions and solutions, with teacher assistance only as needed (Georgia State Department of Education, 1982).

Project SEED is an example of a more structured approach to inquiry learning. Developed in 1963 by William Johntz, a public school mathematics teacher in California, Project SEED has worked successfully with disadvantaged minority students in grades 4 through 6 to increase their classroom participation, raise their academic self-confidence, and increase their knowledge and proficiency in mathematics. The program uses algebra as a vehicle for achieving its goals. Algebra was chosen for two reasons. First, students consider it a high-status subject: you have to be smart to do algebra. Second, because students in the program have not previously studied algebra, it is not associated with a history of failure.

The approach requires a high degree of staff training. SEED specialists work with participating schools, teaching math classes two to four times a week for up to one year. The program trains mathematics specialists to teach SEED classes in grades 4 through 6 using SEED's particular instructional techniques. Regular classroom teachers are usually present during SEED instruction. They have an opportunity to learn to incorporate SEED's approaches into their own teaching through SEED demonstrations, interactions with SEED instructors, and special workshops.

SEED uses a structured inquiry approach to guide students' understanding of algebraic concepts. Lessons are taught to an entire class through a Socratic dialogue. Teachers engage

students through a series of questions that lead them to discover mathematical concepts for themselves. Teachers constantly
monitor students' responses and adjust the pace and content of
the lesson to ensure that students comprehend the problem. As
a staff member explained, "We are constantly monitoring and
getting a reading on the entire class, not only of who is participating but who is understanding. What you do is to continuously adjust the pace of your lesson to know whether you
should do another problem of a particular type or go back over
something you did yesterday or if it is time to move on to something new."

SEED also uses students' natural inclination toward physical and social activity to enhance their engagement in the learning experience and to provide instructors with necessary feedback about students' understanding. As a supplement to verbal
dialogue, students are taught to use hand signals to answer questions and to indicate whether they agree or disagree with a particular answer. SEED instructors also prompt for group responses as another means to promote interest and reinforce
students' learning. By using a variety of kinesthetic responses,
all students have an opportunity to participate actively in the
large group lesson.

Activity-based instruction focuses on using students' own
actions as a vehicle for learning. Frequently, activity-based instruction employs manipulation activities to provide concrete
means of learning new concepts. Activity-based instruction may
be used in conjunction with other approaches, depending on
instructional goals. It is used with inquiry approaches when
learning experiences are structured to promote students' own
exploration and discovery of the underlying nature of phenomena. It may also be used to reinforce learning introduced through
more directive teaching approaches.

Most intervention programs employ some form of activity-
based instruction, involving students working alone or in groups
using actions and/or objects to solve problems. The purposes
for which activity-based learning is used vary among programs.
Some programs, including Operation SMART, Family Math

(a project of the Lawrence Hall of Science), and Hands-On Science Outreach in Rockville, Maryland, use activity-based learning experiences for exploration and development of interest in science and mathematics activities. Others, such as Finding Out/Descubrimiento (a project of the Center for Educational Research at Stanford University), use activity-based formats for traditional curriculum mastery.

Operation SMART, which was developed as an after-school enrichment program for middle school girls, has created a number of curriculum modules requiring students to solve math and science problems through activities based on real-life situations. Students learn that math and science are useful for solving real-life problems and that the process of solving problems can be not only useful but fun. For example, students might be asked to figure out the most efficient route to get to a particular location by surveying the area and drawing a map illustrating their solution. Family Math, which is also an enrichment program, was developed for elementary through junior high minority students and their families to create confidence and enjoyment in mathematics learning. Using everyday materials, Family Math encourages parents and children to talk about mathematics and the difficulties of solving problems. Through the program, children gain confidence and experience in solving challenging problems. Classes begin with familiar math topics; participants are given strategies to solve problems to relieve anxieties and provide successful experiences. Hands-On Science Outreach is an after-school enrichment program serving elementary and early middle school students. Open to all students through grade 6, the program serves a large population of minority youngsters. Classes, which are held for one hour a week for eight weeks, are structured around different science topics geared to students' interests and levels of understanding. The program emphasizes process rather than products: students are not required to learn facts but are encouraged to ask questions as they conduct experiments to solve problems. Activities include learning about reflected light by experimenting with patterns held in different positions before a mirror. Saturday Science Academy helps students to learn about science. Third- through eighth-graders attend classes in science, math, and creative expressions taught by Clark Atlanta University students and professionals from the community. The youngsters express their scientific knowledge through poetry, stories, short essays, and drawings. Some of these pieces were compiled into an impressive booklet (Saturday Science Academy, 1987).

Cooperative learning approaches provide alternative social and goal structures for learning. Cooperative arrangements involve shared goals rather than the individual or competitive goal structures that are more typical of traditional educational approaches. Students assume a greater responsibility for their own learning by working together in small groups; teachers assume a facilitative rather than a directive role.

Finding Out/Descubrimiento uses cooperative goal structures along with an inquiry-based approach to successfully engage students with diverse language backgrounds, experiences, and cognitive abilities in mathematics and science learning. The program focuses on developing thinking and language skills through a series of activities that require students to communicate with each other to solve problems. Students learn basic skills, vocabulary, and concepts along with such science process skills as observation, measurement, comparison, classification, prediction, and interpretation of phenomena. Concepts are taught and reinforced through a variety of activities. Repeated exposure to the same concept through the use of different materials and topics gives students a chance to learn the concept at their own pace and level of development.

In Finding Out/Descubrimiento, students' activities are organized around multiple learning centers. In one classroom, there may be six centers with up to five students working together at each center. Each center has a theme and a corresponding set of curriculum materials — activity cards, hands-on activities, work sheets, and unit tests. The activity cards are written in English and Spanish and include pictographs that clearly structure and demonstrate the tasks to be performed. Related work sheets guide students' thinking and provide a simple recording format. The activities are intrinsically interesting, capitalizing on children's natural curiosity about how the world works and requiring manipulation of materials to solve open-ended problems. Within each group, students are clustered heterogeneously and assigned rotating roles. They take turns as setup person, takedown person, facilitator, checker, safety monitor, and recorder. Assuming these roles fosters a smooth flow of activities and a sense of shared responsibility for learning.

Because most students enter the program without previous experience in cooperative learning, the program systematically trains students how to work together. Students are taught certain norms of behavior, such as having the right to ask others for help when they do not understand what to do and having the responsibility to assist others in need. They are also taught to explain to each other what the task involves and what their results may mean. They learn to apply these norms to further their own work as well as the work of other group members: while students are responsible for their own work, they also have a shared responsibility to assist others in the group. When all members have participated actively in completing the task and the work sheet, they can move on to another learning center.

Because the groups are heterogeneous in language, ability, and knowledge, status differences within groups may arise, impeding group interaction. Teachers confront this potential problem directly by legitimizing differences. As part of students' initial training, teachers explicitly inform them that a variety of different abilities are needed to do well at a particular task and that no one person has all the necessary abilities. Good work habits (for example, persistence, careful work) and reasoning skills are accorded equal status with conventional abilities to read, write, and compute.

Teachers are also provided extensive training to assume their nontraditional role of facilitator rather than director of learning. Moving among the centers, teachers observe and interact only to promote students' cooperative work and to help students reflect on their own activity. Through questioning strategies, teachers stimulate and extend students' thinking and promote discussions within the groups. They also facilitate by providing feedback, delegating responsibility to students for their own activity, and reinforcing cooperative behaviors. Teachers work with the entire class at the beginning and end of the day to support classroom management structure and to extend concepts learned through students' activity.

Minority students have benefited from programs that use direct instruction as well as nontraditional instructional strategies. With direct instruction, the teacher determines the content objectives, pacing, and method of instructional delivery, introduces the lesson, and guides the discussion by focusing student attention on the most important features of the topic. The teacher and students demonstrate and discuss problem-solving approaches. Through discussion and directed questioning, teachers challenge students to propose solutions and defend their ideas. Teachers also provide feedback to correct misconceptions and to reinforce students' understanding of salient concepts and relationships.

Many intervention programs employ direct instruction along with several other intervention approaches. A major focus of such an approach is to teach students not only what to learn but also how to learn. Students are taught learning strategies and study skills to make their own learning more effective and efficient. As students become aware of effective learning strategies, they are also taught to evaluate and revise their use of learning strategies on the basis of their own assessments. The summer residential programs at institutions of higher learning expose students to collegelike lectures, and some of these programs give the participants credit for taking college courses.

The Connecticut Pre-Engineering Program (CPEP), which has centers in Bridgeport, Hartford, New Haven, Stamford, and Waterbury, identifies minority students in grades 6 to 12 who have an interest in and potential for college-level work in math and science and assists them in pursuing college preparatory work. CPEP offers a year-round enrichment program. Students attend after-school classes to supplement the regular school curriculum and receive directed formal instruction in mathematics and science. Saturday and summer programs are also offered and include field trips and presentations by professionals. Additionally, students are provided career and guidance counseling and tutorial sessions. Teachers participate in professional development programs designed to increase their knowledge and awareness of new technology.

A partnership between the University of California, Berkeley, and the Oakland and San Francisco school districts — the Alliance for Collaborative Change in School Systems (ACCESS) — involves university staff who provide planning, coaching, and curriculum development support to teachers and administrators at school sites. The goal of ACCESS is to promote excellence in curriculum, instruction, and standards of college preparatory math and English courses and to enhance the learning and teaching environment. University teaching assistants/mentors provide direct instruction to students in their math and English classes and in after-school work groups. The direct instruction and after-school programs help students to deepen their understanding of course work, to develop problem-solving, writing, and study skills, and to develop an awareness of college requirements.

Tutoring

Tutoring is a vehicle to provide additional academic support to students. The focus of tutoring can be remediation or enrichment — to help students to master previously presented material or to extend and provide a challenge to the information that they have already learned. Tutoring may be either a one-to-one teaching-learning situation or academic-oriented instruction in a small-group setting.

Research and Theory

Tutoring promotes learning through an exchange of ideas between the tutor and the student. Explanation and instruction require that both student and tutor examine and articulate their own thinking. These exchanges are consistent with cognitive theories of formulating and reformatting one's own knowledge within the context of social interactions (Piaget, 1970; Bruner, 1963).

There has been substantial research on peer tutoring (Allen, 1976; Strain, 1981; Bowers, 1991; Vergason and Anderegg, 1991), but relatively little attention has been given to the nature or effects of peer tutoring for minority students or females. The consensus is that the students receiving tutoring learn from their peers, and the students providing the tutorials learn from teaching other students (Gartner, Kohler, and Riessman, 1971); to give students the chance to teach is to give them an additional opportunity to learn (Scribner and Stevens, 1975).

Program Examples

Many middle school intervention programs use peer and/or adult tutoring for remediation and enrichment purposes. With peer tutoring, the tutor may be the same age as the tutored student or older; with both same-age and cross-age peer tutoring, the students receive instructional help and support from each other.

The Teacher Training in Tutoring Techniques program, offered by the Chicago public schools, combines instruction of students in mathematics problem solving with the professional development of teachers. Lead teachers are trained to develop extended-day tutoring centers where students working in small groups support each other as they work on problem-solving strategies. Such an approach helps to reduce mathematics anxiety and raise the mathematics achievement scores of the students. Exhibit 4.1 presents sample items for evaluating a tutorial session.

To assist students with deficiencies in math, science, English, or reading, and to present further challenges for advanced students, the Tomorrow's Scientists, Technicians, and Managers (TSTM) program, established by the Tri-County (Peoria) Urban League in Illinois, provides academic tutorials for students in grades K–12. Tutorial assistance is provided by TSTM members in every subject. In addition, motivational speakers and

Exhibit 4.1. Sample Items for
Observation Rating of a Tutoring Session.

	Low				High
1. Tutor was knowledgeable about subject matter.	1	2	3	4	5
2. Tutor clarified class instruction and offered alternatives.	1	2	3	4	5
3. The pace of the presentation of concepts was generally appropriate.	1	2	3	4	5
4. The methods used by the tutor were appropriate and conducive to learning.	1	2	3	4	5
5. Tutor encouraged tutee to ask questions.	1	2	3	4	5
6. Tutor displayed positive attitude toward tutee(s).	1	2	3	4	5

workshops are held once a month to encourage minority students to pursue careers in math, science, and technology.

MESA uses both peer tutoring and study groups to develop study skills and to increase achievement by helping students improve their ability to understand a wide range of mathematical and scientific concepts.

Test Preparation and Study Skills

Test preparation and study skills training encompasses a number of related approaches. One of these is teaching students strategic knowledge about learning and test taking. With this approach, students are taught strategies to organize their studying as well as strategies to use in testing situations. Another approach is to provide students with direct instruction and practice on specific skills or problem formats that are particularly difficult. By learning effective strategies and mastering skills, students are enabled to anticipate demands and to approach tests knowledgeably and with confidence.

Research and Theory

Learning theory (Skinner, 1953) and cognitive theories (Brown and Campione, 1978) lend support to test preparation strategies by suggesting the positive effects of practice on performance.

The learning strategies emphasized include strategic knowledge, task demands, practice, schema development, and automaticity.

Research shows that females tend to perform better on essay questions and males to perform better on multiple-choice questions (Harding, 1979). Extended answers allow females to develop the context in which a scientific idea is useful, rather than remembering it in isolation (Smail, 1984). These findings suggest that females need training and confidence building for dealing with questions that require recall and speed in marking one single right answer. Research on a number of different test-taking interventions has found that mathematics achievement can be improved through the use of practice problems (Bookman and Iwanicki, 1983) and training in test-taking skills (Benson, Urman, and Hocevar, 1986). Moreover, a move away from multiple-choice exercises to less structured, essay-style assessment would facilitate higher thinking processes and be more equitable for females.

Program Examples

Among the strategies for study skills and test preparation are focusing on test anxiety for minority students and math anxiety for females; helping students, particularly minority students, to brush up on their skills and knowledge in a specific subject; helping students to improve their test performance by improving their study skills and work habits; and teaching students test-taking techniques. Most programs do not seem to emphasize test preparation, though there is a need to help students in this area.

The I Love Mathematics program, conducted by the Golden Spiral Institute in Washington, D.C., was a seminar designed to alleviate math anxiety or dislike of math, to develop proficiency in performing mathematical operations, and to develop an appreciation of mathematics as the key to understanding beauty and truth. The program served students in grades 6 to 12 during after-school hours and on Saturdays. Activities included exercises in self-analysis, principles of success, anxiety management, personal discipline, memory, and developing a blueprint for excellence. The program helped participants to overcome math anxiety, gain math confidence, and build the foundation to succeed on standardized tests and in math courses of all types.

Many competition programs offer test preparation activities. Student competitions provide opportunities for sharpening skills and recognition of accomplishment. Mathcounts, a nationwide mathematics competition program offered by the National Society of Professional Engineers for seventh- and eighth-graders, demonstrates that coaching can be fun, educational, and a way to improve performance. Coaching activities include mock competitions with awards for success and developing students' problem-solving skills by asking and answering each other's questions that they have rewritten from the program's handbook. In addition to skills-building activities, the program also emphasizes the importance of self-confidence for success. An important aspect of coaching is helping students to want to be successful, to believe that they can be successful, and to develop within them the will to prepare, compete, and win.

The Mathematics Pentathlon, which is sponsored by the Pentathlon Institute in Indianapolis, Indiana, and held at various school sites, is an annual tournament of mathematical games held each spring. The events focus on active problem solving and critical thinking skills. During the months of August through December, parents and educators are oriented to the games that constitute the tournament; they then teach the games to children at home or in school and prepare and select those "athletes" who will register for tournament competition. The program also includes a mathematics clinic, which offers professional help in the assessment of learning difficulties in mathematics understanding and specialized instructional sessions.

MESA provides students with tips on study skills, including time management, reading with a purpose, exam strategies (how to study the right material for a test and how to approach tests calmly), group study, and outlining. The Pre-Engineering Summer Workshops for Women and Minorities, conducted by the College of Engineering at Arizona State University, provide a session on test-taking and study skills. Students are instructed on test-taking strategies and provided examples through a practice exercise from an actual exam (see Exhibit 4.2). Instructors demonstrate approaches for improving note-taking skills by pointing out major points of a sample lecture.

Exhibit 4.2. Test-Taking Skills — Sample Educated Guessing Quiz.

Using structural clues, answer the following questions by placing the letter in the blank provided. No penalty for guessing. Value: 1 point each question.

_____ 1. One of the kost crenuelty given reasols for bisorye is:
   a. ilcibelity   b. sevual mroxleks
   c. loss of ilterest   d. loss of yokkuliyatiol
_____ 2. Fimmocrates' tymology categorized mersols according to:
   a. xoby xuilb   b. xefasior
   c. tekmerakelts caused by xoby fukors d. loses
_____ 3. Leural ikmulses that eventually activate the ridft oxyimital lode originate in
   a. ridft eye   b. lect eye   c. ridft ear
   d. ridft side of each retila   e. lect side of each retila
_____ 4. Yokkuliyatiol loss is the major reasol for
   a. sfim   b. jat   c. bisorye   d. sfielb
_____ 5. In the kid-eidtfeeltf celtury, culbs were
   a. always selc-delerateb   b. never from endlalb
   c. usualky from xalhs   d. all from kilild

Source: Arizona State University, 1984, Appendix C.

Teacher Training

Teachers are influential in determining students' participation and performance in mathematics and science. Students who indicate a strong liking for and/or do well in these subjects frequently point to a teacher as an important influential factor. Similarly, students who express negative attitudes and opt out of future mathematics and science course work often attribute their thinking and decisions to a bad experience with a teacher.

In a variety of ways, teachers contribute to differential participation and performance in mathematics and science for minority and female students. For example, during mathematics and science instruction, teachers may give more attention to majority and male students than minority and female students, and, too often, minority and female students infer from such differential interactions that mathematics and science are more essential for males and majority students. Some teachers perceive minority and female students as less able than majority and male students to learn mathematics and science; such perceptions and expectations often result in behaviors on the part of both teachers and students that conform to gender and racial stereotypes. To combat these barriers to academic excellence in mathematics and science, intervention programs often provide workshops, seminars, or other forms of training to help teachers improve the performance of minority and female students.

Research and Theory

Since teacher behavior and attitudes strongly affect student achievement, teacher training and staff development should be emphasized in intervention programs. Guskey (1986) has developed a theory of teacher training that includes three goals: changes in teachers' behavior, enhancement of student learning, and changes in teachers' attitudes and beliefs. An important contribution of Guskey's theory is the order in which he advocates that these three components should be addressed in staff development programs. Guskey believes that such programs should focus first on changes in teachers' behavior; such changes should have a positive impact on student achievement, which in turn should produce changes in teachers' beliefs and attitudes. Irvine (1990) outlines a model of teacher training and staff development designed to improve the motivation and learning of Black students. Building on Guskey's theory, Irvine incorporates Guskey's model of teacher change into a program of staff development that involves teachers, principals, and parents.

Research has shown that important dimensions of teachers' expectations and behavior as they affect science and math achievement are the amount of material taught and the level of teacher-pupil interaction (Brophy and Good, 1974; Persell, 1977). In a study of science classrooms, Kahle and Lakes (1983) found that more opportunities were provided for boys to use science instruments and equipment than were provided for girls,

and Contreras and Lee (1990) found cultural bias in teachers'
treatment of minority students in middle school science classes.
While these studies underline the relationship between teachers'
expectations and effects of the self-fulfilling prophecy, they also
suggest a need for teacher training programs that focus on cultural rather than individual differences.

Program Examples

The format of teacher training programs ranges from school-
based in-service programs to out-of-school workshops and conferences. They may be led by a single facilitator or an instructional team, familiar or unfamiliar to the teacher participants.
They may be designed to train teachers in particular instructional strategies, to raise their awareness of gender differences
and show them how to implement classroom practices that address the needs of young females, or to help them to address
and eliminate the performance deficiencies of minority students
in mathematics and science. Instructional strategies were addressed earlier in this chapter; the remainder of this section discusses teacher training programs that focus on gender differences and racial and cultural diversity.

　　　The Multiplying Options and Subtracting Bias program
holds two-hour workshops designed to help teachers to improve
females' peceptions and participation in mathematics. Workshop facilitators elicit teachers' responses to questions such as
"How do you respond to a female who is having difficulty with
mathematics?" "Under what circumstances would you encourage
or discourage girls who want to quit taking mathematics?" and
"Would the circumstances be similar or different for boys?" The
workshops also use dramatic vignettes to examine the subtle ways
in which teachers treat females differently from males. In one
such vignette, when a female student becomes frustrated and
teary-eyed after struggling with a math problem, the teacher
intervenes, telling the student that she does not have to complete the problem and moving on to help other students. Workshop participants discuss what messages are conveyed by the
vignettes and suggest alternative ways of handling the situations.

Girl-Friendly Science (Smail, 1984) offers guidelines for increasing female participation in the laboratory or classroom by organizing the curriculum to fit females' interests. The book offers suggestions such as the following:

- Organize practical work in mixed groups, not by gender.
- Choose females by name to help with a demonstration.
- Praise females for good ideas as well as neat work.
- Address females' wrong answers and difficulties. Help them to work through problems and encourage them to admit that they do not understand something in a small-group setting rather than in front of the whole class. Also, do not ask a male who understands something to help a female who does not.
- Encourage females to think things out for themselves. Be supportive but do not do it for them.
- Set experiments in context by providing background information about the possible uses and applications of scientific principles in everyday life.
- Link the study of physical science concepts to the human body.
- Use imaginative writing to facilitate the assimilation of scientific principles and ideas.

Project BASE (Blacks for Academic Success in Education) grew out of a desire by the superintendent of the Duval County, Florida, public schools to increase the achievement of minority students to the point where students' test scores could not be predicted by the color of their skin. A team of professionals, inspired and challenged by the goal, planned and implemented the project. The teacher training phase of Project BASE, known as "Making a Difference," has two objectives: (1) to increase teachers' feelings of efficacy — their belief that they have the capacity to affect student performance — which will in turn increase the achievement of their students, and (2) to raise teachers' levels of expectation for the performance of minority students. Components of the teacher training phase include efficacy and expectations, facilitative teaching, and instructional delivery.

The efficacy and expectations component emphasizes that teachers can and do make a difference in the achievement of their students. Teachers with a high sense of efficacy are more likely to be attentive to the individual needs of students and to respond to students in a positive, accepting, and supporting way. Promotion of student achievement also requires that teachers believe in their students' ability to master information, earn good grades, complete school, and go on to institutions of higher education. Minority students will greatly benefit from favorable teacher expectations.

The component on facilitative teaching gives attention to an empowering atmosphere for growth, one in which students are certain of acceptance. Teacher behaviors addressed include helping students feel that they are accepted and respected and eliciting higher-level responses from students. Training includes asking person-centered questions and using response techniques such as clarifying, summarizing, and reflecting feeling. Active listening is emphasized. The Operation SMART Training Guide suggests strategies for asking effective questions (see Exhibit 4.3).

The instructional delivery component focuses on teacher competencies effective in promoting academic achievement for minority students. Among the teaching behaviors that are developed, refined, and observed are positive reinforcement patterns: asking students to extend answers or elaborate on ideas; asking questions that lead students to analyze, synthesize, and think critically; seeking and using student ideas as part of the teaching procedure; nurturing students' creativity and discovery; and encouraging active student participation.

Mathematics, Science, and Minorities, K–6 is a two-year, team-based staff development program. In the first year, the focus was on the factors that contribute to the underachievement of Black and Hispanic students in mathematics and science education and the personal, social, economic, and political ramifications of that underachievement. Skills development was one of the primary activities for the second year. The goal was to increase demonstrated skill in teaching behaviors that affect the performance of minority students in mathematics and science in the areas of persistence, academic deficiencies, teacher anxiety,

Exhibit 4.3. How Should I Ask Girls Questions?

The skill of appropriate questioning takes time to master. The best questions raise other questions and stimulate discussion. They lead neither to praise nor blame, nor do they interrupt the child's flow of experience.

The following kinds of questions and comments are helpful:

"What do you think about that?"
"How do you feel about that, Susan?" (To one girl after another has made a comment)
"What if we . . . ?"
"I wonder what else would be fun to do . . ."

The following kinds of questions should be avoided:

"What do you know about . . . ?" (Such questions can make less experienced girls feel like failures at the start)
A question that requires only a "yes" or "no" answer
A question that relies on prior knowledge
Any question that interrupts girls' conversation

Remember that there's a vast difference between girls asking themselves and each other questions as they work — "I wonder what would happen if . . ." — and the adult authority asking, "Why does this work?" Keep in mind that many girls have already experienced discouragement and failure in science and math and are sensitive to being thought stupid.

As you practice asking better questions, be sensitive to the children's reactions and don't be surprised if you are occasionally ignored. That's the best sign that they are so involved with the activity that your question seems beside the point.

> Asking open-ended questions that lead to inquiry, but do not require the child to put out a "right answer," is very difficult to do. In one instance, a seven-year-old girl tried out the stream bottles and was very excited by the way that the water flowed from the bottle. Sarah ran over to the adult facilitator, shouting, "Look! Look! Look! at the way the water's coming out!"
>
> The teacher, because she'd been taught to ask questions, said, "Why do you think that happens?"
>
> Sarah stopped dead in her tracks. She couldn't articulate the answer and therefore didn't say a word.
>
> Another girl came over and talked about the water being displaced by air. The teacher supplemented the girl's answer for Sarah. Very soon after that, Sarah left the stream bottles station to pursue something else.
>
> —Operation SMART Trainer

Source: Excerpted from Girls Incorporated. *Seeds for Growth: Operation SMART Training Guide,* pp. 65–66, 1992.

and learning styles. Among the teaching behaviors emphasized were:

- Diagnosing strengths of target students and checking perceptions of deficiencies using a variety of assessment modes
- Identifying learning-style preferences and providing instruction responsive to these preferences
- Using peer tutoring
- Establishing groups for instruction that are not based on skill levels
- Relating content to out-of-school applications and providing real-life experiences
- Providing for a variety of challenging concrete and abstract teaching modes
- Teaching problem-solving skills
- Including role models in instruction
- Providing noncompetitive and cooperative learning options
- Assisting students with short- and long-term goal setting
- Providing opportunities to learn from and cope with failure and success and increasing students' skills in taking responsibility for outcomes of their own behavior
- Including a minimum of three to five hands-on activities for each instructional unit
- Using affective and higher-order cognitive activities and having integrated, interdisciplinary lessons
- Having high expectations for student achievement in mathematics and science (allowing sufficient wait time for student responses, using praise, providing challenges and encouraging independence, eliciting student responses in a variety of ways, discussing wrong answers, and so on)

Parental Involvement

There has recently been an increased interest in the social influences that affect students' participation and achievement in mathematics and science. The family is one of the societal forces that are influential in the learning process: parents who value and have confidence in their children's ability to do well in math and science have a positive influence on their children's attitudes and performance.

Research and Theory

Parents can help their children to improve their performance by acting as teachers, role models, and support people (Clewell, Anderson, and Thorpe, 1988; Parsons, Adler, and Kaczala, 1982). Developmental psychology (Hurlock, 1972; Myers, 1986) emphasizes the significant role of parents in helping their children to develop cognitively and socially. Parental presence and participation ensure a culturally consistent social and academic program for students (Comer, 1984). Additionally, theoretical constructs of home-school relationships hold parental involvement to be integral to the development of sound educational programs for children (Laosa, 1983).

Several research studies lend support to the idea of involving parents in skills development and enrichment intervention programs. Researchers such as Clark (1985), Prillwitz (1983), and Thomas (1986) report that parental encouragement and support are important to participation in mathematics and science. Correlational research has indicated a positive relationship between parental encouragement (Armstrong, 1980) and parental expectations (Parsons, Adler, and Kaczala, 1982) and young females' interest and achievement in mathematics. On the other hand, a lack of significant others, especially parents, who have an interest in math and science or see their relevance in everyday life as well as for students' future careers and lack of direct encouragement from parents have been cited as reasons for the underachievement of minority and female students in these disciplines (Beane, 1985; Clewell and Anderson, 1991; Olstad, Juarez, Davenport, and Haury, 1981).

Program Examples

Parents' expectations and support are a major consideration in most skills development and enrichment programs. Such programs have found that it is important to involve parents early in the program and to maintain positive relationships throughout the period of student participation. Intervention programs use several approaches to promote this type of parental involvement. Initial contact is often through program literature describing the objectives and activities of the program. Parents are invited to orientation meetings. Some programs ask parents to sign a contract stipulating student requirements and pledging to support and actively encourage full participation. Through regular mailings or conferences with program staff, parents may receive information about their children's progress and program activities. They may also be invited to attend the program's year-end awards ceremony and are asked about their perceptions of changes in their children's attitude toward and performance in the academic subjects.

Most programs welcome parent volunteers to share their experiences with students, to plan social events, and to chaperon student activities. A few programs use parents who are employed in math and science fields to stimulate students' participation in these areas. For example, MESA encourages parents and guardians to talk about their math-based careers with MESA students at different schools. MESA considers family involvement a critical part of the support network. Family members promote student achievement by encouraging the students in their studies and by working with other parents to help with such activities as study groups, field trips, and social events. One important task of the parents is to reinforce MESA requirements that students attend regular tutoring and study group sessions and that students study a sufficient number of hours each day (see Exhibit 4.4).

Parents of students in the Operation SMART program chaperon field trips. Several programs extend parental involvement to include communitywide participation. For example, a key component of the Denver Educational Excellence Program (DEEP) of the Denver public school system is the involvement of role models from the business community, who provide students with a clear understanding of the role of a professional through demonstrations and shadow experiences. The program is designed to assist students in attaining skills necessary to be successful candidates for scientific fields.

Exhibit 4.4. MESA Parent's Assessment.

Irene Cox says she believes MESA made a difference by opening new avenues for her children to explore and by backing her up in her role as a parent. "I went along on some of MESA's activities," she recalls, "and I could see that it was giving my kids more self-confidence and helping them work on their own, independently. So in that way it helped me to just be there when they needed me, and just try to spread the love as far as I could spread it. With MESA, I knew I wasn't the only voice telling my children they could make it. And for them, being able to achieve those grades and earning the extra money from incentive awards really made them feel good about themselves. They felt they were not only learning, but helping out to support themselves at home."

Source: "More Than Getting By . . . ," 1982, p. 4.

Some programs also provide instructional training to enable parents to assist their children in learning math concepts. For example, Family Math consists of six sequential workshops aimed at demystifying mathematics for parents and students. Parents and students work together to develop problem-solving skills. The emphasis is a hands-on approach to mathematics to enable students to see the applicability of math to daily life. The goal is to create a positive learning environment where parents and children can work together on various math-related activities designed to include and supplement the school curriculum. This grass-roots approach to teaching and learning math has been found to be an enriching and fun experience for both parents and students.

PART THREE

Intervention Models

While Parts One and Two of this book have focused on the need for and appropriateness of intervention during the middle school years and specific approaches and strategies that have proved successful in increasing the participation of female and minority students in mathematics and science, the next two parts concentrate on delivery systems for these strategies and approaches; that is, how programs are structured and operate to most effectively deliver the benefits of successful approaches to the target population. Although the focus is on programs, much of the information can be applied to the regular classroom setting.

Part Three develops a conceptual framework for viewing programs, describes a program model, and discusses key elements and the ways in which they interact to produce a successful program. This part also considers contextual elements — elements that are not part of the program itself but that affect it — and their effect on program success. Chapter Five presents a conceptual framework for viewing programs and gives a detailed description of the key components of an effective program — goals, design, and content. Chapter Six discusses program outcomes and contextual elements.

5

Conceptualizing Programs:
A Systems Approach

Although the programs described in the previous chapters vary in terms of characteristics such as target population, size, subject matter, duration, and approaches used, they also have many similarities in terms of structure, components, and process. By focusing on the similarities, we have been able to develop a single conceptual framework that is representative of all the intervention programs that we have examined and that provides a mechanism for understanding effective programs and how they work. This framework, which is illustrated in Figure 5.1, is a systems approach. The systems approach emphasizes the interrelationship and interdependence of elements necessary for achieving a goal or goals as well as the relationship between the system and its environment (Schoderbek, Schoderbek, and Kefalas, 1985).

A description using the systems approach is useful because it captures not only individual components of a program, such as program format or administrative structure, but also the relationships of these components to one another, describing how they work together to produce program outcomes. Another important benefit of this approach is that it considers not only how the system interacts with its own components but also how it interacts with other systems within its setting, thus giving a more holistic picture of the processes that contribute to a program's success or failure.

Figure 5.1. Conceptual Framework for Intervention Programs.

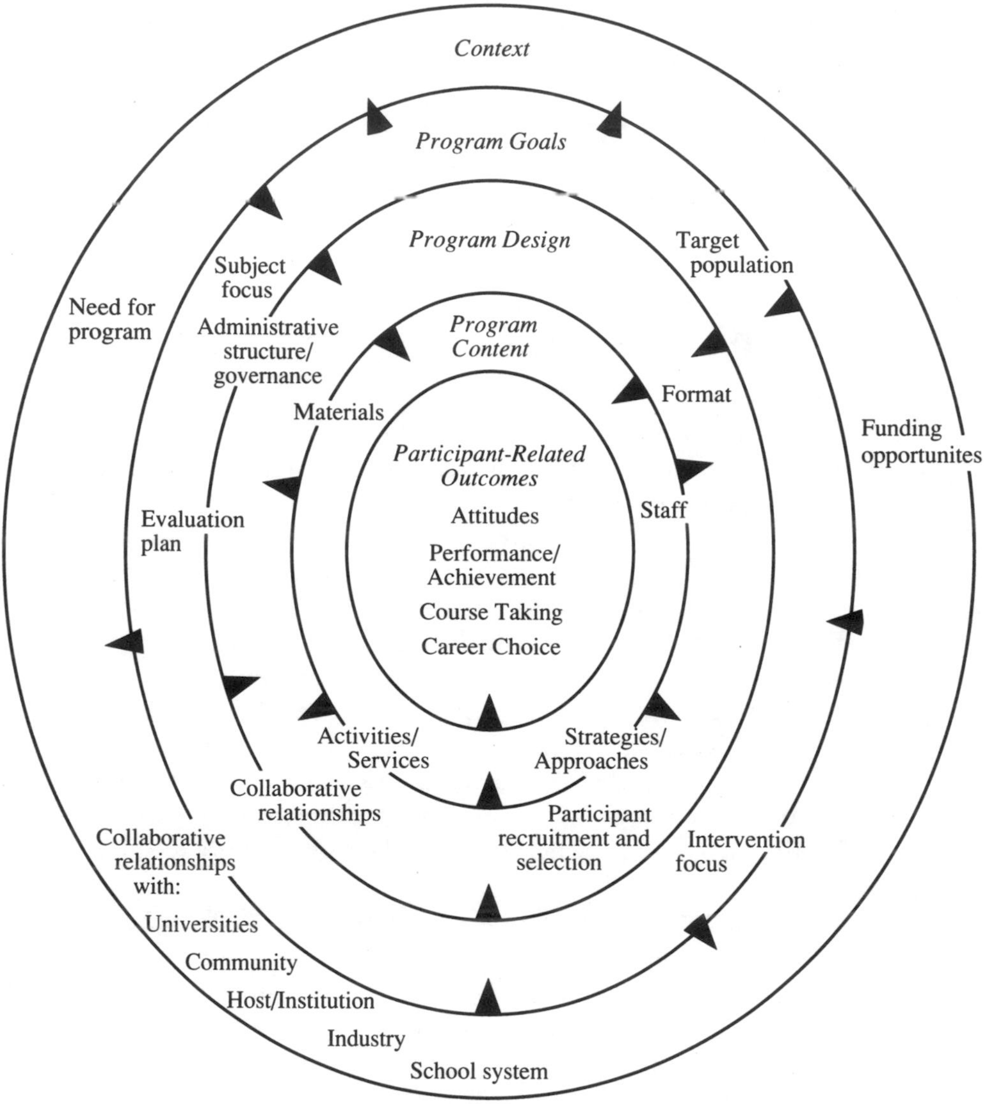

Context

Program Goals

Program Design

Target
population

Subject
focus

Need for
program

Administrative
structure/
governance

Program
Content

Materials

Format

Funding
opportunites

Participant-Related
Outcomes

Attitudes

Evaluation
plan

Staff

Performance/
Achievement

Course Taking

Career Choice

Activities/
Services

Strategies/
Approaches

Collaborative
relationships

Participant
recruitment and
selection

Collaborative
relationships
with:

Intervention
focus

Universities

Community

Host/Institution

Industry

School system

The basic elements of our framework are program goals,
program design, program content, program outcomes, and program context. Program goals drive the design of the program,

because they determine program characteristics (such as target population and subject focus) that define the service delivery system or structure. Program content includes components such as curriculum, materials, instructors, and activities that are delivered to the participants via the service delivery system. Program design and content interact to produce the desired outcomes of a program, which may include changes in attitude or course-taking behavior, improvement in performance or achievement, or choice of a math- or science-related career. The context of a program includes elements that are outside the program but affect it and interact with it. Contextual elements may include the problem that generated the need for the intervention, a program's relationship with its setting, efforts to disseminate or replicate the program, and efforts to institutionalize it.

Key Program Components

This section provides a detailed general description of each of the first three key program components: goals, design, and content. The following section offers examples of these program components as they are embodied in actual programs. (Program outcomes and context are discussed in Chapter Six.)

Program Goals

Programs develop goals to respond to a problem (such as low participation of minority citizens in math and science) and determine the focus, design, scope, and evaluation of the program. For example, a program with a goal of encouraging participants to enroll in advanced math courses in high school will differ in many respects from a program directed at increasing participants' awareness of career opportunities in engineering. Program goals drive the evaluation design and determine many of the other characteristics of a program, such as subject focus, target population (minority versus female students), level (elementary, secondary, and postsecondary) of student served, and intervention focus.

Evaluation consists of measures of effectiveness in meeting

goals. For programs with multiple objectives that contribute to the attainment of an overall goal, each of the objectives can be evaluated. For example, for a program whose overall goal is increasing minority students' participation and performance in mathematics and science through the development of school-based teams, specific project objectives may focus on increasing teachers' content knowledge in these subjects and providing professional development for principals, teachers, counselors, and education specialists. An additional consideration that may affect the program goal is the question of funding: what particular aspect of the problem is the focus of the funding agency?

Program Design

The program design defines the framework within which the program operates. It includes elements such as the format — whether it is held in or during school, after school, on Saturdays, during the summer, or all or some of these; the administrative and governance structure — where the program is located, who has responsibility for monitoring it, whether it has collaborative relationships with other institutions, or whether it operates within a larger framework; duration of program services; what kind of recruitment and selection procedures the program uses; and activities and services offered.

Format. Programs use a wide range of formats, and some combine two or more formats. A program may, for example, offer both in-school and after-school activities as well as a Saturday session and a summer camp.

Recruitment and Selection Procedures. Programs can determine who will participate by the way they recruit and select students. For example, a program that confines its recruitment activities to wealthy, suburban public schools or private schools is likely to recruit a very different type of student than one that recruits in inner-city school systems. One of the accusations leveled at successful programs is that they enroll only the most able students. This practice, known as "creaming," can ensure successful outcomes but does little to expand the pool of potential math and science professionals.

Administrative Structure: Governance and Collaboration. Most programs have some kind of collaborative agreement with other institutions. In some cases, the programs are located within a university or school and have cost-sharing agreements with these institutions. Such agreements encourage a sense of ownership of the program. Most programs have directors who are responsible for monitoring and overseeing program activities. Programs often have advisory boards made up of representatives from industry, higher education, the community, the school district, and so on. These boards usually act in an advisory capacity and help to make policy decisions.

Program Content

Program content consists of the program staff and what the program delivers to the participants — the activities and services offered and the approaches and strategies (including materials) used.

Training. The characteristics and skills of program staff are important to the success of a program. In addition to choosing staff who are sensitive, caring, and competent, many programs offer specialized training for staff, especially instructors. In addition to introducing staff members to program goals and approaches, this training encourages certain behaviors in instructors that have been found to improve teaching, such as having high expectations of students, using hands-on techniques in teaching science, and giving feedback and encouragement. (A discussion of teacher training approaches appears in Chapter Four.)

Activities and Services. Although almost all programs offer academic activities to improve achievement and performance in math and science, not all have activities to awaken students' interest in math or science careers. Activities to enhance achievement include the development of curricula and materials that are effective with target populations, use of innovative teaching and classroom management techniques, and other aids to direct instruction in mathematics and science. Activities to awaken students' interest in math or science careers include exposure to role models, dissemination of career information, internships, field trips, and job shadowing. Activities to encourage enrollment in higher-level math courses and to provide tutoring services and academic counseling also help to prepare students for math and science careers.

Approaches and Strategies. The effectiveness of approaches and strategies depends on a knowledge of the target population and on the application of theoretically sound practices. Strategies that focus on encouraging positive attitudes toward math and science and increasing participants' awareness of careers in these fields include role modeling and career awareness activities, exposure of students to out-of-school science and math activities, and provision of a supportive environment within the program, in school, and at home. Strategies for improving participants' achievement and performance include instructional and tutoring approaches, test preparation, influencing teacher behaviors, providing a positive classroom environment, and providing a positive family and home environment. (Detailed descriptions of activities, approaches, and strategies are provided in Chapters Three and Four.)

Goals, Design, and Content in the Case Study Programs

From the 163 intervention programs in the three-year study that led to this book, 10 programs were selected for in-depth analysis in order to arrive at some conclusions regarding the characteristics of effective programs. The following criteria were used in selecting the programs: they had demonstrated their effectiveness; they had been in existence for at least three years; and they were located in an urban setting. Programs were identified as being effective if they had clearly articulated goals and evidence of having fulfilled those goals. The three-year requirement allowed us to look at programs that had overcome the initial glitches in implementation and were running smoothly. The initial study of the 163 intervention programs focused on urban programs because of the concentration of minority students in urban areas and because national studies of student achievement have suggested that students in urban areas of the country have lower achievement levels than their suburban and rural counterparts.

In selecting programs, we also took care to include a wide range of program types, as well as programs targeted at different groups and with different subject focuses. Geographical distribution of the programs was also taken into account. Programs that were primarily contests, conferences, or workshops were not considered. Because of the timing of the site visits, programs that provided only summer sessions were also eliminated from consideration.

Given the large number of excellent intervention programs included in the initial 163, it was very difficult to arrive at our final selection. Twenty programs were originally selected for site visits, and from this number, 10 were chosen to provide a broad range of delivery models. Because numerous factors had to be taken into account in selecting the final 10 programs, we would like to make it clear that these programs do not by any means represent the 10 most effective intervention programs from among the 163 in the original study. They are, in fact, part of a group of effective programs and have been chosen because they meet the selection criteria and represent a wide range of program types and/or are located in certain geographical regions. Table 5.1 lists for each program its location, subject matter focus, and target population served.

An analysis was conducted across programs for each component of the conceptual framework to determine similarities or dissimilarities among them. The remainder of this section describes these components and looks across programs to identify common as well as divergent characteristics and practices. This approach will enable us to identify common elements or patterns of elements in programs that have proved effective.

Program Goals

The case study programs all have clear, well-articulated goals that are reflected in the evaluation design. These goals divide the programs into two groups: those that focus on increasing the math and science skills of participants ("skills development

Table 5.1. Intervention Program Characteristics.

Program Name	Location	Format	Subject Matter	Target Groups		Ethnicity/ Race	Grade Levels
				Minorities	Females		
Detroit Area Pre-College Program (DAPCEP)	Detroit, Michigan	Year-round program, in and after school, Saturday, summer	Math, science, and computer science	●		Black and Hispanic	7–12
Family Math Program	Berkeley, California	Workshop series	Math	●	●	White, Black, Hispanic, and Native American	K–8
Finding Out/Descubrimiento	Stanford, California	In-school program	Math and science	●	●	Black and Hispanic	2–5
Mathematics, Science, and Minorities, K–6	Washington, D.C.	In-school program	Math and science	●		Black and Hispanic	K–6
Mathematics, Engineering, Science Achievement (MESA)	Berkeley, California	Year-round program, in and after school, Saturday, summer	Math and science	●		Black and Hispanic	7–12

Program	Location	Schedule	Subject			Ethnicity	Grades
Operation SMART (Science, Math, and Relevant Technology)	New York City	Year-round program, in and after school, Saturday, summer	Math, science, and computer science	•	•	Black and Hispanic	1-8
Project Interface (PI)	Oakland, California	Year-round program, after school and summer	Math, science, and computer science	•		Black and Hispanic	7-9
Project MiCRO (Minority Computer Resource Opportunity)	Atlanta, Georgia	In and after school	Math, science, and computer science	•	•	Black and Hispanic	6-8
Project SEED (Special Elementary Education for the Disadvantaged)	Berkeley, California	Year-round program, in and after school and summer	Math	•		Black and Hispanic	4-6
Saturday Science Academy	Atlanta, Georgia	Saturday program	Math, science, and computer science	•		Black and Hispanic	3-8

programs") and those that focus on increasing the participation
of females and minorities in math and science careers ("career
choice programs"). A subset of this latter category contains programs that have as a specific goal the enrollment of minorities
and females in higher-level math courses. The characteristics
of programs by goal type can be summarized as follows:

Skills Development	*Career Choice*
Focus on increasing math and science skills of participants	Focus on increasing the participation of females and minorities in math and science careers
	May focus on enrolling minorities and women in higher-level math courses
Serve younger children	Serve junior high and older students
Focus on improving performance	Focus on career awareness, enrollment in higher-level courses, and performance improvement
Measure success by improvement of participants' performance	In addition to measuring changes in attitude and performance, track students

Family Math, Finding Out/Descubrimiento, Operation
SMART, Project MiCRO, and Project SEED are skills development programs. These programs tend to serve younger children, focus on improving performance and achievement, and
measure their success in terms of whether there is an increase
in their participants' performance. The career choice programs
in our sample include DAPCEP, Mathematics, Science, and
Minorities, K–6, MESA Junior High, Project Interface, and
the Saturday Science Academy. Characteristics shared by these
programs include a target population of junior high and older
students, a focus on career awareness activities and enrollment
of participants in higher-level math courses, performance im-

provement, and some type of tracking of students beyond their participation in the program as part of the evaluation design.

Program Design

Elements of the program design as they are illustrated in the case-study programs are described below. With one exception, the design of our case-study programs did not seem to differ according to whether they had skills development or career choice goals.

Format. Seven of the programs utilize more than one format, and five have year-round activities. Programs with in-school or during-school formats tend to be skills development programs. DAPCEP, for example, combines both in-school and after-school formats and offers a Saturday session as well as a summer camp. Both MESA and Operation SMART also provide year-round activities, including after-school programs, Saturday sessions, summer camps, and workshops or conferences.

Recruitment and Selection Procedures. None of the case-study programs can be accused of "creaming"—that is, selecting only those students who are most likely to succeed. Programs such as Family Math, Finding Out/Descubrimiento, Mathematics, Science, and Minorities, K-6, Project MiCRO, and Project SEED work in regular classrooms with students in the general school population. Of these, all except for Family Math operate in schools with high minority enrollments. Although DAPCEP, MESA, and the Saturday Science Academy at Clark Atlanta University cannot always accept all the students who apply, they do not base selection on grade point average (GPA) or test scores but have developed guidelines for selecting students for whom participation can be most helpful—those with middle-range GPAs and test scores. In all cases where quantitative criteria are used in selecting students, these are combined with qualitative criteria. In describing the program's recruitment focus, one of the MESA staff members said that the target population is students who are "mid-track" (scoring at about the fiftieth percentile on the Comprehensive Test of Basic Skills). "We didn't want to work only with students in the ninetieth percentile," he said. All those who work with the case-study programs understand that by working with students who are not at the top of their classes (rather than those who would succeed whether or not they participated in an intervention program), they are expanding the pool of potential math and science professionals.

Administrative Structure: Governance and Collaboration. All the programs have some kind of collaborative agreement with another institution. Programs such as DAPCEP and MESA have collaborative arrangements with as many as four institutions, representing industry, school systems, universities, and the community. The universities and schools with which DAPCEP and MESA collaborate have made cost-sharing agreements, which encourage a sense of "ownership" of the programs on the part of the institutions. All but one of the programs have a collaborative arrangement with schools or school districts. Also, a majority of the programs (seven) are located at school sites, with half holding sessions during school hours. Each of the programs has a program director who is responsible for monitoring and overseeing program activities, and eight have advisory boards. Seven are part of a larger entity, such as a center or a national office, and six are located at universities.

The high level of collaborative efforts may indicate that these programs have a great deal of support and that they are highly integrated into their environment. The location of many programs at school sites may be a sign of these programs' desire to have their approaches and strategies adopted in the classroom. Some programs, such as Mathematics, Science, and Minorities, K–6, Finding Out/Descubrimiento, and Project MiCRO, have been designed for implementation in the classroom and include a plan to involve and train school personnel from the very beginning of the project.

The prevalence of advisory boards made up of representatives from industry, higher education, the community, the school district, and so on may be another sign of the support and integration that the programs enjoy as well as a strategy for ensuring institutionalization. For example, DAPCEP's eighteen-member board of directors includes six representatives from corporations, six from universities, three from the Detroit public schools, and three parents. The board thus includes representation (and support) from all sectors of society with which the program is involved.

Duration of Services. With the exception of one program, the Saturday Science Academy at Clark Atlanta University, the career choice programs provide longer-term services to students, with MESA providing the greatest continuity into the undergraduate years. (The Saturday Science Academy is part of the Atlanta Resource Center, which has programs for students from elementary through graduate school.) This is logical, since an interest in a career must be sustained over a period of years — well into high school — in order to result in a career choice.

Program Content

The activities, services, and training offered by the case-study programs are described below.

Training. All programs offer specialized training (as described in Chapter Four) for teachers. In addition to introducing staff to program goals and approaches, this training encourages certain behaviors in teachers that have been found to improve instruction. Some programs, such as Finding Out/Descubrimiento, Family Math, Project SEED, Project MiCRO, and Operation SMART, have developed well-defined, replicable training programs for teachers (and other staff and parents). Training focuses less on instructional content than on technique and approach. The introduction of all teachers, other staff, and parents to the objectives of the programs and program approaches is considered vital to the effectiveness of the intervention effort. Exhibits 5.1 and 5.2 describe the training provided to instructors by Project MiCRO and Project SEED, respectively.

Activities and Services. Skills development and career choice programs differ in the focus of activities offered. The former focus on increasing students' knowledge, competence, and skills in math, science, and problem solving. These programs stress the development of techniques and curriculum materials for more effective teaching of these subjects. Project SEED, Finding Out/Descubrimiento, Family Math, Operation SMART, and Project MiCRO have placed a great deal of emphasis on

Exhibit 5.1. Instructor Training in Project MiCRO.

All teachers in participating Project MiCRO schools receive training in computer use and applications in their subject areas. The first year, just before the start of the school year, the entire instructional staff as well as the principal received a three- to five-day preservice training session. In addition to articulating the goals and expectations of Project MiCRO, the training emphasized integration of math, language arts, social studies, and science curriculum objectives into word processing, data-base management, spreadsheet, and simulation activities. Teachers were also instructed in how to make software specifically relevant to the experiences of their students and in the classroom management techniques required to achieve the greatest amount of time-on-task. On-site assistance was provided to teachers during the school year, with each teacher receiving individualized attention three to five days per month.

A "master team" of several teachers and the principal of each of the schools will gradually begin to assume responsibility for training. They will work with new teachers, monitor the quality of the project, assess staff development needs, and provide in-service training.

At present, both preservice and in-service training at each site is conducted by a project trainer, who has expertise in computers and teaching and who adapts strategies to the teachers' particular needs. The site trainer also makes classroom observations and demonstrations, assists teachers in adapting software to their students' needs, and facilitates an effective classroom management system for microcomputer use. Training of teachers for the analytical thinking skills courses has been conducted by the project director. Principals, parent coordinators, one or two teachers, and on-site trainers at each school attended a three-day workshop during the second year of the project. This training has been followed up by site visits by the project director to provide technical assistance to the teachers. During the third year of the project, the site trainer has spent less time on site. The trainers' primary responsibilities during the last year will be to serve as a resource to the master team and provide quality control for the project.

---

the development of curriculum materials, innovative teaching and classroom management techniques, teacher training materials, and other aids to direct instruction of mathematics and science. Exhibit 5.3 describes the classroom implementation model developed by Finding Out/Descubrimiento.

The career choice programs emphasize activities to awaken interest and encourage positive attitudes toward math and science in addition to activities to improve performance. Three of the career choice programs in the sample encourage enrollment in higher-level math courses and offer tutoring services and academic counseling as well. The services and activities

Exhibit 5.2. Instructor Training in Project SEED.

Project SEED instructors must complete a multidimensional training program that builds on their strong background in mathematics. Training focuses on both SEED techniques and how to present advanced mathematical concepts Socratically.

Each applicant must successfully complete an unpaid two-week training and screening program before being hired as a probationary instructor in the program. The training program includes workshops on SEED philosophy, curriculum, and methodology; observation of experienced specialists; study of written guidelines; practice lessons with other SEED staff; and, eventually, teaching parts of lessons with students under the supervision of an experienced SEED specialist. When specialists are able to plan and teach full lessons, they are assigned classes and gradually build to a full teaching load. Although this initial training period lasts approximately three to five months, specialists continue an ongoing training process that lasts throughout their SEED careers.

Project SEED's ongoing staff development program has several facets designed to maintain a high level of success in the classroom. Several times each week, specialists attend workshops in advanced mathematics, Project SEED curriculum, methodology, classroom psychology, and related topics. Observation is another important component of the program. Project SEED is a self-evaluating program, in that specialists at all levels of experience are required to observe and critique each other on a weekly basis. Observers not only provide feedback to the specialists whom they are observing but also gain ideas for their own classes as well, ensuring a high level of quality throughout the program.

provided by the MESA Junior High Program involve parents and include the exposure of middle school students to a university campus and facilities during the academic year and in the summer (see Exhibit 5.4).

Approaches and Strategies. Tables 5.2 and 5.3 show the approaches and strategies used by the case-study programs. (The research and theoretical bases of these approaches are discussed in Chapters Three and Four.) The programs seem to differ somewhat in the emphasis that they place on attitude and career choice strategies such as role modeling and career awareness activities, with career choice programs such as DAPCEP, MESA, Project Interface, and the Saturday Science Academy offering the widest range of these activities. Particularly creative approaches to encouraging positive attitudes and increasing career awareness are DAPCEP's development of video materials featuring peer role models and involvement of students in the Detroit Science Fair (see Exhibit 5.5).

Exhibit 5.3. Classroom Implementation Model
of Finding Out/Descubrimiento.

Elements of the classroom implementation model include the curriculum and materials and the instructional approach called "complex instruction." The curriculum was developed with a Piagetian theoretical framework and is different from other experiential science curricula in that the activities apply science and mathematics to everyday life using problems and materials that are common to most children regardless of language or culture; the instructions and work sheets are presented in Spanish, English, and pictographs; and the purpose of the activities is to enrich the repertoire of each child regardless of developmental level.

The curriculum provides a set of math and science activities for children in grades 2 through 5. Materials include illustrated activity cards with instructions for the task, work sheets to be completed individually by each student, and manipulatives [for hands-on activities]. These activities require individual questioning and experimentation and incorporate many of the characteristics of pure discovery. Learning how to learn, the development of a questioning attitude, and logical thought are emphasized throughout the activities. Children explore and experiment with intrinsically interesting materials and phenomena, and each child takes from an activity what is appropriate to his or her particular stage of development. Multiple learning centers that represent the same basic concept provide the children with several opportunities to grasp a concept, while giving them practice in transferring the concept from one application to another.

While the activities emphasize how children think through a given problem, they also provide children with skills necessary for academic progress. These include making correspondence, sorting, ordering, measuring with and without numbers, using the metric system, comparing, estimating, predicting, making inferences and testing hypotheses, using arithmetic symbols and operations, and understanding relationships. At the same time, language development takes place as students learn new terminology, read directions, and report their results.

The instructional approach, "complex instruction," is the vehicle through which the curriculum is delivered. In addition to the curriculum, this approach encompasses an authority structure with unusual features, a classroom management system, and a nontraditional role for the teacher.

Another innovative approach is the Saturday Science Academy's use of drama and writing to introduce students to role models in science and mathematics as well as to role play their involvement in these subjects. The skills development programs also employ strategies to change attitudes, but these usually take the form of out-of-school experiences and the provision of a supportive environment. None of the programs offers the opportunity for adult mentorship, perhaps because this has been assumed to be more appropriate for high school than for middle school students. Project Interface does provide mentor-

Exhibit 5.4. MESA Junior High Program.

The MESA junior high program provides academic tutoring and study groups, academic counseling, field trips, career awareness activities, role models, science projects, competitions, and parent activities. Many junior high programs offer a summer enrichment program as well.

Study assistance takes place three hours a week after school at the school site. Tutoring is provided by undergraduate students who are math and science majors as well as by peer tutors. During these sessions, students work in a group on projects in math or science. About every six weeks during the school year, students visit the university campus on a Saturday to work on special projects and to use university facilities. The Berkeley program, for example, uses the Lawrence Hall of Science facilities frequently during these Saturday sessions.

Parental involvement is an important component of the junior high programs. There are monthly parent meetings, usually held right after the grading period. The Berkeley program uses these meetings to present awards such as calculators or trips to the theater to students who make the honor roll. Parents talk about their concerns at these meetings, and sometimes professionals, such as adolescent psychologists, give presentations. The Berkeley program also holds a Family Math course at each participating school at least once during the year.

During the summer, the Berkeley program has a prefreshman engineering program sponsored by the U.S. Department of Energy for seventh- to ninth-graders. The program runs for six weeks, during which time the students live on campus and participate in career awareness activities and math classes and work on projects.

Most MESA centers offer activities during the summer, although these vary from center to center. Summer enrichment programs typically last from five to six weeks and consist of skills-building activities (regular classroom-type courses), cultural enrichment (such as art or humanities classes or attending a play), and preengineering activities (such as laboratory research, special expeditions, or research and design competitions).

---

ship opportunities with junior college students serving as mentors to the younger students in the group.

Every program has a component that addresses the improvement of participants' performance. Specific strategies for improvement in achievement and performance include instructional and tutoring approaches, test preparation, modification of teacher behaviors, provision of a positive classroom environment, and provision of a positive family and home environment (see Table 5.3). (As with the strategies to influence attitudes and career awareness, the research and theoretical bases of these strategies are discussed in Chapters Three and Four.)

Instructional techniques common to all programs are the

Exhibit 5.5. DAPCEP Preengineering Classes and Science Fair.

Students in DAPCEP's in-school preengineering classes prepare science fair and engineering projects, take field trips, hear technical speakers, research the lives of minority engineers and scientists as role models, and attend audiovisual presentations prepared by DAPCEP corporate and university representatives. Students also view videotapes on such topics as how to prepare a science fair project and discuss careers in science and engineering using middle school students as moderators.

The Science and Engineering Fair of metropolitan Detroit was first held in 1958; some 25,000 to 30,000 students in grades 7 through 12 from schools in Wayne, Oakland, and Macomb counties participate each year. More than 3,000 of these students actually enter the fair, and 2,000 or more present projects.

In 1977, when DAPCEP began participating in the fair, the participation of Detroit public school students was low. For example, of 2,438 entries, 222 (or 9 percent) were from the Detroit public schools. By 1991, the number of entries had increased to 2,063, or 57 percent of all entries. Data collected through the intervening years show that without the participation of DAPCEP students, the number of Detroit public school entries would be considerably smaller. In 1980, the first grand award winner from the Detroit Public School System in five years was a DAPCEP participant. Of the eight grand award winners in the 1990 fair, three were from DAPCEP. Numbers of first-, second-, and third-place winners who were in DAPCEP also increased at an even greater rate than the increase in participation.

---

use of inquiry and discovery approaches in teaching and hands-on activities. There is very little use of the traditional lecture method; when that method is used, it is combined with the inquiry and discovery approach. The use of cooperative learning methods is less frequent, with three programs specifically mentioning this as part of their strategy. Most programs, however, incorporate some of the characteristics of cooperative goal structures, such as lack of competitiveness, a high degree of interaction among students, and group responsibility for goal achievement. Similarly, although five of the programs specified that they focus on teaching problem-solving techniques (with Project MiCRO having this as its main focus), all the programs, in one form or another, teach problem solving. Four of the programs consciously structure activities to progress from the concrete to the abstract; the other programs achieve this progression indirectly through their use of the inquiry and discovery method.

Six of the ten programs offer some form of tutoring. Since

the purpose of all the programs is enrichment rather than remediation, tutoring services might be called "study groups" or "academic enrichment classes" in order to avoid the unfortunate (and incorrect) association of the word *tutoring* with remediation. Programs that offer tutoring usually offer either cross tutoring (tutoring by older students) or tutoring by adults. The MESA Junior High Program, however, offers three types of tutoring: peer, cross, and adult.

MESA is the only program to offer test preparation. This was a somewhat surprising finding, since it seems a natural focus for intervention. This dearth of test preparation activities in middle school intervention programs was pointed out by Clewell, Thorpe, and Anderson (1987). A possible explanation is that students have not typically been exposed to standardized testing until high school, although the growing prevalence of statewide testing at all grade levels will intensify the need for test preparation activities.

All programs require that their instructors have high expectations of students, give them feedback and encouragement, have a thorough knowledge of their subject matter and of the populations that they will be teaching, and have the ability to accommodate instruction to the students' various cognitive styles, developmental levels, and preferred learning styles. Although all programs seem to be aware of the range of cognitive development present in middle school students, only five specifically said that they give conscious consideration to this. An awareness of the role of language in learning was evident in the one program that works with students with limited English proficiency, Finding Out/Descubrimiento, and in the Saturday Science Academy, which emphasizes oral and written expression.

The classroom environment may also influence learning. All programs have mixed-ability classes; that is, classes with children with varying achievement levels. Some programs use special classroom structures. For example, Operation SMART, a program for girls, has many single-sex classes, and three programs — Finding Out/Descubrimiento, Math, Science, and Minorities, K-6, and the Saturday Science Academy — use cooperative learning structures in the classroom.

Table 5.2. Approaches and Strategies: Attitudes and Career Choice.

	DAPCEP	Family Math	Finding Out/ Descubrimiento	Mathematics, Science, and Minorities, K–6	MESA Junior High	Operation SMART	Project Interface	Project MiCRO	Project SEED	Saturday Science Academy
Role Modeling										
• Mentors – adults										
• Mentors – peer							●			
• Guest speakers	●	●		●	●	●	●		●	●
• Materials	●			●	●	●	●			●
Career awareness										
• Use of media and promotional materials regarding careers	●									
• Job shadowing	●									
• Internships and preceptorships	●	●			●	●	●			●
• Field trips	●			●	●	●	●			
• Guest speakers	●	●			●	●	●			●
• Career counseling	●	●			●	●	●			●

	1	2	3	4	5	6	7	8	9	10
Exposure to out-of-school math, science, and computer science activities										
• Field trips	•				•	•	•			•
• Science projects	•				•	•	•			•
• Competitions	•		•		•		•			
• Science and math clubs			•			•	•		•	
• After-school classes			•		•	•	•	•	•	•
Provision of a supportive environment										
• Parental involvement	•	•	•	•	•	•	•	•		•
• Teacher and counselor education and training	•	•		•	•	•	•	•	•	•
• Rewards, prizes, certificates of recognition	•				•	•	•			•

Table 5.3. Approaches and Strategies: Achievement and Performance.

	DAPCEP	Family Math	Finding Out/ Descubrimiento	Mathematics, Science, and Minorities, K-6	MESA Junior High	Operation SMART	Project Interface	Project MiCRO	Project SEED	Saturday Science Academy
Instructional approaches										
• Inquiry and discovery method	•	•	•	•	•	•	•	•	•	•
• Socratic method	•								•	•
• Lecture method					•					
• Team-assisted instruction, cooperative learning			•	•						•
• Activity-based instruction, hands-on activities	•	•	•	•	•	•	•	•	•	•
• Progression of instruction from concrete to abstract			•	•		•		•		
• Focus on problem-solving techniques		•	•	•	•	•		•		
Tutoring approaches										
• Peer tutoring	•				•					
• Cross tutoring					•	•	•			
• Tutoring by adults					•					
Test preparation					•					

	1	2	3	4	5	6	7	8	9	10
Teacher behavior										
• High expectations	•	•	•	•	•	•	•	•	•	•
• Feedback and encouragement	•	•	•	•	•	•	•	•	•	•
• Attention to varying stages of cognitive development	•		•	•	•		•	•	•	
• Accommodation to learners' cognitive styles and locus-of-control orientation	•	•	•	•	•	•	•	•	•	•
• Awareness of the role of language in learning										
• Knowledge of subject matter	•	•	•	•	•	•	•	•	•	•
• Knowledge of target population	•	•	•	•	•	•	•	•	•	•
Classroom environment										
• Cooperative learning	•		•	•	•	•	•	•	•	•
• Status treatment	•	•	•	•	•		•	•	•	•
• Mixed-ability classes			•		•		•	•		
• Single-sex classes										
Family and home environment										
• Parent-child classes and activities	•	•		•		•				
• Parent contract	•				•	•				
• Other parental involvement	•			•	•	•	•	•	•	

A family and home environment that is supportive of student involvement in math and science can be achieved by focusing intervention activities on parents. Parental involvement in the program can take many different forms. DAPCEP involves parents in the policy-making process by including them on the program's advisory board. Family Math, Project MiCRO, Mathematics, Science, and Minorities, K–6, and Operation SMART offer classes for parents and their children. Project Interface and DAPCEP ask parents to sign a contract stating that they will review their children's homework and engage in other activities that will help improve their children's achievement in math and science. Other programs involve parents through workshops, monthly meetings, and volunteer activities. Project MiCRO even has a parent coordinator to encourage parents to become involved with the program.

6

Determining Program Outcomes

The outcomes of an intervention program are a result of the program's process and one of the means by which the program is evaluated. Contextual elements influence every component of a program. This chapter discusses types of outcomes (with a focus on participant-related outcomes) and measures of them, suggests how they can be used in evaluation, and gives examples of outcomes and outcome measures from the programs in our case studies. The chapter also describes types of contextual factors and how they affect programs, with examples from our case-study programs. The chapter closes with a discussion of the dissemination and institutionalization of the programs in our case studies and a summary of what we have learned about characteristics of effective programs.

Participant-Related Outcomes

All the programs that we looked at measure their goal attainment at least partially in terms of participant-related outcomes, such as the development of a positive attitude toward a math or science career, an increase in performance or achievement levels in math or science, the enrollment of participants in higher-level mathematics or science classes in high school, or progress along the career path toward a math or science career.

Attitudes

The development of a positive attitude toward math and science is an outcome that all programs strive for, although not all use it as a specific measure of success. The most prevalent method of measuring this is through a survey of participants or their parents or teachers. The Saturday Science Academy, for example, surveys students, parents, and teachers to ascertain whether students' attitudes toward science and math have changed after exposure to the program. Project MiCRO surveys its participants regarding their feelings about computers and the use of computers in school and compares their responses to those of nonparticipants.

An indirect method of assessing whether participants maintain a positive attitude toward math or science is to look at their participation in the programs and their enthusiasm in class. If they attend regularly over a period of time, as one project administrator stated, "we know they're positive."

Performance and Achievement

While increasing performance and achievement levels in math and science is a goal of all the programs, it is the special focus of the skills development programs. Three of the five skills development programs (as well as one career choice program) use pre- and posttests to measure student progress in raising scores. Project SEED, Project Interface, and Finding Out/Descubrimiento use pre- and posttest scores on the Comprehensive Test of Basic Skills (CTBS) to measure change. These scores are also compared to those of a similar cohort of nonparticipants. Finding Out/Descubrimiento also collects achievement data from a number of other tests. Project MiCRO has developed its own instrument to measure computer literacy of participants, using pre- and posttests administered to both participants and a control group.

Another way of measuring changes in performance is monitoring participants' grade point averages as well as their grades in math and science subjects in school. This is one of the measures used by MESA and Project Interface.

Enrollment in Higher-Level Math and Science Classes

This outcome is of interest primarily to the career choice programs. Measuring this outcome involves tracking students into high school to ascertain their curriculum track and then their choice of math and science courses. Programs that continue their services to students beyond the junior high school years, such as DAPCEP, MESA, and Project Interface, are best able to measure this outcome. For example, Project Interface looks at the number of seventh-graders who move into prealgebra as eighth-graders, into algebra as ninth-graders, and into geometry as high school sophomores, as well as the total number of partici-. pants who enroll in college preparatory classes. MESA uses similar benchmarks.

Progress Toward a Math or Science Career

For intervention aimed at the middle school level, the most reasonable method of assessing students' progress in math and science is to track their movement into an academic curriculum in high school and their enrollment in higher-level math and science courses. Some programs, such as MESA and DAPCEP, also track participants into college to determine the number majoring in math and science subjects. This type of tracking is a time-consuming, expensive procedure that is likely to produce very low response rates, but the results can be a very strong proof of a program's efficacy.

Other Types of Outcomes

Programs often produce outcomes that are not participant-related and that are not related to the programs' stated goals. These outcomes, usually termed *spillover effects,* can take many forms. The most common are products that have been created as part of the program process, such as curricula, instructional materials, training manuals, or workshops. These are often used in dissemination activities and serve to extend the influence or effect of the program. Examples of these are given in the discussion of dissemination and institutionalization later in this chapter.

Other types of spillover effects are changes in a system or systems resulting from the operation of a program and changes in attitudes caused by individuals' exposure to the program. For example, the participation of DAPCEP in the Science and Engineering Fair of Metropolitan Detroit dramatically increased the representation of Detroit public school students as well as the number of winners from that system. In addition, DAPCEP's training of Detroit public school teachers has had a lasting effect on the way these teachers approach their science classes. Operation SMART has increased teacher awareness of sexism in the classroom. Project SEED, in working with engineers as instructors, has influenced the way some engineering firms think about disadvantaged minority students as learners of mathematics and as future engineers.

Contextual Factors

The context within which a program develops and operates includes its geographical location, its setting, the economic situation in the community, the school system, its relationship with other entities, and a host of other factors. These contextual factors can affect all aspects of a program, from its goals to its outcomes. For example, a program developed in an area in the Southwest where there is a concentration of engineering industries that are experiencing difficulty in finding engineers might formulate its goals to correspond to the local problem and develop an intervention program to encourage Hispanic and Native American children in the area to opt for careers in engineering. The industries in the area might be a source of funding as well as providing advisory board members and opportunities for field trips, internships, and summer jobs for participants. They might even provide instructors and role models from among their employees or provide equipment to be used in teaching. The contextual factors discussed in this section are a program's relationship with other entities, its location and setting, funding opportunities, and labor market demands.

Relationships with Other Entities

An important contextual factor that affects a program is the way it interacts with its host institution, community, school districts, university system, local or state governments, and other entities both outside and within the program setting. This includes not only whether the program has collaborative arrangements with other institutions but also the nature of these relationships, as well as the program's relationship with entities within the program setting.

Industry. Some of the programs that we studied depend on industry for funding, in-kind contributions, and participation on governing boards. Programs that have a marked degree of involvement with industry are DAPCEP, MESA, Project Interface, and Project SEED. Corporate contributions make up a large share of MESA's funding, and corporations make significant donations of staff time, facilities, and equipment to the program. While industry can provide a great deal of financial and in-kind support for most programs, its involvement is especially important for career choice programs because of its ability to provide valuable work experience through internships and job-shadowing programs.

Schools or School Districts. All but one of the programs are involved with schools or school districts. The relationship ranges from tangential (Project Interface and the Saturday Science Academy) to intense, with the program being held in the classroom during class hours and funded by the school district (Finding Out, DAPCEP, Mathematics, Science, and Minorities, K–6, Project SEED). This relationship enhances the probability of the program's institutionalization.

Universities. Six of the ten programs are involved with universities. In four of these cases, the program was developed by university faculty and/or staff and is run from the university. In the other two cases, the universities are part of a group that works with the program. Program collaboration with a university provides resources such as use of university space, personnel, and equipment. DAPCEP works closely with six universities in the Detroit area. These institutions make contributions of faculty time, equipment, and physical facilities for Saturday classes and a summer program held at the participating universities. Programs with a strong research orientation, such as Finding Out/Descubrimiento, are often based at a university.

Community. Involvement with the community in which a program is located is an important element of its operations. Eight of the ten programs that we studied have some type of interaction with the community, ranging from the use of community facilities (Saturday Science Academy, Project Interface, Operation SMART, Family Math) to community funding and support of the programs (Project SEED, Family Math). In addition to providing support for a program, community involvement encourages parental involvement. For example, Project Interface is housed in a Baptist church in an Oakland, California, community and has used its location to attract and involve parents of participants.

Other Affiliations. Seven of the ten programs—Finding Out/Descubrimiento, Family Math, MESA, Mathematics, Science, and Minorities, K-6, Saturday Science Academy, Project MiCRO, and Operation SMART—are part of a larger framework, such as a national office or research center. Being part of a larger organization or center provides both material support and a broader support base.

Location and Setting

A program's geographical location and its setting—economic, political, and so on—are contextual factors that also affect the program. For example, programs in the West or Southwest, such as MESA and Finding Out/Descubrimiento, may focus more on Hispanic or Native American students than programs in the Southeast or in Detroit, which may target Black students. MESA was originated because liberals in Berkeley in the 1960s were concerned about the fact that there were few minorities enrolled in engineering programs at the University of California. The fact that Project Interface is located in a Black Baptist church strengthens its ties to the Black community and helps increase parent involvement.

Funding Opportunities

Program goals, design, content, and outcomes are often influenced by the availability of funding. For example, the preference of funding agencies for programs at the high school and postsecondary levels led to an unrealistic focus on activities at those levels during the 1960s and 1970s. Since the 1980s, however, there has been a surge of interest in intervention at the middle school level, triggered by a realization that intervention during later years of schooling may come too late. A host of studies on middle school students and adolescents have been funded by both foundations and the federal government. Additionally, there has recently been much more activity on the part of industry in supporting school improvements through public-private partnerships with schools or school districts, for example.

The mission or philosophy of foundations may shape the focus or scope of an intervention. Developments in the progress of educational research and the resulting political climate may also influence what kinds of programs receive funding.

Labor Market Demands

The recent emphasis on intervention programs to encourage the participation of underrepresented groups in mathematics and science careers is due, in part, to the projected labor shortage in these areas. Recent reports such as the Office of Technology Assessment's *Educating Scientists and Engineers: Grade School to Grad School* (U.S. Congress, Office of Technology Assessment, 1988a) and the National Research Council's (1989) *Everybody Counts* have warned that the need for workers with mathematical and science skills will exceed the national supply by the year 2000. Demographic trends indicate that Black and Hispanic students will make up at least a third of the college-age population within the next two decades. It is logical that an effort must be made to increase the participation of these underrepresented groups in mathematics- and science-related fields.

Other Factors That Affect Programs

In addition to the factors discussed above, the existing knowledge base (regarding both the intervention approach and the target population) and the programs' use of innovative approaches are elements that affect intervention programs.

The Role of Knowledge

The staff of all the programs that were part of this study have a thorough knowledge of the populations that they serve as well as the approaches, strategies, and techniques that are most appropriate and effective for their target populations. Although few were able to point to the theoretical bases of their approaches, their practices obviously have good theoretical support, as can be seen by comparing their approaches with those that theory and research have found to be the most effective (see Chapters Three, Four, and Five).

The Role of Innovation

A characteristic of all the programs studied was that they are innovative in some way. DAPCEP, Mathematics, Science, and Minorities, K–6, MESA, and Project Interface have innovative program designs. Finding Out/Descubrimiento, Family Math, Operation SMART, Project MiCRO, Project SEED, and the Saturday Science Academy have developed unique teaching approaches, curricula, and/or materials for teaching math, science, and/or computer science.

All these programs are different from traditional programs and have responded in an innovative way to the problem of minority and female underrepresentation in math and science. In fact, one of the reasons these programs are effective may be that they are willing to be creative and to take risks. In the absence of generally accepted strategies and designs for effective intervention, they have been resourceful and unconventional in devising solutions to the problem of low minority and female participation in math and science.

Dissemination and Institutionalization

The wish to replicate is a sign of a good program. All except one of the programs have undertaken or have made plans to undertake their replication at other sites. A majority of programs (eight) have developed a product as part of this replication effort. This product may take the form of a curriculum or teaching materials (Finding Out/Descubrimiento, DAPCEP, Family Math, MESA, Mathematics, Science, and Minorities, K–6, Project SEED, Project MiCRO, Operation SMART), teacher or staff training packages (Finding Out/Descubrimiento, Family Math, Mathematics, Science, and Minorities, K–6, Project SEED), or career awareness materials (DAPCEP, MESA). To facilitate replication efforts, most programs maintain complete documentation of program approaches, strategies, and techniques. In Operation SMART, for example, the documentation has taken the form of a handbook that contains a complete description of the project, including lesson plans for activities. An ultimate goal of all the programs is the incorporation of their approaches, techniques, and strategies into the classroom setting. Finding Out/Descubrimiento is training faculty at the California State University in its techniques, and the faculty and program staff train master teachers in school districts where student teachers are placed for field experience.

Characteristics of Effective Programs

By looking at the program elements set out in Figure 5.1 across programs, we felt that we could identify shared characteristics that, by inference, could be used to describe effective programs. A description of these characteristics can be used, together with the more prescriptive information in Chapters Seven and Eight, as a guide to developing effective programs. The remainder of this section summarizes, by program component, the shared characteristics of our ten case-study programs.

Program Goals

Program goals in the ten case-study programs are clear and well articulated. Goals are central to the development of program design and content as well as to the evaluation plan. As noted earlier, the programs can be divided by goal into two groups: skills development programs and career choice programs; the latter may include a subgoal — participation in advanced math courses. Skills development programs and career choice programs often differ with respect to characteristics and approaches. Because of these differences, it is often useful to classify programs by goal type.

Program Design

The programs have established collaborative relationships with industry, school systems, universities, and the community. These relationships have often resulted in cost-sharing agreements to help finance program activities or in-kind contributions such as space, staff, materials, and equipment. Collaboration with schools or school districts helps programs to institutionalize their strategies. A high level of collaborative effort is an indicator of program integration into the environment and of varied sources of support.

An advisory board is another valuable source of support. In addition to program directors who monitor and administer activities, our case-study programs have advisory boards that are representative of the various sectors of society with which they are involved. The primary role of these boards is to provide helpful advice and input into policy decisions; they also assist in fundraising; provide services, in-kind contributions, and valuable contacts through members; and legitimize the programs.

None of the programs targets high-achieving students for recruitment. Those with a goal of expanding the talent pool of potential math and science professionals (the career choice programs) target middle-range students who can benefit the most from their help.

Program Content

All the programs that we studied offer a mix of services and activities that includes academically oriented activities. The type of mix depends on the focus of the program and the needs of the participants. Skills development programs stress the development of techniques, curriculum, and materials for effective teaching of math and science; their other activities involve services that enhance learning, such as tutoring. Career choice programs focus on career awareness activities and on ensuring that students take higher-level math courses in high school. They provide exposure to role models, mentoring, dissemination of information regarding careers, field trips, internships, counseling, and academic tutoring.

All the programs emphasize enrichment rather than remediation in their approaches and use innovation and creativity in designing solutions to the problem of underrepresentation. This often means that multiple approaches and strategies are used. Of these, the most important are inquiry and discovery approaches, including hands-on activities; cooperative goal structures; teaching of problem-solving techniques; and the development of higher-order thinking skills.

In addition to these specific teaching approaches, the programs use strategies and techniques that are appropriate to their target populations. For example, they take into account participants' cognitive and physical stages of development, learning styles, and linguistic needs. The activities are student-centered and require high levels of student involvement; they often involve classes of mixed-ability students.

Training of teachers and other staff is offered to introduce staff to program objectives, strategies, and approaches. Instructors in these programs have high expectations of students, give students feedback and encouragement, and have a thorough knowledge of their subject matter and of the populations that they are teaching. They also have the ability to accommodate instruction to students' cognitive and learning styles. A high level of parental involvement is characteristic of these programs, which strive to attract, involve, and work with parents of participants.

In short, with one exception, our case-study programs embody in practice those effective strategies and approaches described in Chapters Three and Four. (The exception is the lack of test preparation activities, which are offered by only one of the programs.)

Participant-Related Outcomes

In all the programs, goal attainment is measured, at least in part, by participant outcomes. These outcomes are described in terms of attitude change, increase in performance or achievement, enrollment in higher-level courses, or progress along the math and science career path. Many programs use a combination of outcome measures to assess efficacy.

The development of a positive attitude toward math and science, an outcome that all programs strive for, is not always used as a specific measure of success. The most prevalent method of measuring attitude changes is surveys of participants, parents, or teachers. Skills development programs, which have an increase in achievement and performance levels as their special focus, often use pre- and posttest scores as measures. Other measures include monitoring participants' grade point averages and grades in math and science subjects.

Enrollment in higher-level math and science classes is an outcome of interest mainly to career choice programs. This outcome can be measured by tracking students into high school to ascertain their curriculum track and choice of math and science courses. For programs targeting middle school students, progress toward a math or science career is difficult to measure, since it involves the tracking of participants into college, which is a costly, time-consuming, and risky process.

Program Context

The programs are supported by a mix of resources from the various entities with which they are involved. This increases their stability, since they are not dependent on any one source of funding. This mix of resources is encouraged by the involvement of various constituencies, such as industry, universities, school systems, and the community. Collaborative agreements and the inclusion of representatives from several sectors of society on advisory boards are strategies used by programs to achieve this involvement.

All the case-study programs undertake dissemination activities and strive to replicate their programs elsewhere. Documentation of activities, the development of workshops, presentations at conferences, articles in journals, and the development of instructional materials are some of the dissemination methods used by the programs. Many of them have a long-term goal of institutionalizing program practices into the classroom setting. Developing teacher training programs and collaborating with school districts are two effective ways of encouraging institutionalization. (Both dissemination and institutionalization of intervention practices are discussed in greater depth in Chapter Nine.)

PART FOUR

Guidelines for
Successful Implementation

This fourth and final part of the book presents a guide to implementing a program in mathematics, science, and/or computer science and discusses issues of institutionalization.

Chapters Seven and Eight describe the steps that go into planning, developing, and implementing a program, covering such topics as goal setting; designing a program format; choosing appropriate program activities, strategies, and instructional materials; developing recruitment strategies and selection criteria; selecting, training, and involving staff; obtaining funding; developing and implementing a management plan; and designing an evaluation. Examples from the case-study intervention programs are used throughout the chapters to illustrate key points.

Chapter Nine suggests ways of disseminating program findings and strategies through workshops; training sessions; development of videos, curricula, and materials; technical assistance to schools or school districts; and other approaches. This chapter also discusses the problems inherent in institutionalizing a program, explores the possibilities for successful adoption of intervention practices, and identifies factors that encourage successful institutionalization.

131

7

Planning and
Developing Programs

The process of conceptualizing and planning a program is a lengthy one that involves many steps. The planning process can be thought of as the foundation on which the program rests. Thoughtful, careful, and informed planning can help to ensure a prompt start-up as well as a smooth developmental period for a program. One of the hallmarks of the systems approach is a well-thought-out plan for developing and managing a system — in this case, a program. Having a good plan laid out before the program begins allows the director and staff to concentrate on the important issues in running the program. It helps anticipate requirements that may arise while the program is in progress and helps avoid crises.

Just as important as good program planning is effective implementation to ensure that the program is carried out in the most efficient manner possible. Effective implementation involves following the program plan as initially conceived, monitoring the timely accomplishment of tasks, and making the adjustments that the operation of a program (no matter how well planned) in a real world invariably necessitates.

This present chapter outlines the steps for planning and developing a program and implementing the key program components of our model, beginning with the definition of the problem and ending with a guide for selecting, training, and involving staff. Examples from the ten case-study programs are provided.

For each major step of the process, we provide a set of questions to guide you in completing that step.

Focusing on the Problem

Almost without exception, intervention programs have been established as a response to perceived problems. In the case of
many of the programs discussed in this book, the realization
that certain groups are severely underrepresented in mathematics, science, and engineering (MSE) fields was the catalyst
for the intervention effort. With some programs, the problem
was perceived as poor performance in the classroom; with others,
the focus was on the low enrollment of certain groups in MSE
majors in college; and with still others, the problem was pinpointed as an absence of these groups among MSE professionals.
The way in which each program defined the problem gave each
resulting intervention effort its focus and character.

Project SEED was born of the experiences of William
Johntz, a teacher of minority students in general math classes
at Berkeley High School. Johntz realized that by the time his
students reached high school, they were convinced that they
could not do math. Although they responded well to instruction in algebra using the discovery method, he was aware that
by the ninth or tenth grade, they lacked the basic skills to be
successful learners of mathematics. This made Johntz consider
using the same method with sixth-graders, and a program was
launched.

The idea underlying MESA was conceived when a group
of university professors, secondary school teachers, students,
and other professionals expressed concern about the small proportion of engineering students enrolled at the University of
California who were members of historically underrepresented
groups. A survey of minority students at the University of
California, Berkeley, revealed that a higher number of students
than expected had been interested in math and science in high
school but had not taken the courses required for acceptance
into a college-level math-based major. This finding resulted in

the establishment of a precollege program to help underrepresented minority students complete three or four years of high school math.

Operation SMART was established when it became clear to the national office of Girls Clubs of America, Inc. (now Girls Incorporated), that girls needed a background in math and science if they wanted to get jobs and pursue careers. Because the main mission of Girls Incorporated is to help girls develop a capacity for economic independence, the organization could not ignore the technological revolution that was taking place. The national office approached IBM, which provided a senior forecaster from its Executive Loan Program to conduct a needs analysis and offer recommendations regarding a basic design for the project.

Mathematics, Science, and Minorities, K–6 was developed to put into practice the ideas expressed in a book published by the Mid-Atlantic Center for Race Equity (Beane, 1985). The program's goal was to involve all the school districts in the Washington, D.C., metropolitan area in a four-year project to implement the research findings of the center regarding factors that affect minority participation in math and science by integrating the practices described in the book into the school system.

Once a problem is perceived, some research is needed to verify that it does, indeed, exist. This can take the form of structured research, such as a survey, as in the case of MESA; information gathering through interviews, as was used by Operation SMART in its needs analysis; or information gathering through observation and trial, as in the case of Project SEED. Other methods of verifying the existence of a problem include reviewing data, such as test scores, enrollment figures, and so on, that document the problem; talking to others who are knowledgeable about the problem; and looking for situations where a similar problem has been identified.

The accurate identification of the problem is the first step in developing a successful program. It is essential to the formulation of appropriate program goals and to the design of an effective delivery system.

- What is the problem as you perceive it? (Be very specific.)
- What evidence do you have that there is a problem as you have identified it above?
- How do you think the problem could be addressed through a program? (Mention the target population to be served, grade levels included, subject matter focus, and other components.)
- How can your proposed program contribute toward solving the problem? (List all the beneficial outcomes you can think of.)

Setting Program Goals

Once the problem has been accurately defined, setting goals should not be difficult. For example, Project Interface defined the problem as the fact that few Black students in the Oakland, California, school district were enrolled in college preparatory classes. One of the main barriers to enrollment in college prep classes was Black students' inability to qualify for the academic track because of poor performance in math and science courses. One of Project Interface's primary goals, therefore, is to increase the number of minority junior high school students who can succeed in college preparatory courses in senior high school. The program proposes to accomplish this by offering intervention in math and science. This goal also dictates that the target population for intervention should be junior high school minority students.

Skills Development Versus Career Choice Goals

As we saw in Chapter Five, there are two main types of program goals: skills development and career choice. The skills development goal is to increase the math and science skills of participants; the career choice goal is to increase the participation of a group or groups in math and science careers. The way the problem is perceived dictates the type of goal. For example, the founders of MESA saw the problem as underrepresentation of minority groups in the engineering profession. MESA, therefore, evolved into a program with career choice–type goals. Project SEED, on the other hand, perceived the problem to be the poor performance of minority high school students in math classes. This program, therefore, developed skills development-type goals.

Objectives

Goals are broad statements that describe a program's purpose. They may be broken down into a set of objectives that describe goals in more specific, operational terms and that are easier to measure. For example, the overall goal of Operation SMART is to help girls acquire an attitude of scientific inquiry toward everything they do. This, as stated, is a difficult goal to measure. The program's objectives, however, are (1) to enable Girls Incorporated clubs to offer programs in math, science, technology, and computers; (2) to help young people become aware of math and science concepts embedded in everyday life and help staff encourage an attitude of inquiry throughout club activities and approaches; (3) to provide girls with access to resources in the community that can increase their interest in math and science; and (4) to determine how clubs and schools can best work together to increase girls' interest and involvement in math and science. These objectives are certainly more measurable than the program goal.

The long-range goal of the Saturday Science Academy is to significantly increase the pool of students interested in pursuing careers in computer science, engineering, mathematics, and the natural sciences. Specific objectives are improving students' problem-solving and thinking skills; improving their self-concept and confidence in their ability to be successful in these fields; helping them to develop positive attitudes toward these fields; increasing their desire to pursue MSE careers; increasing their knowledge base and understanding of science and mathematics; and improving their precision and power in oral and written communication skills.

As the examples above illustrate, goals are global, whereas objectives are specific statements of how goals will be measured and operationalized. Objectives are very useful in conducting an evaluation because they provide measurable outcomes for determining whether a program is fulfilling its goal or goals. For example, in the case of the Saturday Science Academy, it would be difficult to evaluate just how this program has significantly increased the pool of students interested in pursuing careers in computer science, engineering, mathematics, and the natural sciences without specific, measurable objectives for which we can utilize measures such as test scores, attitudinal surveys, or some of the other evaluation tools discussed in detail later in this chapter.

Target Population

Goals should specify the race or ethnicity of the target population for intervention, the age levels to be served, and the subject matter. As the example of Project Interface shows, a good definition of the problem should result in the specification of the target population and the selection of the subject matter for intervention.

In some cases, the identification of the target population may precede the definition of the problem, as in the case of Operation SMART, where the target population is that served by Girls Incorporated. In other cases, the opposite is true: Project SEED and MESA targeted populations by the age level at which intervention was found to be most effective.

Identification of Programs with Similar Goals

It is often helpful to identify programs with similar goals in order to assess the effectiveness of their intervention approaches and to consider the appropriateness of their approaches to a particular situation. It is possible to learn from both the successes and the failures of others.

Publications that list intervention programs in mathematics and science, such as *Intervention Programs in Math, Science, and Computer Science for Minority and Female Students in Grades Four Through Eight* (Clewell, Thorpe, and Anderson, 1987) and *Equity and Excellence: Compatible Goals* (Malcom and others, 1984), are helpful in identifying similar programs. Published evaluations of programs as well as descriptive materials such as brochures, final reports, and videotapes can also be helpful. Visiting programs, telephoning project directors, and attending workshops conducted by other programs as part of their dissemination activities are other ways to become familiar with similar programs.

Questions to Guide You in Setting Program Goals

- Is your program focus developing math and science skills or increasing careers in math and science among underrepresented minorities and/or women?
- What is the purpose of your program, including objectives? (This is your goal statement. Respond in light of the problem that you have identified.)
- Do your objectives adequately express your overall goals?
- Are your objectives specific and measurable?
- Is your target population already chosen because of the problem identified or the nature of your organization?
- What is your target population? (Include race or ethnicity, sex, and age or grade levels.)
- What is your subject matter focus?

Choosing a Program Format

A program may take place during or after school hours, on Saturdays, during the summer, or a combination of some or all of these. Often, the program format is a result of the program's affiliation. For example, Project SEED, DAPCEP, Finding Out/Descubrimiento, Project MiCRO, and Mathematics, Science, and Minorities, K–6 are either funded by or affiliated with schools or school districts. DAPCEP's collaboration with area universities provides it with the opportunity to use the campuses for its summer program and on Saturdays; MESA's ties to area campuses enable the use of campus facilities and equipment for Saturday classes. All these programs have activities that take place during school hours in the classroom, although they also offer after-school and out-of-school activities.

Other factors that affect the program format are the time required to complete the intervention, the age level of students, the location of the program, the availability of transportation, and the availability of facilities. An intervention approach that requires the intensive involvement of students might use a format that combines a highly concentrated summer session with after-school and all-day-Saturday sessions during the school year. Programs that serve younger children may find it necessary to operate during school hours or on Saturdays and/or during summers, since parents may not wish their young children to walk home at dusk. Programs that target older middle school children may find that their participants need to work at jobs during the summer. These programs might consider offering stipends during the summer or not scheduling activities in the summer months. A program located in the community, such as Project Interface, may be more accessible to its participants for after-school activities than a program at a distant university, which may instead offer Saturday classes and transportation. Many programs use more than one format, combining both in- and after-school programs, Saturday sessions, summer camps, and workshops or conferences.

Questions to Guide You in Choosing a Program Format

- What facilities and resources are available to you?
- When and how often can you offer activities that will draw the target population you wish to attract? (Think in terms of convenience of scheduling, safety, availability of transportation, and location.)
- Does your format provide sufficient time to get the job done?

Choosing Program Activities

The first consideration in choosing program activities should be the purpose of the program and how these activities further its goals. As with program format, activities offered by a program are often the function of the time available, its affiliations, location, goals, and format, the age of participants, and the avail-ability of transportation, facilities, and equipment. In the 163 middle school intervention programs that we studied, by far the most prevalent activities were experiences involving hands-on activities followed by direct instruction. Other frequently offered services or activities were counseling, the use of role models, guest speakers, tutoring, and field trips and tours. Career choice programs tend to offer more activities involving role models, career information, internships, field trips, job shadowing, and other career awareness activities.

Programs that are conducted near major science museums, university science facilities, industrial plants, and so on can take advantage of their locations to offer field trips. A program's affili-ation with industry, such as MESA's with engineering, facili-tates the availability of role models, job internships, and field trips. The location of DAPCEP in Detroit, where there is an annual science and engineering fair, provides the opportunity to build activities around this competition.

Approaches and Strategies

Closely tied to activities offered are the approaches and strate-gies used in the program. Chapters Three and Four discuss effec-tive approaches and give an overview of their theoretical and research foundations, while Chapter Five describes the approaches used by the case-study programs. These chapters provide good sources of information regarding effective strategies and ap-proaches. As is evident from these chapters, choice of approaches and strategies should be based on a knowledge of those that are effective for the target population as well as an awareness of the supporting theoretical and empirical research.

Instructional Materials and Activities

There are several curricular and instructional materials devel-oped by intervention programs that have a proven track record. For example, Multiplying Options and Subtracting Bias offers workshops and videotapes that address the problem of mathematics avoidance among females. Many of our case-study programs have developed their own materials or have assembled a composite set of materials from several sources. Operation SMART provides a manual for setting up hands-on science activities and a research tool kit to assist girls in assessing their attitudes about science, math, and technology. Finding Out/Descubrimiento uses an extensive set of materials in English and Spanish that were created to facilitate the program's work with language-minority children. DAPCEP offers a middle school preengineering curriculum guide for use in its in-school program as well as videotapes that are used as teaching, motivational, and career awareness tools.

If a program decides to use the instructional materials that are available instead of developing its own, it should choose materials appropriate to its target population and goals. In any case, racist or sexist materials have no place in an intervention program (or a school, for that matter). Materials should be screened carefully for racism or sexism.

Extracurricular activities and experiences that can enhance the effect of the regular school offering for minority students and girls include visiting programs, conferences, and support networks such as Expanding Your Horizons, Scientists-in-the-Schools, Share-a-Day-with-a-Scientist, Girls + Math + Science = Choices, and Women and Mathematics. Materials developed by the Family Math program are excellent resources.

Questions to Guide You in Deciding on Program Activities

- Given the purpose of the program, which activities are most likely to result in positive outcomes? (Take into account goal type, appeal, and appropriateness for target population.)
- What facilities and resources are available to you to carry out these activities?
- What constraints (time, staffing, format, scheduling, financial, and so on) may affect your choice of activities?
- Given your goals and the target population, which approaches

and strategies would be most effective in carrying out the activities?

- What resources or constraints affect the choice of approaches and strategies?

Developing Recruitment and Selection Strategies

An effective strategy to recruit and select program participants involves a number of tasks.

Identifying Characteristics of the Recruitment Pool

Once the target population has been chosen, the program must decide what additional characteristics it wishes participants to have. For example, does a program wish to work with economically or academically disadvantaged minority students? Does it prefer to focus its efforts on students who are of average ability but who demonstrate potential to improve? These determinations will help a program decide where to focus its recruitment efforts. Project Interface targets underachieving minority students in the seventh, eighth, and ninth grades in the east Oakland schools who are not currently enrolled in college preparatory math classes but who demonstrate potential to achieve. Some programs, such as Project MiCRO, Project SEED, Finding Out/Descubrimiento, and Math, Science, and Minorities, K–6, provide services to all students in a class, a school, or a school district. In such cases, the programs apply selection criteria to the schools rather than to individual students.

Identifying Recruitment Sources

The major sources of participants for middle school intervention programs are the schools. A program that is interested in recruiting disadvantaged minority students may wish to recruit in inner-city schools with large minority enrollments. Counselors and teachers can be very helpful in identifying potential participants, and programs should try to establish and maintain ties with such contacts in target schools. Project Interface works closely with counselors and mathematics teachers to identify potential participants. Schools that participate in the MESA program identify eligible students, who are then interviewed by program staff as part of a selection process. The Saturday Science Academy sends application forms and information flyers to principals of local schools, who in turn distribute them to teachers. Other sources of participants are other intervention programs, community-based organizations, and churches.

Establishing and Maintaining Relationships with Recruitment Sources

Once a program has established a relationship with a recruitment source, such as a school, it should maintain that relationship through periodic mailings of information about the program in the form of brochures, evaluations, or final reports; through regular visits to publicize the program; and through invitations to counselors to visit the program. Some programs (DAPCEP, Saturday Science Academy) include staff from local schools on their governing boards or selection committees; others (Finding Out/Descubrimiento, MESA, DAPCEP, Project MiCRO) use teachers in local schools as program staff and provide training for them. Program administrators should explore ways in which the program can collaborate with recruitment sources to the mutual benefit of both parties.

Developing Specific Recruitment Strategies

Recruitment materials such as posters, brochures, flyers, and videotapes can be mailed periodically to schools or other recruitment sources to be distributed to potential participants or their parents. Videotapes may be shown at workshops or conferences attended by counselors, other school personnel, or parents. Presentations may be prepared for parent-teacher association (PTA) meetings or other occasions when program personnel may have access to counselors, teachers, students, or their parents.

Radio or television spots may be used to publicize the program. Recruitment materials should state the purpose of the program, the characteristics of the students it wishes to recruit, program requirements for application, the procedure for applying to the program, benefits to be derived from participation, and other particulars, such as when and where the program is offered.

Evaluating Recruitment Efforts

A record should be kept of all recruitment efforts to determine those that are most successful. A successful recruitment effort should attract a larger number of applicants than there are places for participants; a relatively large proportion of the applicants should also fit the profile of students sought by the program. Programs should review their recruitment techniques annually; this helps them to identify those strategies and sources that provide the biggest return for their effort. A review also helps program administrators to adapt to changes that may have occurred in their recruitment sources, to identify new sources of potential participants, and to identify new recruitment strategies.

Developing Selection Criteria

Most programs wish to select participants who need intervention but will be able to successfully complete the program. After determining the characteristics of the students that they wish to serve, they choose criteria that they feel are indicators of those characteristics. The most common are standardized test scores, grades, teacher or counselor evaluations, and qualitative measures of noncognitive characteristics such as persistence, community service, and so on. Most programs use a combination of quantitative and qualitative criteria to select participants.

Although effective programs have been accused of "creaming" — that is, selecting only those students who are most likely to succeed — we did not find that any of the programs we studied were guilty of this practice. MESA targets sixth-, seventh-, and eighth-grade minority students who are either college-track or "mid-track" (scoring at about the fiftieth percentile on the Comprehensive Test of Basic Skills). DAPCEP's selection criteria include a minimum GPA of C+, interest in math and science, and a teacher or counselor recommendation.

Programs that select schools or school districts rather than individual students also develop selection criteria. Mathematics, Science, and Minorities, K–6 selects schools where there is a large minority population (at least 20 percent), where teachers and principals are committed to improving minority performance and participation in math and science, and where activity-based science and math programs are not currently being used effectively. The program has also developed criteria for choosing the teachers who will be on school teams. MESA invites applications from area schools that are interested in establishing a partnership. The program requires that a school be willing to provide resources such as space and release time for one faculty member, indicate faculty acceptance of the program, and have a high minority enrollment.

Developing the Selection Process

The selection process should be clearly defined to ensure fairness and effectiveness in choosing the appropriate body of participants. Some programs, such as the Saturday Science Academy, have selection committees with representatives from the community, the public schools, and the university. The Saturday Science Academy tries to select a good representation of local schools, and applicants not selected for a particular session are given priority for the next scheduled session.

Monitoring the Selection Process

It is important that programs assess their selection criteria and process to determine whether they are effective in enrolling the type of participant who successfully completes the program; it is just as important to ensure that they are selecting students who are in need of the intervention provided. New programs often find that it takes a few years to fine tune this process. Records (such as application forms) that make it possible to compare students who were rejected with those who were accepted may provide valuable insight as to the efficacy of the selection process.

Questions to Guide You in Recruiting and Selecting Participants

- Given your target population, what additional characteristics do you want participants to have?
- Where are you most likely to find students with these characteristics?
- How can you establish and maintain contact with the best recruitment sources for these students?
- Has a system been established to maintain frequent contact with feeder institutions (through mailings, visits, or other means)?
- What are the most effective recruitment strategies within the constraints of your project?
- How effective, overall, have your recruitment efforts been? Are you attracting enough applicants? Do these applicants have the characteristics of students you are seeking to recruit?
- What are the most effective tools and measures for identifying the type of student you want as a participant in your program?
- What is the most equitable and efficient process for selecting students?
- Is your selection procedure (including criteria) working? Are you getting sufficient numbers of students who fit your profile? Is your profile realistic?

Selecting, Training, and Involving Staff

The selection, training, and involvement of staff in the implementation and planning of a program require the following activities.

Identifying Required Characteristics

Many programs begin their recruitment process for instructors and other staff by defining the characteristics and qualities they require. Mathematics, Science, and Minorities, K–6 selects teachers for its school teams who have demonstrated success in teaching underachieving minority students, enjoy mathematics and science, and are willing to share with colleagues and parents.

Family Math leaders share characteristics such as these: they enjoy their work; they think of themselves as learners as well as teachers; they are adventurous and confident; they have a positive philosophy about math and teaching; they want to influence parents, the community, the school, and other teachers; they are ingenious in seeing possibilities and making adaptations; they are entrepreneurial in making things happen; and they understand the power of collegiality. The Saturday Science Academy looks for instructors who have the ability to relate warmly and positively to students as well as a natural instinct to create. Instructors are also required to be experts in the subjects that they teach, and many have worked previously in other intervention programs or with youth in the community. Surprisingly, Project SEED does not require that its instructors have prior experience in teaching: it recruits mathematics specialists, many of whom work for corporations and have been granted release time. The program does, however, require that instructors be able to relate well to the students.

Although none of the programs that we studied stated specifically that it recruited staff of the same racial or ethnic background and gender as the participants, we observed that many of the staff did, indeed, share these characteristics. Although some of the literature on effective programs recommends that staff be of the same racial or ethnic background and/or gender of the participants in a program because they can thus serve as role models, the evidence is inconclusive. It seems to be more important that staff be effective in their jobs and that they relate well with students in the program. As can be seen from the qualities required for program staff listed above, academic credentials do not seem to be important, although knowledge of the subject matter is.

Identifying Recruitment Sources

Staff can come from a variety of sources. Since working as an instructor for a program is usually a part-time position, many programs employ classroom teachers from local schools, instructors who have been trained in other programs, or graduate students at nearby universities. Project Interface employs college students as tutors, while Project SEED uses mathematicians from corporations as instructors.

Once good sources of instructors and other staff are identified, it should not be difficult to continue to use the same sources for replacements or additional staff. Notices can be posted in teachers' lounges or on university bulletin boards. Word of mouth is also an excellent way to identify good instructors. Asking principals, university professors, program directors, and other instructors for suggestions as to potential candidates can be an effective recruitment tool.

Training

Central to the development of a staff training program is the definition of what staff need to know in order to perform effectively. Establishing criteria for selection and hiring of instructors and other staff helps to ensure that they have certain basic credentials, experience, and qualities. Providing training ensures that staff receive more specific orientation to the goals of the program and to specific materials, techniques, strategies, and approaches used in the program.

Training can take place at the beginning of a program, with subsequent sessions being offered only for new hires, or it can be offered for all staff both at the beginning and at regular intervals throughout the life of the program. Some of the programs that we studied had very well-defined staff and teacher training components that were an important part of the intervention approach. For example, Family Math offers training workshops for class leaders (who are usually teachers and parents) as well as separate workshops for trainers of trainers. Operation SMART considers staff training to be critical, since the behavior and teaching approaches required by the program do not come easily or naturally to many teachers. Programs that use classroom teachers as instructors, such as Math, Science, and Minorities, K–6, Project MiCRO, DAPCEP, and Finding Out/Descubrimiento, have staff who provide intensive training for these teachers. Project SEED, which uses mathematicians as instructors in the classroom, instructs them in the program's teaching techniques and then allows them to work with a seasoned instructor for as long as it takes for them to feel confident.

It is important to monitor and evaluate a training program to assess its effectiveness. Attention must be given to the adequacy of training for preparing staff—the timing and length of the sessions, the effectiveness of the materials, the quality of instruction, and the completeness of the content. Regular feedback from staff regarding how well the training helps them to carry out their duties should be solicited through informal interviews or surveys or as part of a formative evaluation.

Professional Development

Although related to training, professional development differs in that it focuses not on programmatic needs but on the development of staff as professionals. Many programs offer staff the opportunity and funding to attend a limited number of workshops or conferences in their chosen fields. This practice not only revitalizes staff and improves their skills but also contributes to high staff morale by implying that the program values and supports staff members as the professionals that they are.

Involving Staff in Implementation and Planning

Most of the programs in our case studies hold regular staff meeting as a means of encouraging staff involvement and input into program planning and implementation. During these meetings, staff members may discuss problems that have arisen or seem imminent, contribute to problem solutions, or offer suggestions for improving the program. A yearly staff retreat to discuss long-range planning is a regular feature of many successful intervention programs.

Involving program staff in implementation as well as long-range planning benefits the program in many ways. It obtains valuable input from professionals who know the program well; it encourages staff ownership of the program (and thus improves performance); and it helps to boost morale.

Questions to Guide You in Selecting, Training, and Involving Staff

- What characteristics (including background preparation, credentials, and personal qualities) do you wish your staff to have?
- What are the best sources for locating staff with these characteristics?
- What information do staff members need to do their jobs, and how can this best be provided?
- How often do staff members need training?
- How effective is the training that the program provides?
- What professional development opportunities are most important to staff?
- What are the most effective ways of involving staff in implementation of the program as well as long-range planning?
- What do staff think about the program and its administration?
- What is the morale of staff?

8

Funding, Managing,
and Evaluating Programs

There are a number of activities that, while not part of the program process, are central to the effective functioning of a program. These include obtaining funding, developing and implementing a management plan, and designing an evaluation. The activities discussed in this chapter will help program administrators in identifying sources of funding and obtaining grants, assist them in setting up an efficient system to monitor the timely and effective accomplishment of tasks, and guide them in the development of an evaluation plan. As in the previous chapter, there are questions to guide the reader in carrying out the activities described in this chapter. Examples from the ten case-study programs provide illustrations from actual programs.

Obtaining Funding

During the 1960s and 1970s, most intervention programs were funded with local funds and addressed local needs. As the efficacy of these programs came to be accepted and they gained national acclaim, the federal government and foundations became more willing to support similar efforts. Funding for programs is now available from a variety of sources, including federal, state, and local government agencies; school districts; foundations; and industry. Of the programs we studied, most were started with funding from foundations and have continued supporting their activities through funds from a combination of sources, usually foundations and industry, with in-kind contributions from sources such as universities, schools, and industry.

Identifying Funding Sources

Once the idea and plan for a program have been developed, it is time to approach funding sources. It is a good idea to determine beforehand the funding interests of local and national foundations and to pinpoint those that are interested in your type of program. *The Foundation Grants Index* (Kovacs and Goldman, 1989) is a good source of this information; it also contains application information for each foundation. The *Commerce Business Daily* and the *Federal Register* publish requests for proposal (RFPs) released by the federal government. At the state and local levels, talking to department of education officials or district superintendents may provide leads to funding opportunities. Identifying the funding sources of programs similar to yours is another way of finding funding opportunities.

Local businesses, especially those that require workers with good skills in mathematics and science, are an excellent source of support. If the companies are large, they may have established a foundation through which grants can be made to educational projects. In the past decade, business-education partnerships have become more common. Almost all of our case-study programs have some sort of relationship with industry.

At this stage in the search process, you should have a pretty good idea of the type of program that you wish to implement, your reasons for doing so, the target population, and the approximate cost of the project. Your funding requests should state these points clearly. Being vague and imprecise when talking or writing to potential funders will not help your cause. Also, be prepared to make changes in your plan to accommodate funding philosophies, constraints, needs, and so on.

Writing the Proposal

The initial contact with foundations usually does not require more than a letter with an abstract describing the proposed project. If foundations are interested in your concept, you will be invited to submit a full proposal. Requirements for proposals vary. Most federal RFPs are very specific as to the format and content of proposals, while most foundations are not.

In writing a proposal, applicants should demonstrate a good grasp of the problem and familiarity with related research as well as with approaches to solving the problem; give a good rationale for their particular approach; and present a well-thought-out plan for carrying out the project (work plan and time line). Evidence of the capability and experience of key staff members (especially the project director) and the capacity and resources of the organization for supporting the endeavor is also very helpful. Some funding agencies require a well-designed evaluation as well as a dissemination plan. It also helps if the budget for implementing the program is reasonable and within the range funded by the agency.

Questions to Guide You in Obtaining Funding

- Have you set up a network or system to collect information on potential funding sources? Is this updated periodically?
- Are the funding sources that you have identified appropriate?
- Is your proposal within the range, philosophy, and focus of the funding source or sources?
- Does your proposal address all the requirements (both explicit and implicit) of the funding agency to which it will be submitted?
- Does your proposal give a clear picture of the problem to be addressed, how you propose to address it, and your capacity to undertake the work?
- Do you have a plan to ensure continued funding of your program?

Developing and Implementing a Management Plan

The development and implementation of a successful management plan call for setting up an administrative and governance structure that is appropriate to the program. It is also important to schedule project activities and tasks to ensure that the day-to-day operation of the program functions smoothly.

Administrative Structure and Governance

Most programs are directed by a project or program director who is responsible for monitoring and overseeing program activities. If the program is large and has several sites, a coordinator who is responsible to the project director may be appointed to oversee each site. The role of the program director may vary according to the size and structure of the program. In a number of programs, the project director reports to an advisory board that is responsible for policy decisions, oversight, and guidance. A program may also be part of a larger entity, such as a center, a national office, a school district, a university, or a nonprofit organization. In such cases, the overall management structure of the program (as well as the budgeting process) must conform to that of the parent institution, and the project director may report to the person who has jurisdiction over the unit in which the program is housed.

Several of the programs that we studied have advisory boards made up of representatives from industry, higher education, the community, and the school district. For example, MESA's partnership model requires a board of directors comprising representatives of every sector of the education community in the state as well as some representatives of industry. It also has an industrial advisory board made up solely of representatives of industry. Project Interface's board of directors is made up of representatives of the public and private sectors who are responsible for the direction and management of the project. The program director is responsible for external relations, fundraising, and a capital campaign drive, while a full-time program manager is responsible for the day-to-day operation of the program.

Scheduling Activities and Tasks

Because intervention programs are often part of a larger entity and must conform to the management and budgeting procedures of their parent organizations, this section focuses on establishing a plan for the day-to-day operation of the program. Developing a management plan involves breaking major activities into tasks and subtasks within a time frame that gives beginning and end dates for each and shows the relationships among tasks. Exhibits 8.1 and 8.2 illustrate how charts and diagrams can be helpful in conceptualizing a management plan. The activities of a hypothetical program in Exhibit 8.1 are enumerated in outline format to correspond with the Gantt chart in Exhibit 8.2; this allows for concise recording of the data on the chart. If there is a large staff, it might also be useful to develop a staffing plan that shows the number of hours (or percentage of time) each staff member works on each task. These tools are useful in ensuring that the project runs smoothly and in monitoring the timely completion of tasks.

In scheduling tasks, attention must be given to their interdependence. If one task, such as implementing the selection process, cannot be begun until a number of other tasks are completed, it is important to ensure that the starting dates of these other tasks are set far enough in advance to allow them to be completed before the selection process begins. For example, implementation of the selection process may depend on the completion of the recruitment process as well as the development of selection criteria and the selection process. Recruitment, which requires a long time, should be scheduled to begin some months before selection of students is to take place. Since this activity will take longer than either the development of selection criteria or the development of a selection process, its proper scheduling assumes greater importance. The other two tasks, which will take less time, can be carried out simultaneously with recruitment.

Allowing sufficient time for the completion of each task is another important consideration in scheduling. It is probably best to be conservative in the allocation of time for each task to allow for unforeseen events. A periodic review of the Gantt chart or other management tools can facilitate the monitoring function.

Exhibit 8.1. Activity Chart of a Hypothetical Program.

  I. Recruitment of students
     A. Identify targets for recruitment
     B. Identify recruitment sources
     C. Develop recruitment strategy and materials
     D. Implement recruitment activities
     E. Evaluate recruitment efforts

 II. Recruitment and hiring of staff
     A. Identify type of staff needed
     B. Identify recruitment sources for staff
     C. Develop recruitment strategy and recruit staff
     D. Interview and hire staff
     E. Evaluate staff recruitment efforts

III. Selection of students
     A. Develop selection criteria
     B. Develop selection process
     C. Implement selection process
     D. Monitor and evaluate selection process

 IV. Staff training
     A. Identify areas where training is necessary
     B. Develop training program
     C. Conduct training
     D. Monitor and evaluate training

  V. Program implementation
     A. Instructional component
        1. Develop curriculum
        2. Choose instructional materials
        3. Develop courses
        4. Conduct classes
        5. Monitor and evaluate instructional component
     B. Career awareness component
        1. Identify career awareness activities to be used
        2. Develop schedule for activities
        3. Identify and mobilize resources for activities (guest speakers,
           transportation for field trips, and so on)
        4. Conduct activities
        5. Evaluate career awareness component

 VI. Conduct evaluation
     A. Design evaluation plan
     B. Implement evaluation plan
     C. Use results of evaluation to improve program
     D. Evaluate evaluation plan

Exhibit 8.2. Gantt Chart.

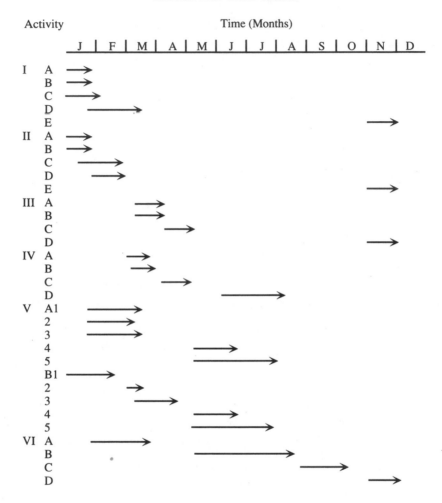

Questions to Guide You in Developing and Using a Management Plan

- Is the staffing plan reasonable? Have you allocated enough time for staff to get the job done?
- Are tasks broken down in sufficient detail to provide a useful monitoring tool?
- Are time lines reasonable and based on the work plan presented in your proposal?

- Does your scheduling of tasks take into account the relationship among tasks?
- Have you communicated the information contained in both the time line and the staffing plan to key staff?
- How realistic and useful was the plan in actually managing the program? What changes are necessary to increase its usefulness?

Designing an Evaluation Plan

Program evaluation has become increasingly prevalent within the last ten years. Some funding agencies require that the applicant submit an evaluation plan with the proposal. Today, rather than being an afterthought tacked on at the end of a program to justify its existence, evaluation is a useful component that is put into place during the planning stage and carried out periodically until the program's end. Evaluation helps program administrators and staff to understand what is effective about a program. It assists them in making decisions about allocating resources or making improvements in the program. It also provides assurance to the funding agency and to the general public that the resources provided were used responsibly. Finally, it provides documentation that might assist in securing additional funding.

The Role of Program Goals and Objectives in Evaluation

As discussed earlier, objectives and outcome measures assist a program in formulating evaluations, especially summative evaluations. Programs with skills development goals are less difficult to evaluate than those with career choice goals because the former do not require tracking, which can be costly and risky (because of the probability of a low response rate).

Finding Out/Descubrimiento, a skills development program, evaluates participants through the Comprehensive Test of Basic Skills (CTBS), the Language Assessment Scale, the Cartoon Conservation Scale (which measures intellectual development across Piagetian-based tasks), and a test measuring participants' grasp of program content. Participants' pre- and post-test scores are compared each year. The program also assesses the effects of the program on students' social interaction through analyses of sociometric measures. Effectiveness of the teacher training model is tested by pre- and postprogram observations.

MESA, a career choice program, maintains a sophisticated data-collection system that enables it to track its participants to determine the number and percentage who go on to college as math or science majors. This is the main evaluation criterion for the precollege programs. Some skills development programs have felt the need to document their students' progress beyond the intervention period and have tracked them over a long period of time after they have left the program. Project SEED, for example, conducted a longitudinal evaluation of six groups of former SEED students and six comparison groups to ascertain both the long-term and the short-term impact of the program on their mathematics achievement.

Types of Evaluation

The main types of evaluation are preformative, formative, summative, and process evaluation. Preformative evaluation takes place during the planning stage. It evaluates program decisions on such issues as target population and subject matter and helps develop a systematic evaluation plan. Formative evaluation is ongoing and conducted at frequent intervals throughout the life of the program. It helps to improve the program by identifying potential problems and successes and providing early feedback that enables program staff to make needed changes. Summative evaluation usually occurs at the end of a defined period, such as a year, and measures the overall quality and effectiveness of a program to determine whether it is fulfilling its stated goals and objectives. Process evaluation, also known as documentation, describes the process through which the program reaches its goals. It documents changes in the program as well as difficulties encountered and how these were overcome.

Project MiCRO conducts both a formative and a summative evaluation. The formative evaluation assesses the effectiveness of preservice and in-service training of teachers, classroom implementation, and instructional materials development. Training workshops are evaluated by participants, and their comments are used to plan future training. Site trainers and principals conduct regular classroom observations, and the results are used to monitor project implementation and plan future training. The formative evaluation also documents the way the delivery system works, thus also functioning as a process evaluation. The summative evaluation compares pre- and post-test data on computer literacy and analytical thinking skills for both group participants and a control group of nonparticipants that have been matched for size, racial composition, standardized test scores, geographical location, and prior experience with computers for each project site.

Types of Data Collected

Evaluation can be quantitative, qualitative, or both; some of the best evaluations combine the two methods. Quantitative evaluation involves the collection and use of data such as test scores, grades, change in the number of students taking advanced mathematics courses, increases in the number of science majors, and so on. Qualitative evaluation assesses the effectiveness of a program or its components through data such as participants' opinions as to whether their attitudes toward science have changed since their participation, an observer's judgment as to whether a class was effectively taught, or an interview subject's feelings as to whether the program has made a difference in the way students approach the learning of science.

Project Interface uses a combination of qualitative and quantitative data to evaluate its effectiveness. These include students' scores on the CTBS, the subjective judgment of participants (measured by surveys), data on junior high school participants' attrition, and data on the transfer rate of junior college students.

Data Collection

Some of the most common techniques used in conducting an evaluation are questionnaires and surveys, interviews, observations, standardized tests, and documents and records. Questionnaires and surveys are relatively inexpensive and can be used with a large number of people. It is, however, difficult to obtain in-depth information from surveys, and the response rate may be low. These methods may also be inappropriate for certain groups, such as young children or students with limited English proficiency. Interviews are ideal for collecting in-depth information. They allow the interviewer to probe to elicit information on sensitive, ambiguous, or difficult topics. This technique, however, is very labor intensive and therefore expensive. Interviewers must be skilled and report their findings in an unbiased manner. Responses may be difficult to summarize. Observation provides information about the contextual factors affecting the program. It also allows evaluators to double-check responses acquired by other means. Here again, it is expensive and requires skilled and unbiased observers. It is potentially disruptive, and data may be difficult to report in any meaningful way.

The use of standardized tests to gather data may be appealing to some evaluators, but it may be inappropriate for some intervention approaches, such as role modeling and dissemination of career information, or for short-term interventions. Finding an appropriate test may also be a problem. Documents and records are easy to handle and relatively inexpensive. They may reveal information not available from other sources. They are good for obtaining background information. Interpretations and explanations, however, may be lacking.

An especially helpful evaluation text is *Evaluating Intervention Programs* by Barbara Gross Davis and Sheila Humphreys (1985).

Questions to Guide You in Designing an Evaluation

- What kinds of evaluation will be most helpful to your project? Why?

- What are your evaluation obligations to your funders?
- What evaluation methods and techniques will you use? Why?
- Will you use an outside evaluator?
- How will you use your evaluations?
- If you are conducting a formative evaluation, is a system in place to ensure that the findings contribute to program improvement?

9

Disseminating and
Institutionalizing Programs

This chapter discusses two activities that may seem peripheral
to the actual implementation of a program but are vital to its
continued success. In some ways, an effective program cannot
be considered successful until it is institutionalized. Dissemination is one of the tools by which institutionalization may be
achieved.

There are many reasons why a program might wish to
disseminate its strategies and approaches. It is natural for a good
program to want to publicize its success; since most programs
are funded to respond to a problem, it might be argued that
a program with a particularly effective solution has an obligation to share its discovery with others; and dissemination of
findings contributes to the body of knowledge on a particular
practice.

Dissemination may be required by the funding agency
as part of the grant that supports the program. Many requests
for proposals now ask for a dissemination plan as part of the
proposal. As mentioned in the previous chapter, dissemination
is also a way to ensure continued funding for a program by publicizing its successes to possible funding sources. Almost all of
our case-study programs have some dissemination activities.
Project SEED, MESA, Finding Out/Descubrimiento, and Family Math have secured additional funding to carry out dissemination activities. In addition to helping to obtain funding for

the program, dissemination assists in the institutionalization process.

Dissemination Methods

Program findings, approaches, and strategies may be disseminated through traditional academic routes, such as presentations at conferences and articles in scholarly journals. These often describe the program as a research project and focus on the program evaluation. Annual conferences of associations such as the American Educational Research Association, the American Association for the Advancement of Science, the National Association for Science, Technology, and Society, and the Society for the Social Studies of Science may offer panel sessions on intervention programs. Publications such as *Science Education*, the *Journal for Research in Mathematics Education*, and the *Journal for Research in Science Education* publish articles on research featuring intervention programs. Staff members of Finding Out/Descubrimiento, for example, have published widely and presented several papers on various aspects of the program. More often, however, programs disseminate their methods through nonacademic outlets. The most commonly used dissemination methods are workshops, training programs, technical assistance, and materials development.

Workshops and seminars for educators who wish to replicate programs are widely used as dissemination tools by intervention programs. Workshops, based on the Saturday Science Academy model, are held for science educators who wish to start their own programs at other historically Black colleges. Usually, these workshops focus on components of the programs that are capable of being replicated at another site, such as teaching strategies and hands-on activities. Training programs offer more in-depth knowledge about program strategies and approaches. Training can be combined with technical assistance, as in the case of Finding Out/Descubrimiento's training program for elementary school teachers, which includes assistance from the training staff during the school year. As part of a statewide dissemination process, this program has also received funding to train university faculty and, together with university faculty, train master teachers in the school districts where student teachers are placed for field experience. DAPCEP has conducted inservice training for the middle and high school teachers who teach DAPCEP students. The training of teachers also contributes to the institutionalization of program strategies.

Materials developed in the course of a program are excellent dissemination tools if they are made available to educators. As mentioned in Chapter Seven, several of the case-study programs have developed materials in the form of curricula, texts, videotapes, activity charts, and other instructional aids. These materials have been made available to the general public or at least to those wishing to replicate the programs. Development of materials is part of the dissemination plan of some of the programs. Mathematics, Science, and Minorities, K–6 is developing instructional packages as part of its dissemination phase. Operation SMART has produced several publications and kits to assist in the replication of its programs. Finding Out/Descubrimiento's bilingual materials are an invaluable asset to the school districts with which the program works. The widespread popularity of Family Math's materials is an important factor in its successful dissemination.

Although wide dissemination cannot ensure the institutionalization of a program, it certainly increases the chances of this taking place. By providing exposure of the program model to the educational community, a good dissemination plan can awaken the interest of educators who might wish to incorporate elements of the model in their schools. Training programs and instructional materials can help to pave the way for the institutionalization process.

The Final Goal: Institutionalization

An intervention program cannot be considered truly successful until it has achieved some level of institutionalization. This may take the form of the incorporation of strategies and approaches developed by the program into regular classroom practice in a school district or several school districts. Or the techniques may become part of a state's teacher education curricula so that all teachers will use them. Whatever form institutionalization takes, there should be a concerted effort on the part of the program to bring this about. Unfortunately, achieving institutionalization is difficult. That there is so little known about effective ways to encourage the process only increases the difficulty.

When one considers the number of excellent intervention approaches and strategies that have emerged from intervention programs in mathematics and science, it is amazing how few have become part of regular classroom practice. Strategies such as the use of role models, which have been commonplace among intervention programs for years, have just recently been discovered by schools. The difficulty of institutionalizing practices that have proved effective in intervention programs may be due to a number of factors.

One factor may be that intervention programs are perceived as remedial programs for special students, though, in reality, their practices may improve education for all students. Educators often do not see the application of strategies developed in these programs to the regular classroom setting. Another factor may be the general resistance of educational systems to innovation. Since this resistance has been the subject of some research, we will spend the rest of this chapter reviewing pertinent literature on the topic, identifying factors that encourage institutionalization, and describing steps taken by the case-study programs to become institutionalized.

Implementation Research

In framing the issues that surround the question of institutionalization, a look at the body of research known as "implementation research" might be particularly helpful. Much of this research concerns the problems inherent in introducing a new concept or policy into a system or systems. As a term that emerged in the work of policy analysts in the early 1970s to describe the putting into practice of the Great Society's reform policies, *implementation* has often been coupled with the word *problems,* as in *implementation problems.* The work of the first generation of implementation analysts focused on defining the problem of policy implementation and sketching its parameters. The second generation analyzed the relationship between policy and practice (McLaughlin, 1987). Much of this research is relevant to the problem of institutionalization, since this process also involves the introduction of a new concept (usually preceded by a policy) into a system, usually the educational system.

What findings from implementation research can help us to understand the difficulties faced by educational innovations (that is, intervention practices) when they seek to become a part of regular classroom practice? Most analysts who have examined the subject of implementation agree that it is extremely difficult to bring about. Two broad factors on which success rests are the system's capacity and resources to implement the change and the attitudes, motivations, and beliefs with which implementors undertake the task (McLaughlin, 1987).

Cohen (1987) addresses the latter factor in his attempt to explain the slow pace of instructional reform. He points out that the European and American scholastic inheritance supports traditional practices in education; that popular practices of teaching and learning, which are mainly traditional in character, also support traditional approaches in the schools; and that the social organization of schooling is such that communication about practice is difficult. This last point is particularly pertinent to the problem of institutionalization of intervention practices. According to Cohen, the educational system in the United States is organized in such a decentralized and fragmented way that it can hardly be called a system. Cohen claims that communication about progressive reforms is especially limited, since these reforms spring from academic intellectuals in elite institutions, which maintain even less communication with the rest of the educational system.

If one applies Cohen's argument to intervention practices, it might be stated that these practices develop in enclaves as far removed from the educational system as are elite institutions — intervention programs for special populations. There seems to be very little communication between these programs and the schools. There is also a tradition of ignoring educational practices that originate in institutions that serve "special populations" as well as the feeling that these practices must be somehow remedial in nature. Perhaps this tradition goes back to the time when minority students, girls, and disabled students were segregated from the so-called normal population of students. If Cohen's reasoning is accurate, then the institutionalization of intervention practices cannot be achieved without a tremendous struggle.

Given the difficulty of introducing intervention practices into the schools, what factors encourage institutionalization of these practices? In their study of federally mandated programs to promote innovative practices in education, Berman and McLaughlin (1976) focused on the process of innovation and factors that affect it. They divided the process of innovation into three stages: initiation, where they identify the motivation for the project as either opportunism (in response to funding opportunities) or problem solving (responding to a perceived need); implementation, an organizational process that involved interactions between the project and its setting; and incorporation, the continuation of a federally sponsored project after the end of federal support.

Berman and McLaughlin found that the main factors affecting innovations were the institutional setting, particularly the organizational climate and staff motivation; the implementation strategy that local innovators used to install the project; and the degree and scope of change required by the project relative to its setting. Project outcomes depended primarily on internal factors and local decisions. More specific factors that encourage implementation and continuation of an innovation are as follows:

- Initiation based on problem solving; that is, in response to a perceived local need
- A flexible implementation strategy that promotes adaptation to the institutional setting
- A critical mass of project staff to build support and morale
- Staff training keyed to the local setting
- A supportive local organizational climate (including staff attitudes)

- Strategies to promote teacher change that involve staff training, frequent and regular meetings, and local development of materials rather than reliance on outside consultants
- The perception of an innovation as central to the school district's priorities
- Innovations involving a comprehensive area of curriculum or requiring an overall change in teacher behavior
- Projects that integrate training-induced change with expectations for classroom behavior
- Values and goals implicit in the project that are congruent with those of the project staff
- Projects that replace existing practices rather than supplementing the existing curriculum
- Projects that emphasize training rather than the introduction of new technology
- Training that focuses on practical issues of the classroom rather than on theory

Institutionalization in the Case-Study Programs

Some of the case-study programs either have been institutionalized or are well on their way to becoming so. Several of the programs have built-in plans for continuation. Mathematics, Science, and Minorities, K–6 has as its ultimate goal the institutionalization of the practices and strategies that it has developed. The program has involved and trained personnel in five school districts from the district level to the school level and has developed instructional packages to facilitate the process of institutionalization. Project MiCRO is working with state superintendents of education in three southern states to urge them to replicate the project on a statewide basis. As part of this plan, there has been a careful and systematic documentation of the implementation process.

Finding Out/Descubrimiento has been implemented in more than a hundred classrooms and ten school districts around the nation. It has received funding for statewide dissemination that includes working with colleges and departments of education on selected California State University campuses to train university faculty in the theory and research underlying complex instruction. Program staff and faculty then train master teachers in school districts where student teachers are placed in their classrooms. These student teachers are then trained by the university faculty and supervisors in the theory and practice of complex instruction. Both cooperating teachers and student teachers who are placed in their classrooms thus have the opportunity to apply the principles of complex instruction in their teaching.

Another example of effective institutionalization is Project SEED, which now operates in three school districts in California as well as in Philadelphia, Dallas, and Detroit. Funding comes from community development grants, corporations, and school districts. Project staff feel that the program not only has influenced teachers' pedagogical techniques and knowledge of mathematics but also has given teachers higher expectations for low-income minority students: "We find that the teachers with whom we work have different expectations for their students, ask them more questions, and expect more from them."

Family Math has achieved institutional status through its successful dissemination, which has been facilitated by the inservice program as well as other products, such as the Family Math book, which has been translated into Spanish and Swedish (Stenmark, Thompson, and Cossey, 1986, 1987, 1988). As of June 1990, the program had reached well over 100,000 parents and children all over the United States as well as in Australia, New Zealand, Sweden, Canada, and Costa Rica. The program has become part of the regular offerings of schools, county offices of education, state departments of education, institutions of higher education, and science centers.

Given the difficulty of achieving permanent status or influencing classroom practices, the programs that are the subjects of our case studies have done very well. This has been due to the effectiveness of their methods, the efficacy of their dissemination activities, and, above all, their tireless efforts to make a lasting contribution to the body of knowledge concerning effective practices in the teaching of mathematics and science. It is hoped that the obstacles to institutionalization of intervention practices that are now present in the educational system will be removed in the not too distant future. These intervention programs represent a valuable resource to education; the system cannot afford to continue to ignore their contributions.

And what does the future hold for intervention programs? Once institutionalization is achieved, will the need for these programs recede? It is our opinion that there will always be a place for intervention programs, for several reasons. First, because they are not part of the regular educational system, they can experiment freely with innovative techniques. Second, they can develop and focus their strategies on the needs of one segment of the population. Third, they can address aspects of a problem that are not solely achievement-related. Intervention programs can be considered education's laboratories for innovation and change.

APPENDIX A

Case Studies:
Ten Effective Programs

This appendix describes the ten effective programs that were selected for in-depth study. The case studies are based on site visits that included observations and interviews with program staff and participants as well as on a review of materials obtained from the programs. Once the case studies were completed, the staff of each program were asked to review and verify our descriptions, and changes were made on the basis of their suggestions. Since the site visits were conducted in 1987–88, the case studies may not reflect the programs as they are now. We did give all programs the opportunity to update the information in the case studies and received updates from most of them, which we incorporated.

Information from these case studies appears in several chapters in the text. We felt that it was important, however, that the case studies be available to the reader in their entirety, since they provide contextual information about the programs that is necessary for a true understanding of their success. For each of the case-study programs, this appendix presents the program's history; a description of its goals, structure, features, recruitment and selection procedures, approaches and strategies, and evaluation process; a discussion of the unique features of the program; and a description of its efforts toward dissemination and institutionalization.

Detroit Area
Pre-College Engineering Program

The Detroit Area Pre-College Engineering Program (DAPCEP) was begun in 1976 with a grant from the Alfred P. Sloan Foundation. At that time, participating institutions included the University of Michigan, Michigan State University, one Detroit high school, two middle schools, and 245 students. By 1992, the program had expanded to include eight area universities, eighteen high schools, fifty middle schools, and 4,300 students.

Program Goals and Structure

The overall program goal of DAPCEP is to increase the number of minority students motivated and prepared to pursue a science or engineering degree. More specifically, the objective is to increase the number of Black, Hispanic, and Native American middle school and high school students who are prepared academically to choose careers in engineering and technical fields.

Program Structure

The program is governed by an eighteen-member board of directors representing the Detroit public schools, local universities, technical employers, and parents. Participating area universities are: the University of Detroit/Mercy; the University of Michigan, Ann Arbor; the University of Michigan, Dearborn; GMI Management Institute; Lawrence Technological Institute; Michigan State University; Oakland University; and Wayne State University. The board has six representatives from corporations, six university representatives, three school system representatives, and three parent members. An executive director is responsible to the board for the implementation of its policies.

In addition to the board of directors, the program has

several committees to which various functions have been assigned.

- Communications Committee — ensures communication with current and prospective students and their parents; maintains liaison with corporate supporters, teachers at participating schools and universities, and community, civic, government, and professional organizations; publishes *Moving Up* (DAPCEP's newsletter)
- Program and Evaluation Committee: responsible for developing and administering in-school programs, campus activities, and program evaluation procedures; presently developing a comprehensive DAPCEP curriculum that includes expanded offerings to the middle school level
- Finance and Development Committee: works with the executive director to raise, control, and manage the financial resources and property of the corporation
- Executive Committee: transacts routine business between meetings of the board and acts in emergencies
- Audit Committee: responsible for reviewing the books and records of the various standing and ad hoc committees
- Information Systems Committee: responsible for tracking the progress of DAPCEP students from admission to the program through college graduation

The program receives support and funding from many different sources. Major corporations and small businesses supply speakers, financial aid, and summer employment for participants. The Detroit Public School System supports many activities of the program, and the participating universities make in-kind contributions of facilities, support staff, and so on. DAPCEP has also recently received a large grant from the National Science Foundation that was used to revise and upgrade its middle school preengineering curriculum and to develop videotapes and supplementary teaching materials in mathematics.

Program Features

DAPCEP's program offerings consist of three interrelated components: the Summer Skills Intensification Program, the Saturday

Enrichment Classes, and the In-School Preengineering Classes. There is also an after-school tutorial component and an active parents' advisory group. Other activities include participation in the local science and engineering fair.

The Summer Skills Intensification Program. This program — held at Wayne State University; Michigan State University; the University of Michigan, Ann Arbor; the University of Michigan, Dearborn; Lawrence Technological University; Oakland University; and the University of Detroit/Mercy — provides classes in mathematics, computer science, and communications skills for students in the ninth, tenth, eleventh, and twelfth grades.

The Saturday Enrichment Classes. These classes are held at eight area universities — the University of Michigan, Ann Arbor; the University of Michigan, Dearborn; Lawrence Technological University; Oakland University; Wayne State University; the University of Detroit/Mercy; Michigan State University; and GMI Management Institute — and consist of courses in physics; chemistry; laboratory science; technical writing; chemical, civil, electrical, and mechanical engineering; algebra; trigonometry; calculus; and computer science. Students in these classes span grades 6 through 12.

The In-School Preengineering Classes. In these classes, which are held at fifty middle and eighteen high schools in the Detroit Public School System, students prepare science fair and engineering projects, take field trips, hear technical speakers, research the lives of minority engineers and scientists, and attend audiovisual presentations prepared by DAPCEP corporate and university representatives. Students also view videotapes that demonstrate how to prepare a science fair project and present discussions of careers in science and engineering moderated by middle school students.

Classes in science and engineering for middle school and high school students are also part of this program component. Teachers who teach the in-school classes undergo a period of in-service training by DAPCEP staff, who are also available for technical assistance. One staff member describes the key to DAPCEP's in-service training: "It's continuous and takes place throughout the year. We also provide technical support (as well as moral support) throughout the year."

The Science and Engineering Fair of Metropolitan Detroit.
The fair was first held in 1958. Some 25,000 to 30,000 students
in grades 7 through 12 from schools in Wayne, Oakland, and
Macomb counties participate each year. More than 3,000 of these
actually enter the fair, with 2,000 or more presenting projects.

In 1977, when DAPCEP began participating in the fair,
the participation of Detroit public school students was low. For
example, of 2,438 entries, 222, or 9 percent, were from the
Detroit public schools. By 1991, the number of entries had increased to 2,063, or 57 percent of all entries. Data collected
through the intervening years show that without the participation of DAPCEP students, the number of Detroit public school
entries would be considerably smaller. In 1980, the first grand
award winner from the Detroit Public School System in five years
was a DAPCEP participant. Of the eight grand award winners
in the 1990 fair, three were from DAPCEP. Numbers of first-,
second-, and third-place winners who were in DAPCEP increased at an even greater rate than the increase in participation. In 1992, 238 or 46 percent of all gold ribbon winners were
DAPCEP students.

Other Activities. Tutorial services are offered at Wayne
State University by college students who are specially trained
to be tutors and are former DAPCEP participants. There is also
a Summer Bridge Program, which helps students to gain practical experience by giving them the opportunity to work in an
engineering-related firm the summer before they enter college.

Recruitment and Selection Procedures

After fifteen years of operation in the Detroit area, the program
does not need to recruit extensively. The summer program at-
tracts an applicant-to-acceptance ratio of 4:1, while the Saturday program's ratio is 3:1. For some of the in-school programs,
the principal decides who will participate; in others, administrators, teachers, and/or other staff may be involved in recruiting students. Selection criteria include a minimum of a C+
GPA, interest in math and science, and the recommendation
of a teacher or counselor.

Approaches and Strategies

   Enrichment, Not Remediation. The focus of DAPCEP classes is enrichment rather than remediation. This approach is reinforced by the fact that classes are held at area universities and are conducted by university professors, some of whom are also deans of the colleges of engineering. Students feel a sense of pride in being a part of this program. The successful involvement and competition of DAPCEP students in the Metropolitan Detroit Science and Engineering Fair also emphasizes the enrichment aspect of the program.

   Integration into the Public School System. DAPCEP's integration into the Detroit Public School System enables the program to effect change within the classroom and to affect the way teachers teach through the use of a preengineering curriculum guide and other teaching materials and its in-service training for teachers. Its approach to gaining acceptance is described by the executive director: "We started with the principal in a given school by finding one principal who not only cared but had some power. We developed our program in that school over two or three years. After that, the program expanded to other schools. The key is to get the principals to buy into the concept."

   Curriculum Development. With funding from the National Science Foundation, the program has developed a preengineering curriculum guide for middle school students. This guide lays out in a systematic way the courses in science that students interested in engineering should take. The guide also emphasizes hands-on activities and the inquiry method, both of which have proved to be effective with minority students.

   Development of Videotapes. DAPCEP uses videotapes in creative ways—as motivating tools, to promote career awareness, and to supplement mathematics teaching. Developed by program staff and consultants (with funds from the National Science Foundation), these videotapes are particularly appropriate for the age group and the population served by DAPCEP and thus are very effective teaching devices.

   Continuous Intervention. DAPCEP provides intervention throughout the year, as well as throughout the week, including

Saturdays, for students in grades 6–12. Thus, its services cover a broad span, one of the characteristics of an effective program. As a university administrator explained, "What we try to do is offer a number of instructional and motivational activities throughout the school year." The activities in the interrelated components of the program are diversified enough to avoid repetition and boredom on the part of the students. The executive director explained that they "dissect individual programs in order to avoid duplication. The emphasis is on overall growth."

Although early adolescents are only one portion of the 4,300 students served by DAPCEP, its middle school population (3,000) outnumbers its high school enrollment (1,300). The emphasis on hands-on experiences and the provision of peer role models in the videotapes are effective for this age group. The feeling of pride that the program awakens, as well as its high expectations for students, gives them a sense of accomplishment.

Program Evaluation

DAPCEP recently sent a survey to 3,170 participants enrolled from 1976 to 1986 and received 2,154 responses. An analysis of the results revealed that 74 percent of former DAPCEP participants who were in college were majoring in engineering, math, or science; 81 percent who had graduated from college had pursued majors in those fields; more than 80 percent were attending Michigan universities; and many of the graduates were employed by Michigan-based companies. The project staff intend to update this survey monthly and to issue a report annually. They hope to increase the response rate through more sophisticated tracking techniques.

Unique Features of the Program

Multisector Board. The inclusion in the policy-making body of the program of various sectors of society, such as public schools, universities, corporations, and parents, ensures a high degree of involvement and ownership of the program. The Michigan universities, for example, see involvement in DAPCEP as a recruiting device to attract the most promising minority students. Corporations see their membership on the board as a tool to identify and recruit minority talent for their companies. Schools, of course, see board membership as a means for them to effect beneficial change in school-related practices. And parents see board membership as a way to become more involved in and to have more input into their children's education. Although representatives of community based organizations are not included on the board of advisers, the community, especially community-based organizations such as churches, is also very involved with the program. The members of a Detroit Baptist church, for example, helped prepare a proposal that won a National Science Foundation grant for the program.

Development of Curriculum and Videotapes. Supported with funding from the National Science Foundation, DAPCEP has been able to revise and upgrade its middle school preengineering curriculum guide for use in its in-school programs. It is also developing supplementary materials for the teaching of math. Videotapes are another teaching, motivational, and career awareness tool developed by DAPCEP. Since these have been created specifically for the population served by this program, the tapes are especially effective for use with minority students from junior high through high school. Their use of role models, both peer and adult, and their placing of science in an everyday, real-world context are particular strengths of these materials.

The Science and Engineering Fair of Metropolitan Detroit. DAPCEP's use of the Detroit fair as a way of motivating students and creating an aura of excellence for the program is unique. Although other programs have created their own competitions, DAPCEP uses an areawide competition and prepares students in a predominantly minority school system to compete and win.

Dissemination and Institutionalization

Although the program has not made a concerted effort to disseminate its model, it has assisted school systems in cities such as Boston and Washingon, D.C., to develop similar programs. Its summer program was recently the focus of a study for replication purposes by Johns Hopkins University and the MESA program of Baltimore. The program also receives visits from educators who wish to learn more about the model and holds seminars for educators and directors of precollege programs.

Family Math

The Family Math project is an offshoot of the EQUALS program at the Lawrence Hall of Science, a public science center and research and development unit in science and mathematics education at the University of California, Berkeley. EQUALS, which was established in 1977, provides in-service training for teachers of grades K–12 to improve mathematics teaching and learning, with special emphasis on equity issues in the teaching of minority and female students. The idea for a Family Math project that would be separate from the EQUALS activities was born of the need expressed by teachers to supply parents with activities and materials for use in the home with their children.

In 1981, Family Math received funding for three years from the Fund for the Improvement of Postsecondary Education (FIPSE) to develop a prototype program and pilot test it as well as to develop training for teachers and trainers of teachers and to develop curriculum materials. Pilot testing was conducted in two inner-city communities. By the end of the FIPSE funding period, the project had conducted seventeen courses at eleven locations, reaching 364 parents and children; conducted seven training sessions for 322 potential Family Math leaders and trainers of trainers; and developed the Family Math book (Stenmark, Thompson, and Cossey, 1986), which gives the full curriculum and information for conducting Family Math courses. The dissemination and publication of this book were funded by the Carnegie Corporation.

Since the initial period of development, the program has continued to conduct training sessions across the United States and in Australia, New Zealand, Canada, Costa Rica, and Sweden. (Program staff estimate that they reached, either directly or indirectly, approximately 15,144 parents and children between January 1982 and June 1986, and over 240,000 parents and children by January 1992.) The program has received funding under the Women's Education Equity Act (WEEA) to produce a seventeen-minute documentary film on the Family Math classes. It has also received funding from the National Science Foundation (NSF) to present Family Math in-service training and classes together with community-based organizations in minority neighborhoods. More recently, it has received funding from the NSF and the U.S. Department of Education (DOE) to develop and present in-service workshops to prepare participants to present Family Math courses to Spanish-speaking families. The Family Math activities have been translated into Spanish and Swedish (Stenmark, Thompson, and Cossey, 1987, 1988), and Chinese and Russian translations are currently in progress.

Goals and Objectives

The overall goal of the Family Math program is to help families become involved in their children's mathematics education. Specific objectives evolved as the program developed. As reported by Thompson and Kreinberg (1986), these objectives are:

- To provide parents with activities to help their children with mathematics at home
- To provide parents with information about the importance of mathematics in future schooling and work
- To inform families about the equity issues involved in mathematics
- To inform parents that mathematics is important for all students
- To build awareness that mathematics consists of more than arithmetic and rote computations
- To develop problem-solving skills and the ability to talk about mathematics
- To build positive attitudes toward mathematics
- To help parents feel that they can and do make a difference in their children's mathematics education
- To provide an opportunity for all members of the family to enjoy doing mathematics

Program Components

The program has five distinct components: (1) the Family Math
courses for parents and children; (2) the in-service training of
Family Math parent and teacher leaders; (3) the preparation
of the trainers of trainers; (4) program dissemination; and (5)
institutionalization through Family Math sites. These components also correspond to phases in the development of the Family
Math program.

   Description of Courses. A typical Family Math course lasts
from four to eight weeks and works with parents and children
in grades K–8. (Usually, Family Math leaders work with two
or three grade levels at a time.) Classes are usually held once
a week, either on weekday evenings or on Saturdays, and typically last two hours a session. The emphasis is on the development of problem-solving skills (and thus an understanding of
mathematics) through the use of hands-on activities and talking about the process of problem solving. Areas covered by
courses include arithmetic, geometry, probability and statistics,
estimation, measurement, and logical thinking. Important elements of the classes include the following:

- A supportive, nonthreatening environment that encourages
  risk taking so that parents and children feel comfortable doing mathematics
- The presentation of the mathematics content that includes
  explanations as to why children are taught paricular concepts at certain ages, how these concepts are interrelated,
  and why they are important for children to learn
- The modeling of a teaching style to be adopted by parents
  that includes providing early success for learners, encouragement to work at their own pace, extensions of each activity
  that preclude the use of drill and practice, and strategies to
  generate enthusiasm and positive attitudes toward math activities
- A link to career possibilities through the use of role models
  from the community

Leader Workshops. In order to ensure that Family Math classes would continue and grow, the program developed workshops for potential Family Math class leaders, who are usually teachers and parents. These include discussions of the philosophy and goals of Family Math, instructions in how to start a course, what and how to teach, and an opportunity to participate in Family Math activities. Workshops usually last two full days.

Trainer-of-Trainer Workshops. These workshops evolved as a result of the establishment of EQUALS sites in six geographical regions. The staff of each region, in addition to offering EQUALS training, began offering Family Math training, and workshops were created to train these trainers. Training centers have been established at more than thirty other sites, including locations in Australia, Canada, Costa Rica, New Zealand, and Sweden.

Recruitment

The ease of recruiting parents to attend Family Math classes varies. In some cases, Family Math leaders have to limit class enrollment because they are swamped with applicants; in others, especially in cases where a predominantly low-income population is involved, recruitment of parents is difficult. Strategies for recruitment include classroom teachers sending a notice home with the student, followed by a reminder shortly before the beginning of the course; teachers informing parents about the course during parent-teacher conferences or family nights; inviting parents and children to a one-night introductory class; and doing a Family Math activity with students in one or several math classes and encouraging them to bring their parents to the Family Math course. The best strategies involve personal contact. No matter how difficult it is to attract parents to the classes, once they have come, they tend to keep coming back.

Family Math training workshops include strategies for attracting parents to classes. Potential class leaders are encouraged to make extra efforts to reach minority and low-income parents. These special recruiting efforts may include telephoning parents or contacting them at parent-teacher conferences. At the workshops, the leaders stress the fact that Family Math was developed as the offshoot of EQUALS, which is an equity program.

Approaches and Strategies

The program contains and combines elements that have been pointed out in the research as being particularly effective in influencing attitudes toward mathematics and in increasing mathematics learning: parent involvement in their children's education, the use of hands-on activities, a belief that the doing of mathematics increases confidence, and an emphasis on the application and use of mathematics in real-life situations (including career role modeling activities). The program also uses strategies that have proved effective in teaching problem solving. For example, Family Math encourages parents and children to talk about mathematics and about the difficulties of solving a problem. Classes begin with familiar math topics, and participants are given tools — strategies — to apply to the solving of a problem so that the frustration of not knowing where to begin is avoided. The leaders gradually introduce unfamiliar topics or ways of doing math problems only after the learners' confidence is established. Class leaders may spend fifteen to twenty minutes separately discussing with parents concerns or questions about their children's curriculum or learning problems.

Family Math also has the advantage of having developed an excellent tool for teaching — the Family Math book. According to one enthusiastic teacher-parent, the materials for teaching Family Math are "well thought out. They accomplish their goal. You learn so much from them. They are meant to be used more than once, and they are so enjoyable that you don't mind doing them more than once. The challenge is there regardless of your age and regardless of the level of math expertise you have. Adults are challenged as equally as children, and there is no frustration."

Family Math leaders have noticed that junior high students and their parents respond differently to the program than younger students and their parents do. For example, they have found that sending notices about the program home with junior high students may not work unless the students want their parents to attend. A staff member noted that junior high students have more influence over the decision to participate than younger ones do. Leaders have also found the dynamics of interaction between adolescent children and their parents to be different from those between younger students and their parents. One reason for this is that the level of mathematics knowledge required is higher for students in junior high. "I have had parents whose mathematical background is weak make their kids stay home for a week while they come to class to catch up," said one teacher. Once parents and children get involved in the class, however, there is less of a competitive attitude on the part of the parents. In other words, parents of adolescents tend to push their children to "show off" less than do parents of younger students. There is also less family-to-family cooperation in the junior high group, with families tending to be more insular. Parents of older children seem to be more interested in the career aspects of the course, since careers are much more a reality to their children at that age.

Staff

In addition to the EQUALS staff, the Family Math staff is made up of the leaders who have been trained over the years and of the trainers of trainers. A study by Devaney (1986) identified qualities that the leaders have in common:

- They enjoy their work.
- They think of themselves as learners as well as teachers.
- They want to do new things; they are adventurous.
- They are confident.
- They have a positive philosophy about math and about teaching.
- They want to influence parents, the community, their school, and other teachers with their point of view.
- They are ingenious in seeing possibilities and making adaptations.

- They are entrepreneurial in making things happen.
- They understand the power of collegiality and seek it.

A survey conducted by the program in July 1986 found that more than half (57 percent) of those attending the leader workshops were teachers and 42 percent were parents. The majority were well educated and White. Approximately half of the participants went on to teach at least one Family Math class.

Program Evaluation

The Family Math program has been evaluated in a number of ways. Surveys, interviews, and observations have determined the effect of both classes and workshops on participants. The number of people reached by the program and its rapid spread throughout the country and beyond are another indication of its success. Two reports have been prepared by outside evaluators. *The Implementation of FAMILY MATH in Five Community Agencies* (Shields and David, 1988) documents the NSF-funded work with community-based organizations. *The Families of FAMILY MATH Research Project* (Sloane, 1990) reports on in-depth interviews of families from four ethnic groups who have attended Family Math sessions and explores parents' attitudes toward their roles in their children's math learning and how these change over the course of their participation in Family Math classes. The program's success in securing additional funding over the years is a measure of its worth in the eyes of foundations, government agencies, and school districts.

Parents. A survey of first-year participants revealed that more than 90 percent played math games with their children and helped them with homework, more than 80 percent talked to their children's teachers about their math progress, and most sustained the math-related activities that were begun during the courses. A majority of parents (75 percent) indicated that they were able to help their children with math and that they knew more about math and how it was taught following their participation in the program. Follow-up surveys sent to first-year participants showed that the program had long-term effects on parents, most of whom maintained a high level of math-related activity.

A series of in-depth interviews with Family Math leaders conducted by an educational consultant (Devaney, 1986) revealed that parents participating in the program have more positive attitudes toward their children's school mathematics than do other parents because they understand more about the curriculum. The relationship between parents and children also seemed to have been improved by having something fun and important to do together. Sloane (1990) found that parents' attitudes toward mathematics and their role in helping their children with mathematics changed over the course of their involvement with Family Math. The parents were particularly impressed with the opportunity that Family Math afforded them to see their children learning and thinking.

Leaders and Trainers. Evaluations of the leader and trainer-of-trainer workshops were conducted immediately following the workshops, with follow-up surveys sent to participants at a later date. The follow-up surveys indicated that almost half of all participants had conducted or assisted in a Family Math course and investigated other options for continuing their own math education. Recently, the program has surveyed everyone who has ever attended a Family Math leader workshop at the Lawrence Hall of Science, as well as those conducted in New Jersey, Santa Barbara and San Diego, California, and Oregon. The data from the surveys are now being analyzed.

Innovative Features of the Program

The Family Math program has a number of innovative features:

- Parents become teachers of mathematics and collaborate with teachers to instruct classes.
- Teachers become school leaders through involvement in the program.
- The program offers a supportive, nonthreatening approach to learning mathematics.
- Household materials are used to teach mathematics.

- The activities presented in the classroom can be repeated and extended at home.
- Parents learn how to help their children enjoy and understand mathematics.

The Parent-Student-Teacher Linkage. Family Math is perhaps the only program that consciously has parents, children, and teachers working together in a learning environment to do mathematics over an extended period of time. Its success is due in large part to its approach to teaching mathematics, which is best articulated in the Family Math book (Stenmark, Thomas, and Cossey, 1986). The classes are conducted in a supportive, nonthreatening atmosphere, and the class leaders have been trained to model appropriate teaching behavior so that parents will learn to work in this manner with their children both in class and at home.

The Family Math Book — a Unique Resource. The Family Math book emphasizes a problem-solving, hands-on approach to mathematics that eschews the drill-and-practice mode usually used to teach this subject. It outlines activities that are challenging for learners of all ages so that both parents and children can maintain their interest. At the same time, the level of mathematics knowledge required by these exercises is such that both parents and children are able to complete them without frustration. The use of the Family Math book, moreover, does not preclude class leaders developing their own materials for class use, so that leaders develop a sense of ownership that benefits the course.

Built-In Self-Perpetuation. The leader workshops and the trainer-of-trainer workshops as well as the availability of the Family Math book ensure that the program is capable of replication just about anywhere that there are parents, children, and class leaders. One reason for this is the great adaptability and flexibility of the program. The program can fit into almost any time frame, it does not require sophisticated equipment or materials, it can be held anywhere, and it can accommodate participants with a wide range of mathematics expertise and ability as well as a wide range of educational and socioeconomic backgrounds.

Dissemination and Institutionalization

As mentioned above, one indicator of the Family Math program's success is the ease and speed with which it has been disseminated. According to program reports, the in-service program has been presented to more than 2,300 people, who have given more than 600 classes for more than 7,500 families and 15,000 parents and their children. As of January 1992, the program had reached well over 240,000 parents and children. Classes have been held all over the United States and in Australia, New Zealand, Sweden, Canada, and Costa Rica. Other products of the program have been the seventeen-minute documentary film showing Family Math classes and how some families are using the ideas and materials, including the Family Math book, which is widely used by both class leaders and parents in the home (more than 150,000 copies had been sold as of May 1992).

Once the FIPSE funding period expired, the program received funds from other sources to publish the Family Math book (Carnegie Corporation), to put together a film on the program (WEEA), to work with minority, community-based organizations to extend the program (NSF), and to provide a Spanish-speaking program (DOE, NSF). The program has become part of the regular offerings of schools, county offices of education, state departments of education, institutions of higher education, and science centers.

Mathematics, Engineering, Science Achievement

The idea underlying Mathematics, Engineering, Science Achievement (MESA) began to take shape in 1968 when a group of university professors, secondary school teachers, students, and other professionals expressed concern about the small proportion of engineering students enrolling at the University of California who were from historically underrepresented groups — Mexican Americans, Blacks, Native Americans, and Puerto Ricans. A survey of minority students at the University of California, Berkeley, revealed that a higher number than expected had been interested in math and science in high school but had not taken the courses required for acceptance into a college-level math-based major. The MESA Precollege Program, which was designed to help students complete three or four years of high school math, began with twenty-five students at Oakland Technical High School. The program was so successful that the model spread to other college campuses in California, the program typically being housed in a university's school of engineering and outreach activities focused on a set of high schools in the area. There are now twenty such programs in California. The MESA program later expanded its services to students in junior high school. In 1981, additional state funding allowed MESA to launch a program at the university level, creating the Minority Engineering Program (MEP). Recently, pilot programs have been established to expand MESA to the fourth-grade level. And a new initiative launched in 1991 is targeting precollege Native American students, mostly on reservations, to receive culture-based MESA training.

The Minority Engineering Program, which originated at the California State University, Northridge, in 1981, works with minority undergraduates majoring in engineering, and MESA has disseminated that model to an additional twenty college campuses in the state. The junior high program had its genesis in the realization that the high school level may be too late for intervention to enlarge the pool of potential minority engineers. A component of the MESA Secondary Program (MSP), the junior high program focuses on seventh- and eighth-graders (and sometimes sixth-graders). There are now middle and junior high programs in nineteen centers around the state. The governor of California signed into law a bill providing $175,000 annually for the junior high program for the period from 1985 to 1990. Funding has been renewed for 1991 and 1992.

Although the focus of this case study is the junior high program, a description of the MSP is necessary to provide the context within which the junior high program operates. Also, where required for a clear understanding of the junior high component of MESA, elements of the overall MESA program are described. Our case study of the junior high program is based on a site visit to the program at Berkeley. Where observations relate specifically to the Berkeley center, we make this clear.

Program Goals and Structure

The MESA Secondary Program goals are to identify Black, Native American, Latino, and other historically underrepresented students who have interest and some facility with math and science and to keep them on track, motivated, and informed so that they will be eligible for the University of California and the California State University systems when they graduate from high school. More specific goals are

- To encourage students from the target population to acquire the academic skills necessary to major in math, engineering, and the physical sciences at the university level
- To promote career awareness regarding math- and science-related professions
- To create partnerships with secondary schools, universities, industry, engineering societies, and others that involve the sharing of resources to achieve these goals
- To establish educational programs within the public schools

that prepare minority students for careers in mathematics, engineering, and the physical sciences

The MESA statewide office has responsibility for the MSP. Its main duties include:

- Planning, evaluating, and managing the MESA program throughout California
- Reviewing proposals for the creation of new MESA centers and the continuation of activities at established centers
- Developing new services and activities to enrich the existing MESA program
- Organizing and hosting regional and statewide conferences and workshops for representatives from industry, foundations, government, educational associations, minority organizations, community organizations, teachers, parents, students, and MESA staff
- Establishing relationships with industry, foundations, government agencies, school districts, and other entities to stimulate support for MESA
- Maintaining a data bank on MESA students
- Facilitating communication among MESA participants by producing handbooks, newsletters, publications, and reports relating to the program
- Maintaining a library of films, career materials, and other instructional media to assist participating teachers and students

These functions are performed by a staff of fourteen, some part-time, at the statewide office at the Lawrence Hall of Science in Berkeley. The board of directors is made up of representatives from every sector of the educational community in the state as well as some representatives of industry. An important function of the statewide office is facilitating the involvement of the industrial sector with MESA at all levels. This responsibility is shared by the development officers and the statewide director. The main role of the statewide director is to establish organizational policy, to solicit contributions from various sources, including corporations and foundations, and, with the director of programs, to establish program policy. Three regional directors monitor activities of the programs throughout the state.

A very important function of the statewide office is the funding of the various precollege- and college-level programs. MESA philosophy recognizes that it is important that the school or university with which it works should feel some ownership of the program. This feeling is reinforced by cost-sharing arrangements, with MESA funding about 50 percent of the college-level program costs and all of the precollege-level program costs and the schools making in-kind donations of faculty time and facilities. Corporate contributions make up a large share of MESA funding; corporations also donate a tremendous amount of staff time, facilities, and equipment.

The goals of MESA's junior high program are to identify minority students who have the potential to do well in math and to encourage them to take algebra in the ninth grade. These goals were established by the statewide MESA office and are shared by all the junior high programs.

The MSP director and staff of the program are located on a university campus (usually within a school of engineering) and administer the high school, junior high, and, where it exists, the elementary components. In some centers the MSP and MEP are administered separately; in others the two programs share the same director. The junior high program works with area junior high schools (seventh, eighth, and sometimes sixth grades). MESA staff talk with administrators at the local schools, and those who are interested in establishing a partnership are invited to submit applications spelling out the types of resources that the schools are willing to provide. The program looks for schools that are willing to provide space and release time for one faculty member, indicate faculty acceptance of the program, and have a high minority enrollment. The statewide coordinator makes the final decision to accept or reject an application.

Once a partnership is established, the MSP staff interview and select students who meet the criteria for the program. A faculty adviser, usually a math or science teacher at the school, is responsible for assisting with recruitment, advising students, and supervising the undergraduate tutors who go out to the school. Peer tutors, who are advanced MESA students who have excelled in their courses, also provide assistance. During the school year, most activities take place at the school after school hours, although there are field trips and Saturday sessions at the university. There are also summer programs at most MSP centers. The Berkeley junior high program works with eleven schools in two school districts.

Program Features

The junior high program provides academic tutoring and study groups, academic counseling, field trips, career awareness activities, role models, science projects, competitions, and parent activities. Many junior high programs offer summer enrichment programs as well.

Study Assistance. Study assistance takes place three hours a week after school at the school site. Tutoring is provided by undergraduate students who are math and science majors as well as by peer tutors. During these sessions, students work on group projects in math or science. About every six weeks during the school year, students visit the university campus on Saturdays to work on special projects and to use university facilities. The Berkeley program, for example, frequently uses the Lawrence Hall of Science facilities during these Saturday sessions.

Parent Activities. Parental involvement is an important component of the junior high programs. There are monthly parent meetings, usually held right after the grading period. The Berkeley program uses these meetings to present awards, such as calculators or trips to the theater, to students who make the honor roll. Parents talk about their concerns at these meetings, and sometimes professionals such as adolescent psychologists give presentations. The Berkeley program also holds a Family Math course at each participating school at least once during the year.

The Summer Enrichment Program. During the summer, the Berkeley program offers a prefreshman engineering program sponsored by the U.S. Department of Energy for seventh- to ninth-graders. The program runs for six weeks, during which time the students live on campus and participate in career awareness activities, take math classes, and work on projects. Most MESA centers offer activities during the summer, although these vary from center to center. Summer enrichment programs typically last from five to six weeks and consist of skill-building activities (regular classroom-type courses), cultural enrichment (such as art or humanities classes or a visit to a play), and preengineering activities (such as laboratory research, special expeditions, or research and design competitions).

Recruitment and Selection

The MESA junior high program's target population consists of sixth-, seventh-, and eighth-grade minority students who are either college-track or "mid-track." Program staff describe "mid-track" as scoring at about the fiftieth percentile on the Comprehensive Test of Basic Skills (CTBS).

After a school has been accepted as a participant in the program, MESA staff receive a list of eligible students. They then interview students who are interested in participating in the program. In many cases, the number of applicants far exceeds the number of slots in the program; at one junior high school in Oakland, there were 130 applicants and only 30 places. Once students have been accepted by MESA, they must maintain an above-average GPA and participate in a reasonable number of MESA activities.

Approaches and Strategies

All of the interviewees stated that the junior high program uses strategies and techniques that are particularly geared toward their target age group. The stress on parental involvement, the use of peer tutors, the giving of rewards, the holding of competitions as a motivational tool, and the relating of mathematics to the "real world" through hands-on activities are some of the techniques that seem to be particularly effective with adolescents. The students are also taught during the tutoring process to work together to solve problems and to rely less and less on the tutors. This develops independence and self-reliance and assists in the development of the adolescent's sense of identity.

Staff

The Berkeley site has two professional staff members who administer the MESA precollege program, forty part-time tutors, twenty-three volunteer teachers (a MESA adviser for each school), and tour site coordinators who oversee several schools and report to the Berkeley director. Tutors are chosen for their competence in the academic area that they teach as well as their similarity in background to the students that they tutor. Tutors undergo training before they begin working, and training continues at the biweekly tutor meetings during the school year. Advisers are math or science teachers who are given release time in order to work with the MESA program. These teachers are usually volunteers who, in the words of a staff member, "do this because they really want to." Advisers attend regularly scheduled meetings and are trained at special advisers' workshops.

Program Evaluation

The MESA program has a very sophisticated data-collection system for all its centers. The system is administered from the statewide office, and programs are evaluated by the statewide program coordinators, who, in addition to reviewing the data from each program, visit each program at least once a year. Data-collection forms are filled out each year by the individual programs; the information is then coded into the central data base.

MESA is one of the few intervention programs that are able to track their students to determine the number and percentage who go on to college as math or science majors. This is the main evaluation criterion for the precollege programs. According to MESA data, more than 90 percent of MESA Secondary Program graduates have gone on to colleges and universities. Of this group, more than two-thirds have chosen majors in engineering, computer science, and related technical fields. Independent evaluations of the MESA programs have also been conducted by the California Postsecondary Education Commission.

Because the junior high program is very new, its centers had not yet been evaluated at the time of this writing. Evaluation of MESA programs at the junior high level will be based on the extent to which the basic program model is implemented and whether participants are taking the courses that they should to stay on track for math-based college majors. Data collected and maintained on junior high program participants include the following:

- The number of students entering the seventh grade
- The number of students enrolling in target courses
- The number of students taking prealgebra and algebra
- Participants' grades and grade point averages
- The number of students going on to high school MESA programs
- The number of students taking the SAT or ACT and their scores
- The number of students going on to college in math- or science-based majors
- The size of each program over a two-year period

Formative evaluation of the junior high program will be conducted through a student survey as well as through informal meetings with participants and MESA chapter officers.

Other measures of a program's success are its growth and its ability to solicit funds. The MESA Precollege Program grew from partnerships with 3 high schools in 1976–77 to 250 participating junior high and high schools in 1990–91. The number of students served by MESA as well as those who can be considered MESA graduates is approximately forty times what it was in 1976–77. The program's total budget for fiscal year 1990–91 was about $6 million, including in-kind services, about $2.5 million of which was funded by the state of California. Other funding sources include industry, foundations, school districts, the

California State Department of Education, universities, and engineering and educational professionals.

Unique Features of the Program

The Partnership Model. MESA's establishment of partnerships among the various sectors of the community — universities, school districts, schools, industry — is a unique feature of the program. Although other programs may operate along similar models, none other is as widespread or includes as many sectors as MESA. One strategy for achieving partnership is the program's insistence on substantial contributions — either in-kind or monetary — from its participating institutions. This is one way of creating a sense of ownership of the program in participating institutions. This strategy also increases the resources available to the program and relieves the pressure on financing centers, since the burden of funding is shared by several entities.

The "Pipeline" Approach. MESA's activities serve students all along the educational "pipeline," beginning with fourth grade and extending to undergraduates in college. At each point in the pipeline, the intervention approach used is appropriate to the major problem present: at the junior high level, the goal is to increase the number of students who are able and who wish to participate in the academic track and to take advanced mathematics and science courses; at the high school level, the goal is to retain them in the math and science pipeline, where they will take advanced courses and make good grades, take prescribed tests in order to graduate from high school, and enroll in college in a math- or science-related major; and at the undergraduate level, the goal is to retain students in college in a math- or science-related major.

Because MESA is so widespread, this approach has a number of spinoff effects. By increasing the number of minority students who enroll in an academic track and who take advanced courses, the program is enlarging the pool of potential minority mathematicians, scientists, and engineers. Over time, it will increase the number of sections of algebra and calculus courses being offered by schools with high minority enrollments and decrease the number of business math and consumer math courses at those schools. This will, in turn, affect the proportion of college-track courses in participating schools.

The program sees its function of increasing the pool of math and science majors as a very important one. Behind the decision to expand MESA's services to junior high schools was the realization that efforts to increase the pool must take place at an earlier point than high school. The statewide director explained: "It became increasingly clear that to identify kids in some cases in the tenth grade who had an opportunity to be on track for college-level eligibility when they graduated meant basically that by that time, the student probably didn't need our help. We began to realize that we really weren't going to catch anyone who was not going to be okay anyway if we didn't go back to the junior high school levels." The program plans to reduce the number of high schools with which it has partnerships and to add junior high schools that feed into the high schools that are doing a good job. The ratio of junior high schools to high schools offering MESA programs, which is presently one to six, will eventually be reversed.

Evaluation and Data-Collection System

As seen in the section on evaluation, MESA has one of the most complete and sophisticated data-collection and tracking systems of all the case-study programs. This system enables the program to monitor individual centers to assess their effectiveness as well as to determine the long-term success of their overall program. Tracking students is a very difficult, costly, and time-consuming activity. MESA's success in establishing a successful tracking system is probably due to its relationships with the various systems that make up the community. Another factor that has probably facilitated the tracking process is that MESA is so large and so widespread that a large initial outlay for a tracking data base is justified.

Dissemination and Institutionalization

As previously mentioned, MESA has spread throughout the state of California. It is now serving over forty times the number of students that it served initially; it has also expanded its services to include junior high students and college-level students. Outside the state, several programs that use the MESA model have been established. New Mexico, North Carolina, and Washington are three states that have adopted the MESA model and requested assistance from the California statewide office in setting up their models. Other adoptions of the MESA model have taken place without the assistance or approval of the original program.

Project SEED

Project SEED was started in 1963 by William Johntz, a California mathematician, psychologist, and teacher. While teaching general math classes at Berkeley High School, where most of his students were minority students, Johntz realized that by the time his students reached high school, they felt that they could not do math. Johntz began teaching his general math classes algebra using the discovery method, and he saw that they became more involved and more interested, they had more self-confidence — and they learned algebra. He also realized, however, that by the time students are in the ninth or tenth grade, they are "pretty well tracked in terms of what they are going to do."

This realization made Johntz consider using the same strategy with sixth-graders. He wanted to reach students while they were still intellectually open, during the crucial years when lifelong attitudes toward school and learning are established. He obtained funding to develop and test his techniques from the University of California, Berkeley, and the Berkeley School District. The program was a success, and Johntz was soon training university mathematicians and corporate volunteers with strong math backgrounds (such as engineers and physicists) to be instructors in elementary math classes in schools with high minority enrollments. In 1989–90, the program worked with 6,000 minority students, primarily in grades 4 through 6. At the request of the school districts that it serves, Project SEED is expanding to the seventh and eighth grades.

Program Goals and Structure

Project SEED's long-range goal is to significantly increase the number of minority and educationally disadvantaged students majoring in and pursuing careers in mathematics and mathematics-based fields. The project's short-term goals are to increase participants' classroom participation, raise their academic self-confidence, and raise their mathematics achievement scores. Although algebra is used as a vehicle for achieving these goals, Project SEED aims to raise its students' self-confidence about academic endeavors in general. Algebra has been chosen because the subject is new to the students and not associated with past failure, as language arts and arithmetic tend to be. (It is part of the program's philosophy that direct remediation frequently fails because it concentrates on areas where the student has already failed.) As a staff member explained, if young students can do high school algebra, they gain the self-confidence to excel in arithmetic and other areas.

Project SEED's involvement with a district frequently begins with demonstration classes to illustrate the project's techniques. Once funding has been obtained, Project SEED and district staff identify schools with low-income, high-minority enrollments to work with. Participating classes are identified by Project SEED and school site staff. SEED mathematics specialists typically teach discovery math four times a week to fourth-, fifth-, and/or sixth-grade classes, although the program also works with younger and older students. SEED classes are supplementary to the basic mathematics program. The students' regular classroom teachers of the classes are present while the SEED specialist is teaching. SEED involvement with a school lasts at least one year.

Program Features

Project SEED's staff consists of mathematicians and scientists trained to teach advanced mathematics using the Socratic discovery method and special techniques developed by the program. Although direct instruction and teacher training are Project SEED's main focus, there are also a number of subsidiary activities carried out by the program.

Mathematics Specialists' Training. Project SEED instructors must complete a multidimensional training program that builds on their strong background in mathematics. Training focuses both on the SEED techniques and on how to present advanced mathematical concepts Socratically.

Each applicant must successfully complete an unpaid two-week training and screening program before being hired as a probationary instructor in the program. The training program includes workshops on SEED philosophy, curriculum, and methodology; observation of experienced specialists; study of written guidelines; conducting practice lessons with other SEED staff; and eventually, teaching parts of lessons to students under the supervision of an experienced SEED specialist. When specialists are able to plan and teach full lessons, they are assigned classes and gradually build to a full teaching load. Although this initial training period lasts approximately three to five months, specialists continue an ongoing training process that lasts throughout their SEED careers.

Project SEED's ongoing staff development program has several facets designed to maintain a high level of success in the classroom. Several times each week, specialists attend workshops in advanced mathematics, Project SEED curriculum, methodology, classroom psychology, and related topics. Observation is another important component of the program. Project SEED is a self-evaluating program: specialists at all levels of experience are required to observe and critique each other on a weekly basis. Observers not only provide feedback to the specialists that they are observing but also gain ideas for their own classes as well, ensuring a high level of quality throughout the program.

Teacher In-Service Training. As a spinoff of the SEED classes, regular classroom teachers observe the techniques and procedures employed by the SEED specialists in their classrooms on a daily basis, have an opportunity to talk with them and discuss these strategies, and learn to incorporate the ideas into their own teaching approach. SEED staff see this as an ideal vehicle for in-service training in both pedagogical techniques and mathematics.

In addition, SEED has developed special in-service training programs for classroom teachers, usually presented through model lessons, seminars, or workshops. These programs incorporate observation of experienced SEED teachers followed by discussion with SEED staff about both methodology and mathematics. Often, arrangements are made for the teachers to use what they have learned in their own classes, with supervision from SEED specialists.

Other Activities. SEED has a small peer teaching program where students are trained in teaching using SEED techniques. There are also some after school programs that students attend voluntarily for follow-up instruction.

Approaches and Strategies

Project SEED's approach is based on three basic postulates:

- Educationally disadvantaged children do poorly in school because they believe that they are inferior and because their teachers have low expectations of them.
- The most effective way to counter this feeling of inferiority is to help them to experience success.
- At-risk children will learn high school and college algebra if it is taught by someone who is highly trained in mathematics and the discovery method.

By helping disadvantaged elementary school children to experience success in a high-status subject, the program improves students' self-esteem and, ultimately, their overall academic achievement.

Teaching Techniques. Specific SEED techniques involve a number of strategies that make it possible to teach advanced mathematics to disadvantaged elementary school children. The teaching format, the Socratic discovery method, deemphasizes traditional lecture techniques and concentrates on leading students to discover mathematical concepts for themselves through a series of carefully developed questions. The technique also provides immediate feedback on whether students are learning the material.

Student Involvement. Another strategy is to involve students in their own learning process. Students are encouraged to participate through hand signals, which let the instructor know whether they agree or disagree with or are not sure about a particular answer. Other specific strategies include the teacher making deliberate mistakes, students chorusing out the answer, having students indicate answers on their fingers, having a student who has made a mistake call on another student for help, and exploring the thinking behind "wrong" answers so that a student is given credit for a thoughtful answer even though it may be technically incorrect.

The Project SEED techniques seem to be particularly effective for young students, because, as an instructor put it, they "keep them kinesthetically involved in the learning process. If you have thirty students, you just can't call on them individually very many times in a forty-five-minute period. Having them show answers on their fingers and use their hands and chorus out the answers gives them a chance to participate in almost every minute of the class." Being able to do high school mathematics gives the students a sense of competence and accomplishment. "I don't think we would be as effective if we used all the same techniques but just taught regular arithmetic," says a staff member.

Staff

The staff is made up of the mathematics specialists who teach the classes and a small core of administrators. In some cases, corporations have provided release time for their employees to work as mathematics specialists in the program. The program's use of corporate volunteers allows the corporations to become integrally involved in public education. Project SEED uses instructors with strong math backgrounds because elementary school teachers often lack the in-depth mathematical training to guide students through conceptual discovery of algebraic topics.

The program does not require that its instructors have prior experience in teaching. It does require, however, that instructors be able to relate well to the students and communicate their love of mathematics. "It's really interesting," said an administrator in the program. "It's a common opinion that corporate researchers are very stiff and formal and not able to relate to young students. But over the years, we've had a number of corporate release-time people teaching, and what seems to happen is that they ask such interesting mathematics questions that the students really pick up on the math. The students become very excited, and the classes have been very successful."

Program Evaluation

Project SEED has been evaluated many times. Recently, a summary of five consecutive evaluations from 1975–76 through 1979–80 was prepared by an outside evaluator. Students in the evaluation, who came from more than ten states and 19 school districts, were from minority and low-income backgrounds. Among the findings of the evaluators were the following:

- SEED students significantly outperformed control classes at all grade levels tested (grades 4–6).
- SEED students consistently showed an average mean gain of about two months' growth for each month of instruction.
- The program has a remarkably uniform effect on students, regardless of initial achievement patterns.
- In the areas of computation, concepts, and applications, SEED students consistently outgained control students on each of the nine subtests of the CTBS for all grade levels.
- The five-year evaluation results show a remarkably consistent record of achievement for children whose previous levels of achievement were considerably below national norms.
- In all states at all grade levels, SEED students made greater gains than their control counterparts.

The evaluators concluded after five years of studying the program that Project SEED had the "best results we have ever seen by any program."

   A more recent in-depth analysis, was undertaken by the Research and Evaluation Department of the Dallas Independent School District in November 1989. The evaluators conducted a multiyear longitudinal study of the effects of SEED instruction on students' mathematics achievements and attitudes, using experimental and comparison groups of students matched by sex, ethnicity, race, socioeconomic status, and pre-SEED instruction achievement level. The groups consisted of students who had received SEED instruction in the fourth, fifth, and sixth grades beginning in 1985, 1986, and 1987 and matched comparison groups that had not received SEED instruction. The major findings of that study are as follows:

- SEED instruction positively affects students' attitudes toward mathematics. The study showed some significant increases in enrollment of SEED students over non-SEED students in advanced mathematics courses at the middle school and early high school levels.
- SEED instruction affects students' overall performance. The rate of grade repetition in the study was significantly lower for SEED students than for non-SEED students.
- SEED has immediate and positive effects on students' mathematics scores as measured by the Iowa Test of Basic Skills (ITBS). Students who had taken only one semester of SEED scored more highly on all mathematics sections of the ITBS than did non-SEED students.
- SEED has a cumulative effect on students' mathematics scores. Not only did SEED students outperform non-SEED students on the ITBS after only one semester of SEED instruction, but also the margin between their scores increased significantly for each additional semester of SEED instruction. These gains are maintained for at least two years after SEED instruction has ended.

The program also administers a questionnaire to classroom teachers at participating schools. Results of these evaluations show that teachers find SEED teaching methods to be extremely effective (81 percent) and would like to see this kind of instruction in more classrooms (100 percent). Many of the teachers also said that they had incorporated several of the SEED techniques into their everyday teaching.

In-service training programs have also been evaluated favorably by the school districts where they have been held. An evaluation in Boston found that "Teachers agreed that SEED methods were effective, that student attitudes and achievement were enhanced by SEED methods, and that they adopted many SEED methods in their teaching of math."

Unique Features of the Program

Three of the unique features of Project SEED are its teaching technique, its teaching of high school math in elementary school, and its teacher training model.

The SEED Teaching Technique. As described above, the SEED teaching technique combines group feedback with Socratic questioning. The constant involvement of students through signs and the chorusing of answers is another unique feature of this technique. Critical to the effectiveness of the program is the use of teachers with a strong background in mathematics. They impart to their students their love and understanding of the subject as well as sharing their excitement about it.

The Teaching of Advanced Mathematics to Young Students. Students participating in SEED classes are proud of being able to do high school– and college-level mathematics. This is a motivating strategy that also results in a sense of achievement that they are able to do advanced math successfully. As a staff member said about this strategy, "There is something magic about their being able to say, 'I am doing high school mathematics.'"

The Teacher Training Model. The SEED teacher training model employs as a basic strategy a system of modeling, observation, discussion, and supervised practice. Having teachers observe other teachers and critique their techniques is an ongoing practice of the model. As this practice was described by a SEED administrator, "You are continuously getting feedback from another adult about what you are doing as well as suggestions about ways you might do it better. There is no egotism involved. If you see someone else doing something that you like, you grab it and run with it."

Dissemination and Institutionalization

Project SEED now operates in three school districts in California and in Philadelphia, Dallas, and Detroit. Funding comes from community development grants, corporations, foundations, and school districts. Since the beginning of the project, it has operated in fifty school districts.

Project staff believe that the program has had effects on the institutions with which it has come in contact. They feel, for example, that they have given corporations a meaningful vehicle through which to become involved with the public schools. The program has also done demonstrations for state legislatures in Michigan, California, Massachusetts, and New Jersey: "Anything you can do that convinces the people in power that certain segments of the population should not be written off is helpful."

The staff also feel that in addition to influencing teachers' pedagogical techniques and knowledge of mathematics, the program has also given teachers higher expectations for low-income minority students: "We find that the teachers with whom we work have different expectations for their students, ask them more questions, and expect more from them." This is confirmed by teachers themselves in the surveys. Finally, many of the people who have worked with Project SEED now run intervention programs or continue to work in the education of at-risk students. They have continued to disseminate SEED practices by incorporating the training and techniques in their new activities.

Finding Out/Descubrimiento:
The Program for Complex Instruction

The Program for Complex Instruction, under the direction of Elizabeth G. Cohen, has been located in the School of Education at Stanford University since 1978. Its goal is the design of intellectually demanding instruction for academically heterogeneous classrooms. Complex Instruction was originally used in conjunction with a bilingual (Spanish-English) math and science curriculum called Finding Out/Descubrimiento for elementary school students, developed by Edward DeAvila (DeAvila and Duncan, 1980a). For many years, Finding Out/Descubrimiento has been a primary example of a multiple-abilities curriculum that can be used for implementing Complex Instruction. In the past three years, additional materials have been designed for the middle school grade levels.

As part of its instructional activity, the program has developed, implemented, and evaluated an innovative instructional approach, a curriculum and materials (Finding Out/Descubrimiento), and a model for teacher training and organizational support. Although the seminal research was funded through several sources, including the National Science Foundation, monies to create and document an effective model for dissemination and implementation were obtained from the Walter S. Johnson Foundation (1982–83).

The Program for Complex Instruction was designed to teach thinking skills to children in the second through fifth grades using concepts of math and science. Developed from an interdisciplinary base in psychology and sociology, the program was concerned not only with effective instruction but also with the uniformity of implementation between classrooms and with the organizational support necessary to ensure the survival of the model over time. During the year 1982–83, when the implementation process was documented and the project's training and

organizational development components were evaluated, the
project was involved with ten schools in three school districts.

Goals and Structure

The primary goal of the program is the proper implementation
and survival of an instructional approach to the development
of higher-order thinking skills useful for heterogeneous classrooms in which a wide range of academic skills and cultural,
racial, and linguistic characteristics are present. Specific program objectives are as follows:

That students will:

- Gain in the understanding of the concepts contained in the
  instructional materials
- Gain in ability to hypothesize, observe, analyze, make in-
  ferences, and generalize (skills essential to scientific process)
- Strengthen their basic skills
- Improve their linguistic proficiency

That teachers will:

- Learn how to manage multiple learning centers while maintaining high rates of task engagement
- Learn how to use cooperative student groups and roles in
  managing complex instruction
- Learn how to stimulate thinking, give specific feedback to
  students, and treat status problems
- Learn how to make the transition from direct supervision
  to delegation of authority while managing complex instruction
- Learn how to conduct effective team meetings
- Learn how to utilize systematic collegial evaluation

That administrators will:

- Learn how to provide organizational support for teachers
  and for the program to enable it to survive over time
- Monitor program success using yearly evaluation data

The program model is the result of several years of research, development, and evaluation activities undertaken by the program staff. During the phase of the project documented here, program staff trained teachers and school staff from participating schools and gave feedback and technical support during the year.

Program Components

The program model has three components: the classroom implementation model, the teacher training model, and the model for organizational support.

The Classroom Implementation Model. Elements of the classroom implementation model include the curriculum and materials and the instructional approach called "complex instruction." The curriculum (Finding Out/Descubrimiento) was developed with a Piagetian theoretical framework (DeAvila, Havassy, and Pascual-Leone, 1976) and is different from other experiential science curricula in that the activities apply science and mathematics to everyday life using problems and materials that are common to most children, regardless of language or culture; the instructions and work sheets are presented in Spanish, English, and pictographs; and the purpose of the activities is to enrich the repertoire of each child regardless of developmental level.

The curriculum provides a set of math and science activities for children in grades 2 through 5. Materials include illustrated activity cards with instructions for the task, work sheets to be completed individually by each student, and materials for manipulative activities. The activities require individual questioning and experimentation and incorporate many of the characteristics of pure discovery. Learning how to learn, the development of a questioning attitude, and logical thought are emphasized throughout the activities. Children explore and experiment with intrinsically interesting materials and phenomena, and each child takes from an activity what is appropriate to his or her particular stage of development. Multiple learning centers that represent the same basic concept provide the children with several opportunities to grasp a concept, while giving them practice in transferring the concept from one application to another.

While the activities emphasize how children think through a given problem, they also provide children with skills necessary for academic progress: making correspondence, sorting, ordering, measuring with and without numbers, using the metric system, comparing, estimating, predicting, making inferences and testing hypotheses, using arithmetic symbols and operations, and understanding relationships. At the same time, language development takes place as students learn new terminology, read directions, and report their results.

The instructional approach, "complex instruction," is the vehicle through which the curriculum is delivered. This approach encompasses an authority structure with unusual features, a classroom management system, and a nontraditional role for the teacher. Classes are organized into learning centers (usually six or seven to a classroom) where no more than five children engage in an activity related to the central theme and concepts of a particular unit. Different groups of students work with different materials and perform different tasks. According to sociologists, this kind of classroom organization represents a highly differentiated instructional technology (Cohen, 1986). In such a classroom, direct supervision by the teacher is impractical and inefficient. A much better approach is for the teacher to delegate authority to working groups of students. This delegation of authority by the teacher is accompanied by a system of cooperative norms and assigned roles:

> This system allows children to manage and monitor their interactions at the learning centers. For example, children have the right to ask one another for help when they do not understand a step in the task; children who seem to understand have the duty to provide assistance. Children attempt to explain to each other what the task entails and why certain things might be happening. When turns need to be taken, children are concerned that everybody in their group gets the opportunity to con-

tribute. It is the responsibility of the student acting as facilitator to see to it that members of the
group use the cooperative norms that have been established. When substantive or procedural decisions
need to be made, for example, extending an experiment or calling the teacher when the group is
at an impasse, opinions are elicited from each child
and a resolution is reached [Lotan and Benton,
1990, p. 55].

After the initial orientation and before the final wrap-up,
the teacher is no longer the focal element in the classroom. Instead, the teacher facilitates student group interaction, moving
from center to center and helping students with their work and
giving information only when absolutely necessary. Often, the
teacher asks questions that stimulate and extend students' thinking about their tasks and reminds them how to apply the cooperative norms and use the roles productively so they can complete their tasks.

The Teacher Training Model. Complex instruction requires a teacher to function as a professional decision maker
as well as a member of a team. In addition to becoming familiar
with the activities and principles underlying this approach to
learning, teachers must do the following:

- Master techniques of classroom management
- Gain mastery of methods for providing effective feedback,
  stimulating and extending student thinking, and raising the
  expectations for competence of low-status children
- Understand how to hold children accountable for their work
- Learn how to work effectively in collegial teams
- Learn how to observe and evaluate individual classrooms

The training includes a one-week practicum in which children are brought in so that teachers can practice their management and teaching skills. In addition, a one-day workshop is
scheduled in January to develop the more difficult skills—giving
specific feedback to individual students and assessing compe-

tence of low-status students. Collegial evaluation is also an important part of the teacher training system.

Teachers receive two full weeks of training before school begins. The principles of classroom management in which they are trained come from organizational theory. When the complexity of instruction or technology increases, the authority of the supervisor must change in order to maintain organizational effectiveness, and delegation of authority must take the place of direct supervision (Cohen, Intili, and Robbins, 1979; Perrow, 1961). Students' behavior is controlled by the establishment of new norms regarding behavior in cooperating groups and by the placing of students in roles that facilitate the work of the group. Evaluation methods are based on the theory of authority and evaluation developed by Dornbusch and Scott (1975).

The Organizational Support Model. School districts that participate in the program are required to send for training a team of at least two teachers from each school, the school principal, and a school staff member who can fill the role of supportive evaluator, making systematic observations of teachers prior to providing specific feedback. The team also includes a liaison person from the district as well as a district official responsible for collecting achievement data.

During the training, members of the team are instructed in how to provide constructive feedback and support to decrease the isolation of classroom teachers. Since each classroom teacher must work with an assistant or credentialed colleague, during implementation trained teachers make systematic observations and give feedback to their assistant or colleague. Principals are instructed in how to provide support for teachers as well as how to provide coordination to solve problems beyond the scope of the classroom team. Supportive evaluators are trained in using systematic methods of observation, evaluation, and constructive feedback to the teaching team. District personnel are instructed in carrying out evaluation using achievement tests. Also, during the initial year of implementation, each classroom receives three feedback visits from center training staff. This model of organizational support builds in collegial problem solving and evaluation, school and district support for the classroom team, and a schoolwide problem-solving capacity.

Approaches and Strategies

The three program components and the curriculum are based on theories as described below.

The Classroom Implementation Model. Cohen, Lotan, and Leechor (1989) tested the following hypothesis: (1) Given the uncertainty of the task from the students' point of view, when the technology of the classroom is more differentiated, the teacher is less likely to use direct supervision. (2) Given the uncertainty of the task from the students' point of view, the more frequently the teacher uses direct supervision, the lower will be the rate of lateral communication among students. (3) Given the uncertainty of the task from the students' point of view, the extent to which students talk and work together will be positively related to the average gains on achievement tests, especially on measures of conceptual learning and problem solving. A corollary to the third hypothesis is that given the uncertainty of the task from the students' point of view, the extent to which students talk and work together will be positively related to a variation of the distribution of the achievement scores from the pretest to the posttest.

Applying organizational theory, the researchers viewed the classroom as a collective (Lazarsfeld and Mendel, 1961) and analyzed the connection between the operation of the classroom as an organizational and social system and learning outcomes of a class of students. The classroom situation is a highly uncertain one from the students' point of view because solutions and outcomes are not immediately obvious (students are encouraged to hypothesize, use trial and error, and discover scientific principles). According to Perrow (1961), when the uncertainty of technology increases, two necessary changes should be made to maintain or increase organizational productivity: increased delegation of authority to workers and more lateral communication among workers.

As described in a previous section, the classroom management model encourages teacher delegation of authority as well as lateral communication among students. This communication — students talking and working together — enhances learning as measured by achievement tests. The communication among students, however, is not sufficient by itself to achieve these gains. The question of status must be taken into account as well, since children of lower status may not have the same access to interaction as do those of higher status. Thus, the model also tests the following hypotheses: (1) Students of higher social status will have more access to task-related interaction than students of lower social status. (2) Interaction will help the student to learn more, as measured by achievement tests. The implications are clear, therefore, that if it can be shown that peer interaction on science tasks simultaneously improves learning outcomes but activates status problems, it is necessary to use some of the simple status treatments for the classroom in order to achieve the benefits of interaction without the drawbacks of status effects.

High levels of interaction are encouraged at the learning center level, although students are rarely assigned to work together toward a joint project. Rules for peer interaction are that each student has the right to ask anyone at the learning center for help and each student has the duty to assist anyone at the learning center who asks for help. These rules have been effective in stimulating interaction among students, especially since the tasks are highly challenging and always novel.

The program designers were aware that for maximum benefits to be derived from the high levels of peer interaction, problems of status would have to be dealt with. They applied a sociological theory on expectation states to explain differential rates of participation in the program curriculum. This theory holds that people tend to use available status information about each other in organizing new and unknown situations and that this tendency produces observable differences in the new situation (for a recent review of this theory, see Berger, Rosenholtz, and Zelditch, 1980). In other words, peers in an interactive situation will assign high status to certain individuals (good readers, for example) because of certain characteristics even though those characteristics may not be required

by the task at hand. These high-status individuals tend to interact at a higher rate than low-status individuals, thereby increasing their learning opportunities. The program designers avoided
this effect by having the teacher point out all the different abilities that are relevant to doing well at a particular task. Children are made to understand that no one student will be good
at all these abilities and that each child will be good at at least
one of them.

The Curriculum and Materials. The curriculum, developed within a Piagetian theoretical framework, is distinct from
other experiential science curricula in at least three ways: the
activities draw on the application of science and mathematics
to everyday life using problems and materials common to most
children, regardless of language or culture; the task instructions
and work sheets are presented in Spanish, English, and pictographs; and the purpose of the activities is to enrich the repertoire of each child regardless of developmental level. This means
that there is no one right answer to many of the tasks. Their
open-ended quality allows children functioning at different levels
of cognitive development to complete tasks somewhat differently.

The purpose of this curriculum is to promote what Pi-
aget calls *horizontal decalage,* rather than to accelerate the transition from one Piagetian substage to the next. (Decalage is the
extent to which the children have applied or have had the opportunity to apply various strategies characteristic of their level
of development to the broad spectrum of elements or situations
defining the total level.) Some researchers suggest that although
"lower-class" children may have the intellectual machinery necessary to perform at levels equal to their middle-class counterparts, they lack practice in applying these various sets, strategies, or schemes across a wide variety of situations.

The Teacher Training Model. In addition to learning the
basic principles and underlying research on which the program
is based, teachers are trained in special classroom management
techniques. They learn to delegate authority to students while
maintaining control of the classroom by monitoring work sheets
and giving feedback to individuals and groups. Students take
responsibility for themselves and for other members of the group

(typically, there are six groups operating simultaneously, with four or five children per group). Because students take over the job of helping each other, the teachers are free to carry out more demanding tasks, such as treating status problems, stimulating thinking, providing feedback to students, extending activities, and asking higher-order questions. Collegial evaluation based on theories of authority and evaluation is also an important part of the teacher training system.

Model of Organizational Support. The theories underlying the organizational support model come from theories of technology and structure that hold that when tasks become more uncertain, it is necessary for the staff to develop interdependent work relationships. Thus, the project requires teaching teams for each classroom and specifies methods of achieving efficient and effective team meetings, providing collegial support and constructive feedback to teachers, solving problems in a collegial manner, and solving schoolwide problems.

Program Evaluation

The program has been evaluated with student achievement data from the CTBS, the Language Assessment Scale, the Cartoon Conservation Scale (which measures intellectual development across Piagetian-based tasks), and a test measuring students' grasp of the program content. Consistent pre-post test score gains were found for all important measures. The program has been able to repeat achievement results over a number of years.

The effects of the program on students' social interaction have been assessed through analyses of sociometric measures collected in 1982–83. These analyses revealed that the classroom environment of participating classrooms showed fewer social isolates and fewer sociometric stars than were present in other classrooms.

Effectiveness of the teacher training model was tested by a comparison of systematic teacher and classroom observations before and after implementation of the teacher training model. Measures of teacher success in implementing the new system of management and instruction were an increase in the percentage of students in small groups; a low rate of teacher disciplining; and an increased level of teachers' questioning, giving feedback to individuals, and stimulating children's thinking by extending activities. The teacher training model was shown to be effective by all of these measures.

Unique Features of the Program

Theoretical and Research Base. As described above, the Finding Out/Descubrimiento program model applies sociological theory to theories of learning. Its grounding in theory as well as its heavy focus on the research aspect of the project makes it unique among intervention programs.

Design to Ensure Continuation. From the very beginning of the project, one of its goals was to develop not only an instructional program but also a model that "incorporates the necessary conditions for proper implementation and survival over time." To this end, the project staff added three components to the instructional model to make it self-sustaining: activities training to help teachers become familiar with the learning activities and the principles underlying this approach to learning; management and instruction to assist teachers in managing multiple learning centers and in learning how to hold children accountable for their work while at the same time allowing them to use one another as resources in learning; and organizational support to create the necessary teamwork that provides a schoolwide and districtwide support system for the implementation of the instructional model. Also important in the continuation of the program is the development of curriculum materials as well as thorough documentation of the different processes involved in program implementation.

Focus on the Multilingual, Multicultural Classroom. The instructional methods and curriculum developed by the program are ideal for use in the heterogeneous classrooms increasingly prevalent in some areas of the country. The instructional approach, with its emphasis on hands-on activities, small-group learning, and peer interaction, allows teachers to simultaneously teach children performing at different grade levels as well as children whose proficiency in English may be limited (or nonexistent). The project's concern for the low-status child has resulted in the development of techniques for improving expectations for competence of low-status children for intellectual tasks and for increasing their social acceptance by classmates.

When asked about the unique aspects of the program, a staff member replied, "You can find many of these components in many other programs, but we have developed a comprehensive view of intervention in the school that brings them all together. Also, the status treatment is found only in this program."

Dissemination and Institutionalization

Inasmuch as one of the main goals of the program has been to encourage its dissemination and replication, the project staff have made dissemination one of their priorities. The program has been implemented in more than a hundred classrooms in ten school districts around the country. Staff members have also published many articles and presented papers based on the various aspects of the program.

The project is now in its fifth year of a statewide dissemination process. It works with colleges and departments of education on selected California State University (CSU) campuses (the CSU system prepares 80 percent of the teachers in the state). Program staff train university faculty in the theory and research underlying Complex Instruction and, together with the CSU faculty, train master teachers in school districts where student teachers are placed for their field experience. These student teachers are then trained by the university faculty and supervisors in the theory and practice of complex instruction. Thus, both cooperating teachers and student teachers who are placed in the classrooms of cooperating teachers have the opportunity to learn how to address the needs of the students in heterogeneous classrooms and how to teach conceptual thinking and problem-solving skills using math and science concepts.

The program has received funding from the Stuart Foundations of San Francisco for its dissemination and from the Car-

negie Corporation of New York for documentation and evaluation of the dissemination efforts. The program is also expanding its focus to include older students. As middle schools move
away from tracking, there is a need for strategies that will enable teachers to be successful in educating students with diverse
backgrounds and a wide range of previous academic achievement. To meet this need, it is working collaboratively with five
middle schools, with the assistance of the Carnegie Corporation, to develop and field-test curricula in social studies/language
arts, math, and science for middle school students. The goal
is to test the generalizability of the principles that have been
so effective at the elementary school level. As before, the program will focus on curriculum, instruction, and issues of access.

Mathematics, Science, and Minorities, K–6

Mathematics, Science, and Minorities, K–6 was developed by the staff of the Mid-Atlantic Equity Center (MAEC) and mathematics and science supervisors from five school districts to put into practice the ideas expressed in the book *Mathematics and Science: Critical Filters for the Future of Minority Students* (Beane, 1985). The program sought to involve all the school districts in the Washington, D.C., metropolitan area in a four-year project to put into practice the research findings of the center regarding factors that affect minority participation in math and science, integrating these practices into the school system. Planning began in the spring of 1985. In the summer of that year, school districts were invited to identify a maximum of eight schools each to participate in a two-day conference to introduce the participants to the philosophy and goals of the program and strategies for achieving the goals. They were then asked to submit school intervention plans based on individual school needs. Twenty schools in three school districts — the District of Columbia, Prince George's County (Virginia), and Montgomery County (Maryland) — were selected for the follow-up program. As the school districts worked with the model that was conceptualized in late spring of 1985 by MAEC and the Mathematics, Science, and Minorities, K–6 advisory board, they maintained its core components, supplemented by the districts' own mathematics and science curricula.

The location of the program within the Mid-Atlantic Equity Center enabled it to make use of center resources. During the first three years of the program, the project director was an MAEC staff member. In the fourth year, the program hired a consultant to serve as director. MAEC also engaged the many outside consultants who ran training workshops for participants and shared other resources with the program, such as staff time, equipment, and facilities. The participating school districts shared funding responsibilities with MAEC by providing release time for teachers and other school personnel involved in the project, training facilities, and facilities for some team meetings.

Goal, Objectives, and Structure

The program goal was to increase Black and Hispanic student participation and performance in mathematics and science through the development of school-based teams that were competent in developing, recognizing, and nurturing young minority students' positive attitudes toward and participation and performance in mathematics and science. Project objectives were to increase teachers' content knowledge in selected mathematics and science topics and to provide professional development for principals, teachers, counselors, and education specialists so that they could be able to do the following:

1. Develop school-based intervention programs to increase minority students' interest and performance in math and science
2. Correlate mathematics and science concepts, focusing on process skills and using hands-on activities
3. Recognize factors that are most likely to affect minority students in mathematics and science instructional settings
4. Demonstrate behaviors based on these factors that will positively affect minority students' attitudes, performance, and participation in mathematics and science
5. Provide minority students with information and experiences in the application of mathematics and science concepts and skills
6. Implement school-based intervention programs first among team members and later throughout the entire school

   The program depended heavily on the involvement of school personnel at every level. In addition to an advisory board, which set program policy and monitored program activities, a steering committee composed of advisory board members from each school district and the project director worked with the training consultant to develop training and management designs. Each school system had representatives who were directly involved in providing services to the project. Each school had a leadership team made up of the principal, counselors, and teachers. This team attended the training sessions and was expected to implement the intervention plan. The schools and school districts had slightly different organizational structures because of individual school and district differences. The project director was based at the MAEC and had overall responsibility for directing the project.

Program Components

The program was designed in three phases: phase 1, the action research and planning component (1985-1987), phase 2, the action research and implementation component (1987-1988), and phase 3, the dissemination component (1988-1989).

Phase 1. The first year of phase 1 focused on increasing participants' awareness of the factors that affect minority performance and participation in math and science. A result of the first year was the development of school intervention plans by each school as well as the identification of factors that the participants felt were most germane to the successful implementation of the plan: learning styles, academic deficiencies, teacher expectations, persistence, and teacher anxiety. It was decided that these five factors would be emphasized in the training sessions in year 2.

Year 2 concentrated on teacher behavior change and its impact on the classroom. The development of team identity, which involved the clarification of goals, roles, and functions of members and skill development, focused on behaviors affecting the five factors listed above. The building of teams within the participating schools to facilitate the implementation of the school plan and support one another individually was an important achievement during this year. Peer coaching, whereby teachers on the team observe one another's teaching and provide feedback, was also developed during this year.

Year 2 also focused on training and staff development. These were delivered via monthly team meetings, school district-level meetings, individual school-level meetings, and specialists' and counselors' meetings. Consultants provided much of the training for these different school personnel. Staff development for specialists focused on enhancing their knowledge of content areas in mathematics and science as well as factors related to minority students' achievements. Counselors focused on assessment inventories and psychological supports. Teachers focused on curriculum issues, teacher behaviors, and elements of the classroom environment.

Phase 2. This phase concentrated on the implementation of the plan as outlined in the school intervention plan developed by and for team members. During this phase, the first attempts at dissemination to other school faculty members took place.

Phase 3. This was the dissemination phase, during which program outcomes and products were disseminated to the entire school, the school district, and the larger educational community. This was facilitated by the development of instructional packages, articles in educational publications and other media, and presentations at professional meetings.

Recruitment and Selection

The twenty participating schools were selected according to the following criteria:

- Teachers and principals were committed to improving the performance and participation of minority students in math and science.
- There was a large minority (non-Asian) population — at least 20 percent — in the school.
- Activity-based science and math programs were not currently being used effectively with minority students.

Teachers selected to be on school teams were expected to

- Have demonstrated success in teaching underachieving minority students

- Enjoy mathematics and science
- Be willing to share with colleagues and parents

Approaches and Strategies

The program advocated approaches to the teaching of mathematics and science that were suggested by the research at the center and described in *Mathematics and Science* (Beane, 1985) as means of improving minority participation and performance in mathematics and science. The following approaches were emphasized:

- The recognition of mathematics as a critical filter to sustaining participation in science
- The belief that all children can learn math and science and can maintain positive attitudes toward these disciplines
- The belief that intervention is most effective at the elementary school level
- The importance of hands-on activities as an effective means of helping students to apply concepts to the problem-solving process
- The relating of math and science to everyday life
- The importance of administrative support and training to assist teachers in presenting effective activity-based science and mathematics lessons in their classrooms
- The belief that the essential resource for change exists within the school district
- The belief that establishment of a good teacher training program designed to improve the teaching of mathematics and science to minority students will result in a higher quality of experience for all students
- Training not only of teachers but also of school personnel, such as administrators, counselors, and others, who influence the educational environment of students
- Teacher education that includes experiential as well as didactic activities
- Professional development programs that model the concepts being taught

Staff

The project staff consisted mainly of school district and school personnel. The role of each staff component of the program was as follows:

Mid-Atlantic Equity Center, American University, advisory board, steering committee

Identify and disseminate resources and research regarding effective educational programs for Black and Hispanic students in math and science; develop overall goals and objectives for the program; facilitate and coordinate interdistrict cooperation; organize school district coordinators; schedule, coordinate, and facilitate bimonthly training

School district

Provide money and material resources for substitutes and consultants; serve on advisory board; provide personnel to help implement project

School district coordinators

Serve on advisory board and steering committee; provide liaison with school districts

Curriculum specialists, supervisors, educational specialists, resource specialists

Participate in workshops and skills development training; make on-site visits to facilitate peer support and observe classroom instruction; provide resources for the school team

School team (principal, counselor, teachers)

Develop local school plans; participate in training and

develop skills in team building and teaching behaviors;
serve as catalysts, dissemina-
tors, and models for pro-
gram development; imple-
ment year 2 plan; provide
school staff with information
about team accomplishments

Team principals

Serve as climate setters,
catalysts, and leaders for
team building; conduct an
inventory of school needs for
math and science resources
and materials and develop
plan for securing them; help
team to accomplish year 2
strategies by providing them
necessary time and
resources; evaluate how successful the math and science
program has been for Black
and Hispanic students

Team teachers

Serve as leaders of school-
based plans; practice in-
structional behaviors related
to enhancing achievement of
minority students; participate in peer coaching;
present progress report to
faculty about goals, directions, and accomplishments
of team

Team counselors

Serve on implementation
team; serve as climate setters; help to increase Black
and Hispanic parent in-
volvement; provide career

education for teachers and
parents; develop self-esteem
workshops for Black and
Hispanic students; assist
school teams to maximize
the use of community
resources

Program Evaluation

At the time of this writing, only evaluation data for phase 1 of
the project were available. Participants were surveyed to determine whether the program was successful in meeting its goals
and objectives for the first year. The survey revealed that 99
percent of participants rated the program as fair or better, with
almost one-fifth rating it as excellent. More than 80 percent of
the participants reported that the training goals were partially
to fully attained. Workshop activities, speakers, and consultants
received high ratings from the participants. Eighty-five percent
reported having adequate information about the factors related
to minority achievement, with a majority saying that they were
now using those factors in planning their classes and in teaching.

The evaluation results of year 2 were not yet available
when the site visit was made. Project staff, however, reported
that the progress made by each school had varied according to
factors such as level of commitment, leadership of the principal,
the past condition of science and mathematics in the school, and
the support from regional offices in each district. The project
planned to hold formal evaluations during years 3 and 4 to measure changes in teacher attitudes and behavior and assess the
effect of the program on students — how student involvement and
achievement have benefited from the program.

Some program effects not documented in the evaluation
have been noted by personnel involved in the project. A cross-
district communication has been established as a result of the
project: "You have school districts as close as these that have
never experienced the professional cooperation of putting a program together. Sometimes districts get tunnel vision about the

way to do things, and they have been seeing other options as a result of the project." Other program effects were described by a staff member: "The way teachers and administrators express themselves now is different. Schools now teach science that did not do so before. I would also hope that the communication between administrators and teachers is different."

Unique Features of the Program

The program had three unique features: the strong research component, the involvement of school districts and schools at all levels, and the use of team building to provide support for implementation of the plan.

The Research Component. The program had a very strong research component: it was developed and planned around research findings regarding minority participation and performance in mathematics and science. Although it had not been designed for research purposes, it could be considered an ongoing research project, since strategies and techniques were constantly being evaluated and fine tuned with the use of research techniques. As one of the project staff explained, "We are using data to continually revise what is going on in the program and testing the actual research model."

The training component relied heavily on the use of outside consultants who were researchers to acquaint school personnel with research findings regarding various topics pertinent to program implementation. These topics included learning styles, the use of hands-on activities, student achievement, and parental involvement.

Involvement of School Districts and Schools. The project stressed the direct involvement and participation of schools from the very beginning, bringing school personnel in on the planning process as well as the implementation process. It also involved schools at all levels through a carefully thought out use of teams as well as a structured approach to the training of school personnel at all levels.

Even though there was input from all levels of school personnel, the approach could be considered a top-down one in

that the decision to participate had been made at the district
level. The program differed from other programs in that the
intervention approaches were being developed from the beginning within the school setting. The project had been planned
to gradually bring about change in the entire school and eventually in the entire school district.

Another unique feature was the cross-district communication that was necessary for the development of the program.
The three districts, although geographically close, had different characteristics in terms of minority enrollment, resources,
and structure: "Each district has a different framework for operating, so what we try to do is keep within the project's philosophy
and within the structure of the school district." There were also
differences among schools that must be taken into account: "Each
school will have its own story. We have given some general techniques to them, but each one develops on its own."

The Use of Team Building. The use of teams that had
different functions and were composed of school personnel at
all levels was another unique feature of this program. The teams
performed facilitating, coordinating, leadership, policy-making,
planning, and implementing functions. Team building was seen
as a major process for developing skills, cooperation, and support for the implementation of the school plan.

Peer coaching was an aspect of the team-building approach. Although this technique had been used in other programs (Project SEED, for example), this program incorporated
peer coaching into the school system, where one would expect
great resistance to such a method. Program staff acknowledged
that teachers at first were unwilling to be judged by their peers,
but they eventually accepted and even welcomed the assistance
and support that peer coaching provides.

Dissemination and Institutionalization

The focus of the dissemination phase was disseminating the practices and outcomes of the project to the schools, the school districts, and the larger educational community. Instructional packages were developed to facilitate this dissemination, and project

personnel also published articles in educational publications and presented papers at professional meetings as part of the dissemination process.

The institutionalization of the strategies and practices developed by the program was the ultimate goal of the project, as was evident from the program design: "A very important goal is that of institutionalizing the program so that it becomes part of the school system and is perceived as essential. We hope that eventually schools of education will make these strategies part of their teacher training." The involvement and training of school personnel from the district level to the individual school level increased the probability that institutionalization at the district level would take place. The gradual and systematic process whereby the practices advocated by the program will eventually spread throughout the participating schools was well thought out and has potential for success. Program staff pointed out that the program had already had some dissemination: "Teachers are talking all the time to other teachers who are not yet involved in the project and are explaining what they've learned."

The Mathematics, Science, and Minorities, K–6 project was an ambitious effort to change schools in ways that would enhance the achievement of minority students. Strong claims can be made for the project's impact on schools. Teams were formed and functioned throughout the life of the project, and teachers incorporated strategies and materials demonstrated in project workshops into their classrooms. The data showed that the behavior of teachers had changed more rapidly than some of their attitudes, which was congruent with human behavior research. The project seemed to renew the skills and enthusiasm of the staff involved (teachers, principals, and counselors) for teaching in general and for working with minority students in particular.

The strongest evidence of this project's success was the overwhelming appreciation of the school personnel and the transformations that occurred in classrooms. Many of the classrooms became alive with plants, insects, and animals and became places where students work on projects and experiments rather than assignments. The "best" classrooms emerged from the project as communities *doing* science and mathematics.

This project also demonstrated the importance of funding. The consultants, meeting sites, parking, lunches, and refreshments were not inexpensive. Even more important than funding, however, were people with commitment and ideas. This project found those people in the university, in the school systems, in the community, and at the MAEC. The ideas generated by this project continue to thrive in the schools and people touched by it.

Though the Mid-Atlantic Equity Center completed its involvement as the coordinating agency in this project in 1989, many components of the project have been institutionalized in twenty elementary schools in the three school districts. For details outlining the research findings, the follow-up, and evaluation of the project, one can refer to two publications available from MAEC. The programmatic elements of the project were guided by the research findings in *Mathematics and Science: Critical Filters for the Future of Minority Students* (Beane, 1985). The follow-up publication, *Opening Up the Mathematics and Science Filters: Our Schools Did It, So Can Yours!* (Beane, 1992), outlines the project configuration in each of the three school districts, recounts the story from the perspectives of teachers and administrators, presents the project's six core components, and describes nine steps for using research and these core components to transform math and science programs in elementary schools.

Saturday Science Academy

The Saturday Science Academy was established at Atlanta University in 1979 as part of the Community Outreach Component of the Atlanta Resource Center for Science and Engineering. It started out serving 110 students in grades 3 through 8 from the metropolitan Atlanta, Georgia, area. Many of these students were from low socioeconomic backgrounds. In working with them, the academy provided an invaluable opportunity for identifying and directing the scientific talents of those who are the potential scientific pool of the future. Since its founding, the program has expanded its services to 200 students per session (or 400 students per year). Although initially funded by the National Science Foundation (NSF), it has received funding from the Minority Institutions Science Improvement Program (MISIP), Rich's Department Store, and the *Atlanta Constitution,* as well as donations from industry and parents. The academy is currently funded by the Atlanta Comprehensive Regional Center for Minorities.

The Resource Center for Science and Engineering (RCSE) was a comprehensive project that combined resources of academic, local, and regional communities to address the problem of underrepresentation of people from minority and low-income groups in science and engineering. Created in 1978 with a four-year grant from the NSF, the center served the needs of precollege students, community education specialists, and doctoral-level students in scientific and technical fields.

The center in Atlanta was the first of a series of centers established in the United States and its territories. The Atlanta center implemented its program activities through three components: the Clark Atlanta University Center Component, the Community Outreach Component, and the Regional Institutions Component. It incorporated the resources of Clark Atlanta University and the three undergraduate colleges in the Clark Atlanta University Center, Inc. (Morehouse, Morris Brown, and Spelman).

The Community Outreach Component of the Atlanta RCSE was created to promote the presence and significance of opportunities in science and engineering in minority communities. This unit contained programs to encourage talented minority and low-income youth to consider careers in science, mathematics, and engineering. It also had programs to increase the awareness of parents, teachers, counselors, and students about career options in science. This component included the following specific elements:

- Saturday Science Academy for elementary and junior high students
- Summer Science, Engineering, and Mathematics Institute for high school students
- Annual counselor workshop for high school counselors
- In-service teacher training in science and mathematics, K–12
- Preparation and dissemination of career information in the sciences
- Public lectures

These programs involved the total community by providing services to a wide range of participants, from city government officials and university professors to elementary school children. The rest of this section focuses on the Saturday Science Academy.

Goals and Structure

The Saturday Science Academy was designed to address specific long-range problems, such as the severe underrepresentation of minorities in engineering, mathematics, and the sciences; students' negative attitudes, beginning in the elementary school years, regarding these subjects; the low proportion of girls (compared to boys) who consider careers in these subjects by the end of elementary school; and the need to augment public school instruction in science and mathematics at the elementary and middle school levels. To address these problems, the program defined its long-range goal as significantly increasing the pool of students interested in pursuing careers in computer science, engineering, mathematics, and the natural sciences. Specific objectives focusing on students are as follows:

- Improvement in problem-solving and thinking skills
- Improvement in self-concept and confidence in ability to be successful in engineering, math, and science
- The development of positive attitudes toward these fields
- Increased desire to pursue careers in computer science, engineering, mathematics, and the natural sciences
- Increased knowledge base and understanding of science and mathematics
- Improved precision and power in oral and written communication skills

As a program administrator put it, the program's main focus is to "turn kids on to math and science, to get them excited about doing math, and to give them confidence in doing math and science."

Classes were originally held on Saturday mornings from 9:00 to 12:00 at the John F. Kennedy Community Center in Atlanta. The academy currently operates on the campus of Clark Atlanta University. Each session runs for ten weeks, and there are two ten-week sessions per school year. Students are grouped in two clusters: third-, fourth-, and fifth-graders in the first cluster and sixth-, seventh-, and eighth-graders in the second. Each cluster has its own faculty team or communication specialist, assisted by a core of graduate and undergraduate science and math majors from the Atlanta University Center institutions.

Program Features

The basic academic program consists of classes in science, math, communication skills (called "creative expressions"), and computer science. Each class is limited to thirty students. Other activities include visits to science centers, nature trail hikes, and presentation of original student skits on the topic of science.

Science classes, which are held in a science laboratory setting, emphasize process skills, concept formation, hands-on science activities, and laboratory-oriented instruction. The inquiry approach is used in teaching science. Math classes develop computation skills and problem-solving strategies, and the instructors use Socratic and discovery techniques in teaching. Computer science covers elementary programming, graphic analysis, and computer-assisted problem solving. Creative expression classes spend half the class time in developing original skits on science subjects and the other half in creative writing. End products of creative expressions classes are the presentation of the science skits and the publication of a booklet of original student writings.

Parental involvement is a key element in the program. Parents participate in the orientation sessions held at the beginning of each ten-week session. They also assist by serving as chaperons on field trips, guides to visitors, hosts at refreshment hours, and presenters at special sessions during the Saturday classes. One instructor stated that the level of parental involvement is a measure that he uses to gauge the success of his classes: "It's one thing for parents to drop their children off at the academy, but to get parents to stay and become involved says a lot more."

Recruitment and Selection

Recruitment is conducted through the local schools. Application forms and information flyers are sent to the principals of the schools, who in turn distribute them to teachers. A few years ago the program attracted many more students than it could accommodate, and it subsequently doubled the number of students served. Recently, program administrators say, they have been able to limit their recruitment activities so that they are able to accept almost all applicants.

Application forms include a rating scale completed by teachers of the applicants and students' essays explaining why they wish to attend the academy. Applications are grouped by grade levels; the program also tries to obtain a good representation of local schools. A selection committee made up of community representatives, public school personnel, and university and academy personnel decides which students will attend a particular session. The use of traditional criteria such as standardized achievement test scores is minimized in the selection process. Applicants not selected for a particular session are given priority for the next scheduled session. As a program administrator explained the selection process, "The main thing we look for is the promise that the kid will come to class."

Approaches and Strategies

The science and mathematics classes use approaches that are known to be successful with minority students, such as hands-on experiences, instruction via the Socratic discovery method and the inquiry method, and group dynamics and peer interaction to stimulate motivation. A mathematics instructor who was trained in the Project SEED technique of teaching described his approach as follows: "The key to my success is movement — the motion, the rapid pace that I use in the classroom. Kids on a Saturday morning have other things they would like to do than be in a classroom. So my job is to keep them interested and motivated. If they are not paying attention, I keep erasing the blackboard or do a voice change from very loud to a whisper. I tell them 'A key ability of a super mathematician is to listen and listen well.'"

Creative expressions classes use the techniques of improvisational theater to help students overcome their inhibitions and shyness and to assist them in working with others. As an instructor describes the philosophy behind the technique, "I think that kids need to have their emotions involved and their bodies involved. Then they remember. Often before the sixth-grade level, kids learn better if things are concrete and not abstract. Improvisational theater is always spontaneous and immediate. The students also have to work with others and be sensitive and to track what the other person has in mind and what they are thinking of as the scene develops. Creative writing involves similar kinds of processes." Teacher attitude is a very important component of the techniques used by the Saturday Science Academy. Program staff feel that "curriculum and materials are not as important as the attitude of the teacher." The teacher should be "someone who can get across the feeling that you are special. The key is to motivate students." Teachers are expected to have high expectations of students, and the staff feel that "positive interactions with the kids are critical." One teacher tells his students, "We are not ordinary mathematicians; we are super mathematicians. And super mathematicians have excellent attendance." Teachers also feel that it is important to let students know at the very beginning that they should not be afraid of getting the wrong answer. Even though they agree that it is important to let students know that they cannot get away with bad behavior, it is also important to avoid embarrassing students in front of classmates.

Many of the approaches described above are appropriate for middle school students. The use of movement and a rapid pace to keep students' attention is an effective device for students of this age group. The creative expressions class, which is held at 11:00 A.M., after two other classes, begins with "a whole lot of movement" before settling down to working in groups of five or six. The use of theater techniques satisfies the middle school students' requirement for the concrete rather than the abstract, as do the hands-on exercises in science. Students also learn to cooperate with their peers by working on group projects in math, science, and creative expressions classes. Early adolescents' need for clear limits is met by teachers' establishing and agreeing on rules at the beginning. Students are given a sense of accomplishment by the publicizing of the end products of classes, such as skits and creative writing booklets.

The program staff feel that "the biggest resource we have to work with is the kids. What we are doing is using some techniques to access the resources that the kids bring with them to class and give them ideas and forms that they can use."

Staff

The staff consists of a project director, an associate project director, seven lead teachers, an administrative assistant, and several student assistants. Most staff members have been with the program for several years. The program also has the help of volunteers — parents of participants or community members. Most of the senior staff have been trained somewhere else. Instructors are required to be experts in the subjects that they teach. They bring other experiences and talents to the classroom as well. Many of them have worked with youth in the community, and the actors who teach the creative expressions classes have been involved with the Atlanta Street Theater, which presents original educational theater for youth in the Atlanta area.

Staff credit the project director with putting together the "incredible talent" represented by the instructors. "There seems to be a perfect match of program and people," said one staff member. The qualities that program administrators look for in an instructor are "the ability to relate warmly and positively to students; also, a natural instinct to create." The program seems to have attracted people who, like the director, believe that "education is exciting, is interesting, is active."

Program Evaluation

The program hired an independent agency to evaluate its activities over the first three years. A stratified random sample of students, representing 10 percent of the 800 students who had attended from 1979 through 1981, was surveyed together with the parents and their regular classroom teachers. Data on students and parents were collected via structured questionnaires administered through home visits and telephone interviews; teacher data were collected through mail surveys. The following are the evaluation results based on the responses of students, parents, and teachers.

Students. Questionnaire results indicated that 100 percent of the students had a more positive attitude toward mathematics as a result of the program, 83 percent had a more positive attitude toward science, and 100 percent felt more comfortable doing math and science. One hundred percent of the students indicated that they enjoyed working in class with teachers and classmates more after their participation in the program, 68 percent said that they assisted siblings or friends with math and science homework, 95 percent said that they were more excited about math and science after participating in the program, and 81 percent indicated a preference for science- or math-related careers after one session in the academy.

Parents. One hundred percent of parents indicated "some change" or "great change" in enthusiasm on the part of their children for doing mathematics and science homework or talking about math and science. The same percentage indicated that they would enroll their children in future sessions of the academy. Ninety percent of the parents indicated that their children's academic performance was excellent or very good after participating in the academy (30 percent had reported their children's performance to be excellent or very good initially). Ninety percent of parents indicated an observed difference in motivation toward math and science on the part of their children after participation. Eighty-seven percent observed a change in attitude for the better on the part of their children regarding math and science; 67 percent said that their children had exhibited anxiety, insecurity, or tenseness toward math and science before their academy experience.

Teachers. One hundred percent of teachers reported markedly more enthusiasm for science and math in academy students than in other students in their classes, increased math and science achievement for academy participants, and observed changes in attitude toward school in general among academy participants.

Unique Features of the Program

Emphasis on Creativity. The Saturday Science Academy's emphasis on creativity and the arts as a means to learning is a unique feature of this program. The program staff believe that "working on the creative part of the child" results in effective teaching. As one staff member explained, "People remember things that they have feelings connected with, and that is why . . . theater is so good in the educational process. I think kids need to have their emotions involved and their bodies involved. . . . In [improvisational theater], the motivation is so great that they automatically apply the discipline of the art form and use it in learning." The end products of science skits and creative writing booklets serve as motivational tools as well as rewards for learning.

Emphasis on Instructors' Attitudes. The program director recruits instructors who he feels possess the personal characteristics as well as the background and experience required for being successful teachers in the program. There is very little training or supervision once the instructor has proved to be an effective teacher. "His attitude is to get good people and then leave them alone," explained a staff member. Characteristics and attitudes expected of teachers in the program are described above in the section on approaches and techniques.

Dissemination

The program's main dissemination activities have consisted of the director's attending conferences and describing the program. The staff have also conducted workshops for others interested in starting programs of their own. Their primary audiences for dissemination have been other historically Black colleges and universities, science educators, and educators from other countries.

At the time of our visit, the program staff were planning to become more directly involved with schools (at that time, three colleges in south Georgia) that wish to replicate the Saturday Science Academy model. They were planning to bring staff from those institutions to Clark Atlanta University for training and workshops and to give technical assistance to them once they have established their programs. The program staff were also planning to hold a regional conference on the education of Black youth.

Project MiCRO

The Minority Computer Resource Opportunity Project, or Project MiCRO, was a project of the Southern Coalition for Educational Equity (SCEE), a nonprofit organization that operates in eleven southern states. It is incorporated in the state of Georgia and was founded in 1978 for the purpose of eliminating racism and sexism from public schools and ensuring the effectiveness of those schools.

The SCEE is the only southern advocacy organization that works exclusively on the issue of education. The coalition works cooperatively with other groups and maintains offices in Jackson, Mississippi (main office); Atlanta, Georgia; Mobile, Alabama; New Orleans, Louisiana; and Pantego, North Carolina. In addition to Project MiCRO, projects have included the Educational Administrators' Leadership Project, whose purpose has been to increase the number and effectiveness of women and minorities in leadership positions in public schools; the Arkansas Career Resources Project, which was designed to increase skills and career options for minorities and single heads of households who are unemployed or underemployed; and the Effective Schools Project, which looks for ways to improve academic achievement in "high-risk" middle and elementary schools. Several of the projects have been replicated and/or institutionalized and serve as models for similar activities throughout the southern states.

Project MiCRO arose from the realization that minority students were at a severe disadvantage when compared to their White peers in their access to and use of microcomputers. Unlike their wealthier white peers, disadvantaged minority children did not have computers at home, they were less likely to have access to computers at school, and when they did use computers, it was typically for drill and practice rather than as learning tools. The program started in 1985 at three project sites: the Austin T. Walden Middle School in Atlanta, Georgia; Pantego Junior High School in rural Beaufort County, North Carolina; and the Paul Lawrence Dunbar Middle School in Mobile, Alabama. The three sites reflected a conscious attempt to test the MiCRO model in three different settings: a small rural school in a farming community where the student body is roughly 60 percent Black; an urban middle school where students are drawn from nearby low-income apartments and are predominantly poor and 99 percent Black; and an urban middle school that serves a large housing project and where the student body is entirely minority (mostly Black) and 85 percent are from single-parent homes.

Initial funding for the project was provided by the Mary Reynolds Babcock Foundation, the Edward Hazen Foundation, the Cummings Engine Foundation, and the Southern Education Foundation. Subsequent funding was received from American Express Project Hometown America; Apple Computer Company, Inc.; Federated Stores/Rich's Foundation; the Ford Foundation; the Hitachi Foundation; Joint Foundation Support; Portman Properties; the Metropolitan Atlanta Community Development Foundation; the Sapelo Island Research Foundation; the Southern Education Foundation; the Tandy Corporation; and the Z. Smith Reynolds Foundation. After the initial input of the SCEE board of directors, the project design, implementation, and monitoring were the responsibility of the project director.

Goals and Structure

The goals of Project MiCRO were to develop a model for providing computer literacy to minority students at the middle school or junior high level and to develop a model program using instructional computing to increase minority students' analytical thinking skills. To accomplish these goals, the program attempted to do the following:

1.   Train teachers to integrate computer literacy effectively into the curriculum

2. Develop a course that teaches minority and economically disadvantaged middle school students analytical thinking skills through the use of instructional computing
3. Familiarize parents with instructional technology to assist them in becoming active partners in their children's computer-based learning
4. Define an effective delivery system for the project and document and disseminate the model, both regionally and nationally

The program structure echoed its goals as follows:

> Phase 1 (year 1): address the first goal — developing a model to increase computer literacy
>
> Phase 2 (years 2 and 3): address the second goal — developing a model to increase minority students' analytical thinking skills
>
> Phase 3 (years 3 and 4): address the replication and dissemination objective of the project

Program Components

The main components of Project MiCRO were teacher training, parental involvement, computer literacy, analytical thinking skills instruction, evaluation, and documentation. The first five components are discussed in this section; the last two are described in the sections on evaluation and dissemination below.

Teacher Training. All teachers in participating Project MiCRO schools received training in computer use and applications in their subject areas. During the first year, just before the start of the school year, the entire instructional staff as well as the principal received a three- to five-day preservice training session. In addition to articulating the goals and expectations of Project MiCRO, the training emphasized integration of math, language arts, social studies, and science curriculum objectives into word processing, data-base-management, spreadsheet, and simulation activities. Teachers were also instructed in how to make software specifically relevant to the experiences of their students and in the classroom management techniques required to achieve the greatest amount of time-on-task. On-site assistance was provided to teachers during the school year, with each teacher receiving individualized attention three to five days per month. A master team of several teachers and the principals of each of the schools gradually began to assume responsibility for training. They worked with new teachers, monitored the quality of the project, assessed staff development needs, and provided in-service training.

Both preservice and in-service training at each site was conducted by a project trainer who had expertise in computers and teaching and who adapted his or her strategies to the teachers' particular needs. The site trainer also made classroom observations and demonstrations, assisted teachers in adapting software to their students' needs, and facilitated an effective classroom management system for microcomputer use. Training of teachers for the analytical thinking skills courses was conducted by the project director. Principals, parent coordinators, one or two teachers, and on-site trainers at each school attended a three-day workshop during the second year of the project. This training was followed up by site visits by the project director to provide technical assistance to the teachers. During the third year of the project, the site trainer spent less time on site. The trainers' primary responsibilities during the last year were to serve as a resource to the master team and provide quality control for the project.

Parental Involvement. Parental involvement was a very important component of the program. The project offered computer training to parents, and parents volunteered to work on project activities or special projects. There was an open house for parents at the beginning of the school year to introduce them to the computer laboratories. At each site, a paid, full-time parent coordinator performed a number of tasks related to involving parents in the program. For example, the parent coordinator held individual and small-group meetings with parents to instruct them in computer use. Parent coordinators also made home visits, taking along a microcomputer, to reach parents who had difficulty going to the school. Every site had a parents' room where parents could learn how to use computers and to practice their skills. Here the parent coordinator was available at all times convenient to parents, including late afternoons and some evenings. Parent training fell into two categories: training parents to work with their children on particular kinds of software and developing the parents' own computer skills.

Parent coordinators also performed multiple functions that assisted the project in achieving a good rapport with the school, the parents, and the community. They submitted monthly written reports as well as weekly telephone reports to the project director, coordinated test administration at project and control sites, assisted in training teachers, assisted principals, and worked closely with the trainers.

Computer Literacy. The first year (phase 1) of Project MiCRO focused on this aspect of instruction, which addressed the first of the two major project goals: teaching computer literacy through the use of computers as tools in all subjects. Here the project's approach was the intensive training of all teachers and the active involvement of parents in their children's education as described above. Students became familiar with microcomputers and used them for a variety of classes and subjects. Much emphasis was given to addressing sex equity concerns, and teachers were alerted to the need to involve more girls in computer use.

Each school established a computer laboratory equipped with roughly twelve computers and a variety of software. There was a schedule for laboratory use to ensure equitable time allocations; each student had a minimum of two hours per week of hands-on computer experience (most students had between three and four hours per week of scheduled time with computers).

Analytical Thinking Skills Instruction. This component addressed the second major project goal: developing a model program using instructional computing to improve students' analytical thinking skills. An interdisciplinary critical thinking skills course was developed and introduced during the second year of the project at all project sites. This course was offered three days per week to a random sample of students in each school. In preparation for the course, MiCRO staff developed a list of specific analytical thinking skills to be taught, as well as ways of incorporating computer programming and logic software into the courses. One or two teachers at each school were identified for training, which included thinking skills, uses of logic and simulation software, and specific pedagogical techniques for teaching thinking skills.

Because teachers of different subjects taught this course at the different project sites, the subject content in the analytical thinking skills courses varied from site to site. At one school, for example, the language arts teacher taught the course; at other schools, it was taught by the science or math teachers. Project staff stressed, however, that the structure was the same, although specific content was flexible.

Recruitment and Selection Procedures

Schools selected by the SCEE had to have a large minority enrollment, positive attitudes toward innovation and parent involvement, and at least one teacher with computer knowledge. Other criteria included strong instructional leadership from the principal, high expectations of students on the part of the instructional staff, and site stability. A great deal of emphasis was placed on district and school staff support for the project, since the SCEE saw this as a partnership between itself and the schools, their districts, and their communities. School districts assumed specific project responsibilities, including release time for teacher training, a room for parent activities, a computer lab, and a teacher for the critical thinking skills course.

Approaches and Strategies

Parents as Active Partners. Project MiCRO involved parents in their children's education through the appointment of parent coordinators, the offering of courses in microcomputers for parents, and assistance for parents to help their children learn. Parents were also given many opportunities to become involved in school activities as volunteers. For example, volunteer parents at the sites organized a variety of informal computer activities for students during lunch and after school.

On-Site Teacher Training. In each school, a site-based trainer offered from three to five days of training every month throughout the school year for each teacher in the school. This staff training involved not only computer use but also the development and adaptation of software tailored to the students' needs and the teacher's subject and the development of sound classroom management practices for computer use. This ensured that computers became an integral part of instruction in all subjects, thereby increasing computer time for students as well.

Teachers chosen to teach the critical thinking skills courses received training in theory, content, and pedagogy involved in teaching analytical thinking as well as the use of the computer in teaching these skills. The teachers were also instructed in lesson design to teach specific thinking skills, such as making inferences or judging credibility, using methods that encourage analytical thinking (modeling, guided discovery, open-ended questioning), and fostering cooperation rather than competition through the use of peer teaching and small groups.

Computer Literacy — an Interdisciplinary Approach. Teachers integrated activities that use computers (spreadsheets, word processing, and data-base management) into the curriculum in many subjects. This ensured computer use by students and an increase in the time spent on the computer. The emphasis here was on the practical application of computers as problem-solving tools rather than as an end in and of themselves.

Analytical Thinking Skills. Project MiCRO's emphasis on the teaching of analytical thinking skills stemmed from the belief that analytical thinking will enhance quantitative performance. The project literature based this belief on the assumptions that there is a cognitive link between analytical thinking and quantitative skills, that analytical thinking is learned behavior, and that analytical thinking skills should be taught directly.

Two levels of analytical thinking that were taught were discrete skills and multistep processes. The discrete skills were observation, recall, sequencing, classification, inference, induction, deduction, and association. The processes were distinguishing between fact and opinion, judging credibility, detecting bias, judging the relevance of information, solving problems, and making decisions. Instructional units were designed around each skill or process and based on a systematic metacognitive approach. Many of the learning activities in the units were microcomputer-based and multidisciplinary. Visible Pascal simulations, such as "The Other Side" and "Robot Odyssey," and logic courseware, such as "The King's Rule," "Puzzle Tanks," and "Mind Benders," were some of the software packages used in the course. Project staff, however, felt that the "canned packages" that were available to teach critical thinking were not entirely satisfactory.

The project's analytical thinking skills course combined the teaching of specific critical thinking skills and processes with teaching behaviors that encourage analytical thinking and the use of metacognition. Teachers who taught these courses had been trained to encourage the desired student behaviors through teacher modeling, guided discovery methods, examples of the skill being taught and behaviors to be avoided, task-explicit positive reinforcement, adequate response time, facilitation of student interaction, and other teaching behaviors that are effective in teaching critical thinking. Students were also taught to use peer teaching and metacognition, which stresses learning about brain functions and becoming aware of how their own thinking takes place.

The approaches described above are particularly effective and relevant for the age group that was served by the program. As the program literature stated, Project MiCRO chose the middle school level because "by early adolescence, learners are able to handle many forms of abstract thinking." The use of peer teaching was an effective strategy for early adolescents, as was parental involvement. The use of microcomputers stressed the hands-on approach to learning analytical thinking skills, also appropriate for this age group.

Staff

The project staff consisted of a project director, three parent coordinators, on-site trainers for each of the project sites, and an evaluation coordinator, who assisted the project director in developing the evaluation design, selecting appropriate evaluation instruments, collecting evaluation data, and interpreting the results. The project director was responsible for coordinating and managing the project as well as for documentation and evaluation.

Program Evaluation

Evaluation used both qualitative and quantitative approaches to answer the following questions:

- Can the project design be implemented effectively?
- Does the project increase performance in analytical thinking skills for those receiving the analytical thinking skills course?
- Does the project result in an understanding of instructional computing for minority students that they would otherwise not have?

Both formative and summative evaluations were conducted.

Formative Evaluation. Formative evaluation assessed the effectiveness of preservice and in-service training, classroom implementation, and instructional materials development. The training workshops were evaluated by participants, and their comments were used to plan future training. Site trainers and principals conducted regular classroom observations using an instrument that had been specially developed for this purpose. Results were used to monitor project implementation and plan future training. The results of the formative evaluation were used as constant feedback for planning in-service training and monitoring the implementation of the project and as a means of documenting the delivery system.

Summative Evaluation. The effectiveness of the project was assessed by comparing pre- and posttest data on computer literacy and analytical thinking skills for the treatment group as well as a control group (matched for size, student racial composition, standardized test scores, geographical location, and students' prior experience with computers) for each project site. All 1987 graduates had posttest scores significantly higher than their pretest scores. Two of the three experimental schools showed significant differences between pre- and posttest computer literacy scores. When compared with control schools, one experimental school had posttest scores significantly higher than its control, while the other two showed scores no different from the scores of their controls. The combined posttest scores of the three experimental schools for visual reasoning and problem solving were significantly higher than their pretest scores.

Surveys of the graduates revealed the following effects of their participation in the program:

- They had higher self-esteem.
- They wanted to work with computers on their first jobs.
- They did not like to miss school on the days the computer was used.
- Their grades had improved.
- They felt that they had achieved greater performance as learners on the computer.

The project director stressed the importance of assessing the long-range effect of programs such as these: "A lot of evaluations are one semester long. That is not long enough to draw any meaningful conclusions regarding a complex project such as this." She also discussed the difficulty of finding an appropriate instrument to test analytical thinking skills. "It was a real handicap not to have standard measures for critical thinking skills," she stated. "How do you assess critical thinking, particularly at this level? There are not adequate instruments to test critical thinking at the level of the students we have."

Unique Features of the Program

Parental Involvement. Although several of the programs described in this appendix stress the importance of parental involvement, only Project MiCRO had paid parent coordinators at each project site to organize activities for parents and encourage their participation. The project's offering of computer training and other classes for parents in exchange for volunteer work was one of its unique strategies for increasing parental involvement.

Site-Based Teacher Training. The presence of an on-site teacher trainer who was available to all the teachers in the school was another unique feature of the project. Having all the teachers in a school undergo training ensured that students increased their use of computers, learned to apply use of computers to several subjects, and increased the amount of time spent on the computers. Having the trainer on site ensured that teachers would use their computer training effectively in teaching their various subjects.

Use of Computers by Every Teacher. All teachers in the schools where the project was located used computers to teach, regardless of their subject area. All received training in computer use and applications in their particular subject. Teachers were also taught how to make software relevant to students' experiences.

Teaching Analytical Thinking Skills. Project MiCRO took a unique approach to teaching analytical thinking skills. This approach combined the direct teaching of specific critical thinking skills and processes with teacher behavior that encourages analytical thinking in students. According to project staff, this was "the only way to effectively transfer analytical thinking skills from one domain to another—for example, from science to mathematics—through the student's mastery of those attributes that generalize to the skills themselves."

The project's approach to using microcomputers to teach analytical thinking skills was also unique. Project staff cited as one of the reasons for using microcomputers that "right now, analytical thinking skills are not being taught in schools. . . . Microcomputers offered a window of opportunity to bring change to this situation. That opportunity meant that you can change lots of things—not only the delivery tool but what you are delivering. Both students and teachers are very motivated by computers, and because they are motivated, they are willing to try new things."

Dissemination and Institutionalization

The project was designed to be replicated by others at other sites. Documentation, therefore, was an important part of the project activity. One SCEE staff member had the responsibility for systematically interviewing, observing, and recording the process of implementing Project MiCRO.

The project director planned to publicize the project at school board and school administrators' meetings at the state and national level. Project materials and results were to be disseminated among organizations and networks concerned with equity and to be reported at national and state meetings focusing on instructional computing. In addition to publishing articles about the program, the project director is to meet with state superintendents of education in Georgia and Alabama to share the results of the project and to urge them to replicate it on a statewide basis.

The project also intended to share some of the lessons it learned regarding the use of microcomputers for instruction. According to project staff, students had to use the computer at least two hours per week in order to attain minimum computer literacy. Students who were taught analytical thinking skills using the microcomputer at least three to five hours per week performed even better on tests than those students who used it twice a week. Project staff felt that Project MiCRO was "on the cutting edge of the way that computers ought to be used" for instruction. Project MiCRO developed a manual on teaching critical thinking skills to seventh- and eighth-graders using science software.

Operation SMART

Operation SMART (Science, Math, and Relevant Technology) is a project of Girls Incorporated (formerly Girls Clubs of America), a national organization with nearly 300 club centers located in 34 states serving girls ages six through eighteen. The first girls' clubs were established more than a hundred years ago for the young women who worked in the factories of the northeastern mill towns and for the daughters of factory workers. Today, Girls Incorporated centers serve 250,000 children yearly, more than half of whom come from families with incomes of less than $15,000 per year and three-fourths from families with incomes of under $20,000. Close to half of the participants are members of minority groups.

Over the years, Girls Incorporated centers have changed their focus from providing social gathering places for girls to fostering girls' achievement and independence by offering education, preemployment, and social welfare programs. Local centers are affiliated with the national organization (which was established in 1945), but affiliates are autonomous and locally funded. The national headquarters is located in New York City; the Girls Incorporated National Resource Center, which compiles and publishes information on topics relating to girls (such as adolescent sexuality and equity funding) and conducts research and evaluation, is located in Indianapolis, Indiana. In addition to Operation SMART, Girls Incorporated has developed a number of other national programs for girls, including a program to prevent adolescent pregnancy, a comprehensive health promotion program, a substance abuse prevention program, a program to help parents and children prevent sexual abuse, and a program to foster girls' sports skills and participation.

The project director for Operation SMART describes its genesis as follows: "In the early 1980s, it was clear to the na-

258

tional office that girls really needed a background in math and science if they wanted to get jobs and pursue careers in this world. The mission of Girls Incorporated is to help its girls develop a capacity for economic independence, so we really couldn't ignore the technological revolution that was going on." Although "at the beginning we thought 'computers,'" both the national and local organizations soon realized that the overriding need was for competence in math and science.

The national office approached IBM, which provided a senior forecaster from its Executive Loan Program to interview staff during 1983 and offer recommendations regarding a basic design for the project. In the meantime, national staff obtained funding for a planning grant from General Electric in 1984 (the General Electric Foundation continued to fund the project during its implementation). Operation SMART began its implementation phase in January 1985 with five local Girls Incorporated centers serving as model sites: Lynn, Pittsfield, and Greenfield in Massachusetts and Syracuse and Schenectady in New York. In 1986, two more centers — the Holyoke and Springfield centers in Massachusetts — joined the project.

Goals and Structure

The overall goal of Operation SMART is to help girls acquire an attitude of scientific inquiry toward everything they do. As project staff describe this goal, "Operation SMART is more a perspective than a set of activities or lesson plans. What we are trying to communicate to girls is a way of thinking and looking rather than a body of information or concepts." Specific objectives of SMART are:

- To enable Girls Incorporated centers and other organizations to offer programs in math, science, technology, and computers
- To help young people become aware of math and science concepts embedded in everyday life and to help Girls Incorporated staff encourage an attitude of inquiry — questioning and exploration — throughout center activities and approaches

- To provide girls with access to resources in the community that can increase their interest in math and science
- To determine how Girls Incorporated centers and schools can best work together to increase girls' interest and involvement in math and science

The structure of the project is a complex one, encompassing several overlapping elements, including program development and research. Program development involved developing the model program and testing it at the seven model sites. The research element involved two phases. In phase 1, Girls Incorporated centers offering activities in math, science, and technology were surveyed to determine the characteristics of the activities that they offered, and six communities that represented the existing range on a whole series of variables (Schenectady, Atlanta, Pueblo, Santa Barbara, Santa Fe, and Detroit) were selected for case study. For phase 2, three communities — one in the midwest, one in the northeast, and one in the southeast — were chosen for intensive case studies, where a sample of girls were identified and followed for a year. The project director described this process as follows: "We asked them to think about and record all of the messages that they get about math and science from their schools, their families, the center, and the media." Phase 2 involved the development of a research tool kit described by one staff member as "a set of fun and challenging activities that girls can use to measure their own and others' attitudes."

Program Components

Structured Sessions in Math, Science, and Technology. These have been organized into modules containing eight to twelve sessions of an hour to an hour and a half each and focusing on various aspects of math and science. In addition to classes in math and science, the Schenectady site offers classes in woodworking, bicycle repair, and computers.

SMART activities emphasize the hands-on approach and minimize the use of paper-and-pencil exercises. SMART leaders have found this approach to be extremely successful for their target populations. As a Schenectady staff member explained, "The more they can touch and feel and experiment and try something out, the better. They don't like paper-and-pencil activities as much." A SMART leader said, "I think one of the things that really turns kids off is that so many of the teachers [in schools] 'do' while the kids watch. The kids like to do things for themselves."

Incorporation and Integration of Math and Science into All Girls Incorporated Programs and Activities. Making training opportunities available to all staff at the centers has been one way of disseminating the Operation SMART perspective and approach so that it can be applied in other areas of Girls Incorporated activities. As project staff explained, "In a lot of ways it was intended that it [Operation SMART] would shape all programs in Girls Incorporated, and that is really happening. There is a whole initiative now called Going Places, which is an attempt by the national organization to design a core program — a set of approaches, standards, and philosophies for what programs for girls really should be."

Career Exploration and Awareness. Field trips, speakers, mentors, and internships as well as special workshops and conferences are some of the approaches that Operation SMART uses to implement this component. The program also raises the consciousness of the staff regarding the importance of supporting participants' aspirations and helping them to examine their own ideas about their interests and their futures.

Involvement of Families. The centers involve families in different ways through Family Math programs and by encouraging parents to volunteer to lead activities and accompany field trips as advisers, consultants, and career role models. Girls Incorporated of Schenectady offers as part of its Operation SMART classes a mother-daughter computer class.

Use of Community Resources. All the model sites have formed relationships with local museums (especially children's and science museums), professional associations, community, business, and four-year colleges, businesses and corporations concerned with high-tech and science industries, and the public schools. Each center has a SMART advisory board, and the project has a national advisory council that includes representatives of these groups. Other formal collaborative relationships exist with the American Association for the Advancement of Science, EQUALS, the Association of Science-Technology Centers, and other organizations.

Approaches and Strategies

Equity and Inquiry. SMART project staff describe the principal approach as a "combination of equity and inquiry — a concern for equity and an emphasis on exploration. I think that every girl has the right to math and science education. This is not just for kids who are interested in math and science education or who are good at math and science. Our job here is to interest everybody in math and science and to make sure that they stay with it."

Age-Appropriate Strategies. Operation SMART has developed different strategies for the different age groups that it serves. SMART classes at the Schenectady center serve different age groups separately. For example, there are separate classes for girls in grades K–2, 3–5, and 6 and above. SMART started working with six- to eleven-year-olds, the youngest age group, by drawing on knowledge regarding the formation of sex-role stereotypes and gender expectations that develop at an early age. Activities with this age group focused on creating positive experiences involving science — experiences that involved the girls' whole bodies and engaged all the senses and that used lots of manipulatives for hands-on activities and avoided pencil-and-paper exercises.

The programs for young adolescents developed strategies that capitalized on what is known about that age group. For example, the project staff's knowledge of the developing ethical awareness of young adolescents led to community service projects focusing on science or technology. Counseling girls about course enrollment is another important strategy for this age group. Combating gender stereotypes and expectations that reemerge in a powerful way during this period is another main concern of the programs for young adolescent girls.

Programs for fifteen- to eighteen-year-olds focus on career awareness and provide in-depth exploration of architecture and engineering, the environment and music, and science and technology. The programs also offer internship and employment opportunities, scholarships to summer programs at universities, and tutoring and leading of courses for younger girls.

Materials. A series of manuals and videotapes focus on planning and implementing a SMART program, staff development, and hands-on science and math activities that highlight the equity and empowerment issues for girls and young women.

Staff

In the SMART manual, the ideal Operation SMART leader is characterized as follows:

- She models scientific inquiry at all times.
- She does not need to have all the answers.
- She exudes contagious enthusiasm.
- She understands and respects children.
- She takes a scientific approach to teaching.

Staff training is recognized as a critical need, since the behavior and teaching approaches required by the program do not come easily (or naturally) to many teachers. The program established collaborative projects with the Museum of Science and the Children's Museum in Boston for training Girls Incorporated staff in scientific inquiry and hands-on science. Project staff also prefer SMART leaders with backgrounds in science, and several SMART leaders have been teachers.

Program Evaluation

The evaluation of Operation SMART was conducted by the Girls Incorporated National Resource Center in Indianapolis. Demonstration sites documented all activities and reactions of both SMART leaders and participants in reports filled out after every activity. Leaders also sent in a monthly log. Because of the nature of the program and the fact that its purpose is different from that of most intervention programs in math and science, it has been difficult to conduct a conventional summative evaluation of the project. The program administration sees the rapid proliferation of SMART programs among Girls Incorporated centers as a sign of success. The research element of the project documented changes in girls' attitudes after participating in SMART. Outcome measures were developed once the program was in place and worked within the various settings.

Unique Features of the Program

Purpose of the Program. Unlike most intervention programs in math or science, Operation SMART has as its goal not an increase in the participation of girls (or minority group members) in math and science careers but a change in attitude leading to the application of a scientific inquiry approach toward everything that participants do. Another unique feature is the program's emphasis on "not being too much like school." As described in a program report, SMART "want[s] to challenge girls to question and explore; to create and build; to observe, record, watch for changes; to think, estimate, guess, get it wrong, figure out why, and try again; to take things apart, dissect, analyze, and understand; to focus, organize, and look for patterns; to make a mess and get dirty; to grapple with ideas and with objects; to take physical and intellectual risks; and above all, to be skeptics and not take anything for granted." In other words, the program seeks to change the girls' perspective rather than persuade or encourage them to make certain career choices. Operation SMART wants girls to feel that "no matter what they do later on they will have gotten comfortable with themselves here and will have had enough experience to feel that they can make some choices that they may not have been able to make before." The program wants girls to know what it is like to "push yourself to the fullest, then go past that point, and then go even farther."

Effect of the Program on Other Girls Incorporated Activities. In keeping with its emphasis on effecting attitudinal change in all aspects of life, SMART seeks to permeate all Girls Incorporated activities with the spirit of scientific inquiry. Centers are taking a hard look at their policies, practices, expectations, and norms to determine whether they reinforce sexual stereotypes or discourage an attitude of scientific inquiry.

A staff member at Girls Incorporated of Schenectady described the effect of Operation SMART on other center activities: "I look at activities that we do, such as cooking and gymnastics, that do not necessarily have anything to do with math or science, and I see that what has happened is that our whole agency is being involved in the SMART approach. Staff members for the different areas have learned to emphasize the math, science, and technology in each of those areas."

Age Appropriateness of Activities. Although many other programs incorporate strategies that are especially appropriate for the age group that they serve, this is often not a conscious and deliberate development. Operation SMART, on the other hand, has consciously developed different strategies and approaches based on the research literature on the different age groups that it targets. For example, six- to eight-year-olds need to confront and challenge sex-role stereotypes, whereas nine- to eleven-year-olds should expand their horizons, ideas, expectations, knowledge, and interests regarding careers and jobs.

Dissemination and Institutionalization

According to the project director, the program moved quickly into replication. Operation SMART is now operating in ninety of the 128 Girls Incorporated affiliates. The Operation SMART materials have greatly facilitated dissemination, as have the careful documentation of project activities at the model sites and the technical assistance provided by the national office.

Operation SMART has developed materials, for distribution to a wide audience, on how to encourage girls ages six through fourteen to "do" science. It has had many requests for help in starting SMART programs from school systems, teachers, state departments of education, sex-equity coordinators, museums, and after-school programs. See the resource list in Appendix B for a listing of some of the Operation SMART materials.

Project Interface

Project Interface is an after-school math and science preparatory program serving two distinct student populations. The larger group is made up of high-potential minority junior high school students who could and should be in college prep classes but are not. They are tutored, counseled, and mentored by the second client group, college students—primarily in junior college—who aspire to professional careers in the sciences and mathematics. The usual load of the project is between sixty and eighty junior high school students and a staff of thirteen to sixteen college students. These target populations were chosen because they are at-risk student populations that traditionally do not receive the support and services needed to excel in school.

The project began under the joint leadership and support of the Allen Temple Baptist Church in Oakland, California, and the Northern California Council of Black Professional Engineers, whose members were concerned about the lack of services available for junior high school students. The project's initial funding came from a two-year grant (1982–1984) from the U.S. Department of Education's Minority Institutions Science Improvement Program. It is now supported solely by funds raised from corporations, foundations, and individual contributions.

Program Goals and Structure

Project Interface prepares underachieving minority students to make the transition from general math and science classes to college preparatory courses. The project serves seventh-, eighth-, and ninth-grade students from east Oakland schools who are not currently enrolled in college preparatory math classes but who demonstrate potential to achieve. Students are recommended by school staff upon the request of parents.

266

The project's board of directors, which is made up of representatives of the public and private sectors, is responsible for the direction and management of the project. The program director is responsible for external relations, fundraising, and the current capital campaign drive; a full-time program manager is responsible for the day-to-day operation of the program, which is housed at the site of a large urban church with a tradition of outreach to the community, the Allen Temple Baptist Church.

The program consists of several critical components to reach one primary goal: increasing the number of promising minority junior high school students who can succeed in college prep work in senior high school and, later, college. This goal is attained by working toward these objectives:

- Increase the number of these students who enter college prep classes in high school and eventually transfer to four-year schools
- Increase the number of junior college students who successfully make the transfer from two-year to four-year institutions
- See that participating four-year college students graduate
- Contribute to the local, state, and nationwide efforts to develop programs that do indeed increase the number of underrepresented students who pursue academic and professional careers in math and science

The project strives to equip its participants with the necessary skills, attitudes, and knowledge to achieve these goals. Students who are admitted to the program participate in rigorous small-group study sessions, go on field trips, have access to academic and career counseling and to role models and mentors, and become eligible for scholarships and other programs.

Program Features

The program's structure is simple and its methodology straightforward. Students attend the program three afternoons each week for the entire school year, and most enroll in a month-long summer academy as well.

Math Strand. The small study groups are the core of the program. They are conducted by college students who are responsible for working with groups of four to six junior high school students. Mondays and Wednesdays are math days; students attend after school for two hours each day. The program works to accomplish three major tasks. The first is to fill gaps in student learning and develop the basic foundation necessary to master current work. The second is to ensure mastery of current classroom work at a grade level of B or better. Once these objectives have been met, program staff begin to introduce students to material that they will encounter later on in the year or next year in a college prep–level course.

Science Strand. Tuesday afternoons focus on science. Students spend fourteen weeks each in chemistry, physics, and biology. The activities and labs are researched and developed by the college students and are planned to spark the natural curiosity of the younger students by involving them in hands-on experiments and labs and to acquaint them with fundamental concepts in each of these three subjects. A writing component is involved as well, because students not only must write up the experiments but are often required to present them to one another and respond to questions. An annual science fair is also held, where students develop projects on an array of topics.

Career Exploration Strand. This component was developed in cooperation with staff at the Harbor Bay Business Park in Alameda, California. Presently, two companies are active participants: Triton Biosciences, Inc., and Integrated Automation. The purpose of this strand is to introduce students to real-world scientists engaged in actual work settings. Students tour the labs and work areas, hear lectures, and observe demonstrations put on by practicing scientists.

Role Model and Mentor Strand. The program has compiled a roster of professionals in the mathematics, science, and engineering fields who share their educational experiences, career paths, and future plans with students. Role models visit at least twice monthly and often three times. In the words of the project director, "They are a critical component in demonstrating that there are paths to success other than crime, entertainment, and athletics."

Computer Literacy Strand. The Xerox Corporation awarded the program twenty computers and five printers to establish an on-site computer laboratory. The lab is staffed by three professional volunteers, and classes at three different levels, running fifteen weeks each, are offered to students in the program on Thursday afternoons and Saturday mornings.

Parental Involvement and Support. Absences are reported to parents to monitor unexcused absences and chronic tardiness. Tutors call their students' homes on the first absence or tardiness; repeated occurrences can result in a parent conference. Additionally, parents and students receive academic and career counseling, and it is parents who must make the request when a student is felt to be ready to make the transition from general math to college prep classes. Parents receive monthly written feedback on student behavior and performance, conferences are scheduled as needed, and parents and students sign a contract committing themselves to the program's goals at the beginning of each year.

Field Trips. Field trips to relevant sites are conducted by program staff as a means of exposing students to the options and possibilities open to them. The trips are often the result of cooperative relationships such as those with Harbor Bay. A joint effort with the IN-ROADS program has resulted in a regular Saturday series, where college students being primed for corporate careers work with Project Interface every other Saturday. IN-ROADS students serve as role models and coaches by taking Project Interface students to a variety of relevant sites, requiring write-ups of the trips, and coaching them on being successful students.

Motivational, Academic, and Career Counseling. Under this component, program participants are provided with information on the courses needed for college preparatory work and careers in math and sciences. Students who make the transition from general math to college prep classes are featured in the project's quarterly newsletter and participate in other activities that bolster self-esteem and self-confidence.

Incentive Awards. Awards are presented on a monthly basis in the categories of effort, scholastic achievement, attendance, and overall excellence. These take the form of certificates and ribbons and are very effective as motivators.

Programs for College Students. A core of activities centers around grooming college students for transfer to four-year schools, graduate schools, and/or the private or public sector for full-time employment. College student tutors participate in twice-monthly sessions with a professional who shares experience and provides motivation in an informal setting, specifically addressing concerns of the college students. Job and career internships and job leads have resulted from the mentoring that comes from these seminars. Staff members meet with tutors once a week for problem solving and planning. In monthly meetings, tutors' goals for their students are discussed and their notebooks are reviewed to confirm contact with parents, quizzes, and homework assigned. The college students' grades and plans for transfer to four-year schools, graduate school, or permanent employment are carefully monitored.

College students are held accountable for their behavior and are treated as professionals. There are penalties for such things as consistent lateness, inappropriate dress, missing work without telephoning in, being unprepared for work, and other behaviors that might cost them a full-time position once out of school. Performance reviews are conducted, and the program has a salary scale to acknowledge seniority and merit among staff.

As a staff member explained, "We have a saying that our college students 'come to go.' We seek a minimum of a year-long commitment to work with the program and the students assigned to them. Indeed, there is a substantial penalty for tutors not giving ample notice if their schedules require them to leave the program. This is necessary because junior high school students become attached to 'their' tutor; some have even dropped out when 'their' tutor left without time to inform the students with whom they worked to prepare them for a new tutor."

Computer Class. The computer classes, originally conducted at a local college on Saturday afternoon, were developed by a Project Interface tutor and some parents. The purpose of the classes is to introduce participants to computer technology and provide them with hands-on experience in the use of computers. Students are instructed in word processing, and the instructor discusses advances in computing and artificial intelligence. The pilot project, which served twenty-seven students, was so successful that the project decided to establish an on-site program that would offer labs four evenings per week and serve all program participants as well as community members and organizations.

Program Components

Parental and Community Involvement. This is a vital component of Project Interface. Located as it is in the community, rather than at an educational institution, the program relies on parental and community involvement for support. For example, parents provided the transportation from east Oakland to a local college for the Saturday computer classes before the on-site lab was established. Parents also contribute to the project newsletter. All parents sign contracts committing themselves to supporting and assisting their children to "put forth maximum effort in school and achieve as much as he/she is able to." The contract requires that the parent perform specific duties, such as "review[ing] my child's homework to see that it is completed."

Project Interface elicits parental input through monthly parent feedback sheets and holds parent workshops throughout the year. Parents are also asked to attend parent conferences when disciplinary problems arise. The project director stated that the program "couldn't really function without our parents' involvement. . . . It is more than just helpful. It benefits children when they see their parents involved in their education and see them concerned about their education."

Many sectors of the community have given hours of volunteer time and energy to the project. The program has also received assistance from local industry. In 1986–87, for example, the Xerox Corporation placed a Xerox employee at full-time salary for nine months with Project Interface to assist the project director in fundraising and public relations.

Relationship with Local Schools. Although, according to the director, the project's "major point of intervention is the child and his or her family," Project Interface has also developed excellent working relationships with the local schools that its participants attend. At the junior high level, the project staff works with counselors or the mathematics department to identify potential participants. The project director also works with classroom teachers to move participants from general to college prep math courses when the program determines that they are ready.

The Junior College Student Component. Approximately fifteen students were tutors during 1985–86. They were all mathematics, science, or engineering majors, and all but four were enrolled in local junior colleges. One goal of the project is to help the tutors to improve their own grades, to encourage them to transfer to four-year institutions, and to assist them in obtaining paid internships during the summer when the program is not in session. A speakers' series exposes them to professionals in math and science careers and provides role models as well as career information.

Tutors receive two kinds of training: professional grooming for the work world and training in pedagogical techniques and approaches. Weekly staff meetings with the tutors assist and reinforce the pedagogical training by allowing them to discuss problems that have arisen in their classes during the week. The speakers' series helps them to better understand what will be required of them in their professions.

Approaches and Strategies

Helping Students Make the Transition to College Prep Classes. The tutorial sessions that form the core of Project Interface's program activities focus on assisting students in making the transition from general to college preparatory math classes and helping them with their science classes. These sessions first concentrate on mastery of basic skills and then introduce new material to prepare participants for the transition. In addition to enhancing academic performance, the sessions increase participants' confidence in their ability to perform at more advanced levels in mathematics and science. Once the project staff feel that a student is ready to undertake college prep classes in math and science, the project director acts as an intermediary between student and teacher to negotiate the change in track. Use of junior college students as tutors serves two important purposes: it provides participants with role models who are close to their own age and stage in the educational process, and it motivates junior college students to make the transfer to a four-year institution.

Community and Home Linkage. With its close ties to the Black community (as exemplified by its location within the community) and its emphasis on parental involvement, the program increases community awareness of the necessity for increasing Black participation in advanced math and science courses. It also effects change within the home by requiring that parents guarantee a supportive environment for their children to work in and promise to become involved in their children's education in specific ways.

Summary. Many of the strategies and approaches used by Project Interface are appropriate for early adolescents. The provision of role models who are close to the participants in age is effective for this age group. The incentive awards for behavior, attendance, effort, and achievement help students to develop confidence, self-esteem, and a feeling of accomplishment. Information on courses for college preparatory work and on career opportunities in math and science enables them to make informed, realistic choices regarding the appropriateness of careers in math and science as well as their own abilities to undertake such careers.

Program Evaluation

The project uses the following criteria to evaluate its effectiveness: students' scores on the CTBS; student course placement; subjective judgment of participants; data on junior high school participants' attrition; and transfer rate of junior college students.

Student Achievement as Measured by CTBS Scores. The Comprehensive Test of Basic Skills (CTBS) is a standardized test of student achievement administered each spring throughout the state of California. In some districts, it is administered only to students in the third, sixth, ninth, and twelfth grades; in Oakland, it is administered to all students in kindergarten through the twelfth grade. The project reports five years of student results on the CTBS test that exceed those of comparable students not enrolled in a support program for at least two of the three grades served. These results have been consistent year after year. A follow-up study on ninth-grade graduates found that 66 percent of them were enrolled in college preparatory math classes in high school; 40 percent of these reported grades of B or better.

Students' Course Placement. Other important measures are the number of students who make the transition from general math to college prep classes each year and the number that proceed along the college prep course. The 1987–88 class placement of students was as follows:

- Twelve of nineteen seventh-graders moved into prealgebra as eighth-graders.
- Eight of seventeen eighth-graders moved into algebra as ninth-graders.
- Fifteen of twenty-six ninth-graders moved into geometry as sophomores.
- Forty-four of sixty-two students moved into college prep classes.

Subjective Judgment of Participants. Responses elicited from junior high school students indicate feelings of pride regarding their achievement and satisfaction with their experiences in the project, as reflected in comments such as "I like learning more," "It makes me smarter," and "I get a chance to learn more about different math skills."

The college students are also surveyed regarding their feelings about the program. Overall, they express the feeling that participation in Project Interface has been a constructive, helpful learning experience. Not only has the project helped them to hone their skills and enhance their academic performance, but participation has given them a sense of pride in having made a valuable, meaningful contribution to youth and the community.

Junior High School Participants' Attrition. The rate of attrition from the program for project participants dropped from about 40 percent in 1984–85 to 16 percent in 1985–86. The attrition rate for programs serving high school students already enrolled in college preparatory courses averages about 50 percent.

Transfer Rate of Junior College Students. A stipulation of the initial grant from the U.S. Department of Education was the use of junior college students as tutors. However, the project has not been under that guideline since the 1983–84 academic term, and it now hires students attending four-year schools as well. While junior college students continue to constitute the majority of students serving as tutors, the mix of two-year and four-year students has enriched the overall project. Now two-year students have role models attending four-year schools and obtain much informal information about the transfer process and life on a four-year campus from their colleagues. The project staff continue to monitor the progress of all these students. Transfer rates for junior college students were five out of twelve in 1982–83, six out of twelve in 1983–84, and eight out of fifteen in 1984–85. Of the fourteen tutors in the program, three are junior college students. In 1986–87, one Project Interface college student transferred from Merritt Junior College to Mills College, one entered the University of San Francisco's law school, one took a full-time position with the Los Angeles Unified School District, and one was hired by the Oakland public schools. The remaining students continued in good standing in their path toward transfer or graduation.

Unique Features of the Program

Project Interface's unique features are its location within the community, the involvement of parents and other community members in its operation, and its use of junior college students as tutors.

Location in the Community. Most intervention program sites are at educational institutions. Project Interface's location at the Allen Temple Baptist Church makes it easily accessible to students and parents. Its location in the heart of the east Oakland community also provides a more comfortable setting for students and their parents, thereby making it easier for parents to participate in activities. Church members also represent a source of volunteer help, and the program has benefited from this. The pastor of the church, who was instrumental in establishing the program, is a very active supporter. Local industry and business have also contributed resources in the form of both money and time.

The program serves students from the community generally, rather than just students who are members of the church. Only about 20 percent of the students in the program have families that are church members.

Involvement of Parents. The director of Project Interface identified the program's main focus for intervention as the students and their families. A key strategy is involving parents in program activities to interest them in their children's education and to influence the family's attitude toward education-related behavior in the home. Monthly parent meetings, attended by between 30 and 50 percent of parents, feature speakers who address issues about which parents have expressed an interest. Parents also take part in fundraising and planning activities throughout the year.

The parent contract, which was developed by the parents themselves, commits them to supporting their children's education by, for example, providing certain conditions in the home, such as a quiet place for children to study and no telephone, radio, television, or other interruptions during the home study hours. Parents also promise to take an active part in their children's learning by requiring at least one hour per day of study time for each academic course they are enrolled in, taking time to meet each of the children's teachers at school, and reviewing homework to ensure that it is properly completed.

The Junior College Student Tutor Component. The program recognizes that junior college students are an at-risk population just as junior high school students are. In addition to using these students' services as tutors, the program strives to encourage them to transfer to four-year institutions, provides them with information about careers in math and science, exposes them to role models and mentors in the form of advisory board members, and assists them in locating paid internships in industry during the summer. In turn, the junior college students act as role models for the junior high participants.

Summary. Project Interface has developed an approach to increasing minority participation in math and science that has many unique features. By focusing its efforts on junior high school students, it has become part of a growing movement to concentrate intervention efforts in math and science at an earlier point in the educational process than has heretofore been the norm. Its location in a church within the community makes the program more accessible to students, parents, and volunteers from the community. Its strategy of increasing parental involvement in students' education as a means of reinforcing positive learning behavior and attitudes in the program, the school, and the home is another unique approach. Its work with another high-risk group, junior college students, to enhance their chances of success in math and science careers is an interesting and unusual component of the program.

APPENDIX B

Resources:
List of Programs and Materials

Many of the programs described in this book offer program descriptions ranging from flyers and brochures to project reports and annual reports and videotapes. In addition, a few programs also offer curriculum guidelines and/or detailed handbooks for implementing the program. The names and addresses of selected programs mentioned in the text are presented below, with types of materials available at the time the study was conducted.

Blacks and Mathematics (BAM)
College of Arts and Sciences
Wentworth Institute of Technology
Boston, MA 02115

Materials available:
  Program information
  Annual report

Cambell-Kibler Associates
Groton Ridge Heights
Groton, MA 01450

Materials available:
  Pamphlets: *What Works and What Doesn't?; Working Together, Making Changes; Math, Science and Your Daughter; Nothing Can Stop Us Now*

Community Ambassador Program
Steering Committee for Minorities Communication
Westinghouse Electric Corporation
Westinghouse Building
Pittsburgh, PA 15222

Materials available:
   Program information (brochures)

Cranbrook Institute of Science
500 Lone Pine Road
Bloomfield Hills, MI 48013

Materials available:
   Program information (flyers, brochures)

Detroit Area Pre-College Engineering Program, Inc.
(DAPCEP)
Rackham Educational Memorial Building
60 Farnsworth Avenue
Detroit, MI 48202

Materials available:
   Newsletter
   Annual report
   Program information (brochure)

Engineering Fair
201 NE 27th Street, Room 125
Oklahoma City, OK 73105

Materials available:
   Program information (letter, handouts)

Engineering Summer Institutes
College of Engineering and Applied Science
Arizona State University
Tempe, AZ 85287

Materials available:
  Annual report
  Application and enrollment information

Expanding Your Horizons
Skyline Community College
3300 College Drive
San Bruno, CA 94066

Materials available:
  Program information (brochure)

Family Math Program
Lawrence Hall of Science
University of California
Berkeley, CA 94720

Materials available:
  Program information
  Curriculum

Finding Out/Descubrimiento
Program for Complex Instruction
Center for Educational Research at Stanford
Stanford University
Stanford, CA 94305

Materials available:
  Program information
  Curriculum

Futures Unlimited Conferences
Consortium for Education Equity
Rutgers, The State University
Kilmer Campus, Building 4090
New Brunswick, NJ 08903

Materials available:
    Program information (handbook, brochure)
    Curriculum
    Bibliographies
    Multimedia packages
    Videotapes: *Futures Unlimited: Women in Technology; Science Teams; Just Between Sisters: Futures Unlimited; Minority Women in Technology*
    Posters

Girls + Math + Science = Choices
Calhoun Intermediate School District
17111 G Drive, North
Marshall, MI 49068

Materials available:
    Program information
    Curriculum

Go Power for Girls
Ames Community Schools
120 South Kellogg
Ames, IA 50010

Materials available:
    Program information
    Bibliographical list of resources

Idaho Science Camp
University of Idaho
College of Engineering
Moscow, ID 83843

Materials available:
  Program information

Massachusetts Pre-Engineering Program (MassPep)
Wentworth Institute of Technology
550 Huntington Avenue
Boston, MA 02115

Materials available:
  Program information kit
  Report

Math Instruction and Science Studies Career Options
Conference (MISS)
Orange Unified School District
370 North Glassell Street
Orange, CA 92666

Materials available:
  Saturday workshops brochures

Mathematics, Engineering, Science Achievement (MESA)
Lawrence Hall of Science
University of California
Berkeley, CA 94720

Materials available:
  Program information (brochures)
  Annual reports
  Newsletter
  Student handbook
  Report: Atwood, N. K., Doherty, W. J., Kenderski, C. M.,
  and Baker, E. L. *Mathematics, Engineering, Science Achieve-
  ment (MESA) Evaluation Report.* Los Angeles: Center for
  the Study of Evaluation, University of California, 1982.

Mathematics, Science, and Minorities, K–6
Mid-Atlantic Equity Center
American University
5010 Wisconsin Avenue, N.W.
Washington, DC 20016

Materials available:
  Program information
  Curriculum
  Paper: Beane, D. B., Cummings, F. D., and Oliphant,
  V. C. "Mathematics, Science, and Minorities, K–6: An
  Intervention Model." Paper presented at the annual
  meeting of the National Science Teachers Association, St.
  Louis, Mo., Apr. 1988.
  Report: Beane, D. B. *Opening Up the Mathematics and
  Science Filters: Our Schools Did It, So Can Yours!* Washing-
  ton, D.C.: Mid-Atlantic Equity Center, 1992.

Mathematics-Science Summer Enrichment Program
District of Columbia Public Schools
20th and Franklin Streets, N.E.
Washington, DC 20018

Materials available:
  Program information

Mentor in Engineering Program
New York Alliance for the Public Schools
32 Washington Place, 5th Floor
New York, NY 10003

Materials available:
  Program information (report)

Mu Alpha Theta Math Contest
Mathematics Department

Hughes Public Schools
P.O. Box 9
Hughes, AR 72348

Materials available:
  Program information
  Contest (math questions)

Multiply Your Options (MYO)
Project to Increase Mastery of Mathematics and Science
Wesleyan University
Middletown, CT 06457

Materials available:
  Program information (brochures)
  Newsletter

Multiplying Options and Subtracting Bias
National Council of Teachers of Mathematics
1906 Association Drive
Reston, VA 22091

Materials available:
  Report: Fennema, E., Becker, A. D., Wolleat, P. L.,
  and Pedro, J. D. *Multiplying Options and Subtracting Bias:
  An Intervention Program Designed to Eliminate Sexism from
  Mathematics Education.* Reston, Va.: National Council of
  Teachers of Mathematics, 1981.

Operation SMART (Science, Math, and Relevant
Technology)
Girls Incorporated
30 East 33rd Street, 7th Floor
New York, NY 10016

Materials available:
Reports
Spinnerets and Know-How: Operation SMART Planning Guide
The Power Project: Activity Guide
Questions: videotape of girls participating in Operation SMART
Operation SMART Research Tool Kit: set of program and evaluation activities
Seeds for Growth: Operation SMART Training Guide
Papers and reports

People in Science
Cranbrook Institute of Science
500 Lone Pine Road
P.O. Box 801
Bloomfield Hills, MI 48013

Materials available:
Program information

Project BASE (Blacks for Academic Success in Education)
Duval County Public Schools
1701 Prudential Drive
Jacksonville, FL 32216

Materials available:
Make a Difference, an in-service training program manual by S. Wilkinson
Project report

Project Interface
Allen Temple Baptist Church
8500 A Street
Oakland, CA 94621

Materials available:
   Program information (annual reports)
   Student handbook

Project MiCRO
Minority Computer Resource Opportunity
Southern Coalition for Educational Equity
Box 22904
Jackson, MS 39205

Materials available:
   Program information (brochure)
   Annual report
   Manual on teaching critical thinking skills using science
   software

Project SEED (Special Elementary Education for the
Disadvantaged)
2336-A McKinley Avenue
Berkeley, CA 94703

Materials available:
   Program information (brochure and videotape)
   Interservice training program
   Discovering Mathematics modules
   Report: Webster, W. J., and Chadbourn, R. A. "The
   Longitudinal Effects of SEED Instruction on
   Mathematics Achievement and Attitudes." Unpublished
   report, Dallas Independent School District, Dallas, Tex.,
   1988.
   Evaluation report: Webster, W. J., and Chadbourn, R.
   A. *Evaluation of Project SEED, 1990–1991.* Dallas, Tex.:
   Dallas Independent School District.

Saturday Science Academy
Clark Atlanta University

240 James T. Brawley Drive, SW
Atlanta, GA 30314

Materials available:
Program information (brochure)
Booklets with writing and drawings by participants
Collection of newspaper articles
Article: Elfner, L. E. "Science Academies: Strategic
Resources for Excellence in Education." *Educational
Horizons,* Winter 1984, pp. 77–78.

Scientists-in-the-Schools
Hawaii Association for Women in Science
Biomed Building T606B
University of Hawaii, Manoa
Honolulu, HI 96822

Materials available:
Program information

Share-a-Day-with-a-Scientist
Hawaii Association for Women in Science
Biomed Building T606B
University of Hawaii, Manoa
Honolulu, HI 96822

Materials available:
Project summary report

Taking the Road Less Traveled
Iowa State University
Women's Center
Ames, IA 50011

Materials available:
Project information (brochure)

Technical Career Counseling
National Technical Association
P.O. Box 1462
Akron, OH 44309

Materials available:
  Program information (brochure)
  Annual reports
  Newsletter

Women and Mathematics
Visiting Technical Women's Program
University of Michigan
Flint, MI 48503

Materials available:
  Program information (brochure)
  Career and educational information: annotated
  bibliography
  Interim reports and summaries of participant evaluation

Xerox Science Consultant Program
Xerox Corporation and Rochester City School District
Building 105-56C
800 Phillips Road
Webster, NY 14580

Materials available:
  Program information

APPENDIX C

Research on Inequities
in Mathematics and Science

The causes of the underrepresentation of women and minority groups in mathematics, science, and engineering fields are varied and complex. A comprehensive review of factors related to the four barriers discussed in the text has revealed three groups of factors that contribute to sex and race inequities in mathematics and science: student factors, school factors, and societal factors. The following table provides a summary of the research literature on these three influences from the 1970s to the present. A brief review of some of these studies is presented in Chapter One. A thorough review of this literature is contained in the monograph *Women of Color in Mathematics, Science, and Engineering* (Clewell and Anderson, 1991).

Research on Personal, Educational, and Social Influences on Math and Science.

Study	Perceptions and Attitudes			Performance			Participation			Professional Knowledge and Awareness		
	Student	School	Society	Student	School	Society	Student	School	Society	Student	School	Society
Aiken, 1970	✓		✓				✓			✓		
Andrews, 1989	✓	✓					✓					
Armstrong, 1980	✓			✓			✓					
Armstrong and Kahl, 1981	✓		✓	✓	✓		✓				✓	
Astin, 1974	✓											
Beane, 1985					✓				✓	✓	✓	
Becker, 1981				✓	✓							
Belenky, Clinchy, Goldberger, and Tarule, 1986				✓	✓							
Bossert, 1981	✓			✓							✓	
Brush, 1980	✓										✓	✓
Campbell, 1986		✓							✓			
Casserly, 1975		✓	✓					✓				
Chipman and Thomas, 1984												
Clark, 1985						✓		✓				
Clewell and Anderson, 1987, 1991	✓	✓	✓	✓	✓	✓	✓	✓	✓	✓	✓	✓
Clewell, Anderson, and Thorpe, 1988	✓	✓	✓	✓	✓		✓	✓	✓	✓	✓	✓
Cocking and Mestre, 1988				✓	✓						✓	✓
Coles and Griffen, 1987				✓	✓							
Connor, Schachman, and Serbin, 1978			✓	✓								
Davis, 1986				✓								
DeAvila and Duncan, 1980a, 1980b				✓	✓							
Dweck, 1986				✓								
Eccles-Parsons, 1984								✓				

Ekstrom, 1985

Ethington and Wolfle, 1987

Fauth and Jacobs, 1980

Fennema, 1976

Fennema and Sherman, 1976

Fox, 1976

Fox, Brody, and Tobin, 1985

Garcia, Harrison, and Torres, 1990

Gilligan, 1982

Gore, 1980

Granvillle, 1986

Graybill, 1975

Gross, 1988

Hale-Benson, 1984

Hall, 1981

Hart and Stanic, 1989

Haven, 1972

Hensel, 1989

Howe and Shayer, 1981

Howe, quoted in Harden and Dede, 1973

Iker, 1980

Jacobowitz, 1983

Jacobs and Eccles, 1985

Johnson, 1981

Johnson, 1986

Jones and Wheatley, 1988

Kahle, 1982

Kahle and Lakes, 1983

Kelly, 1981

Kelly and Smail, 1986

Kenschaft, 1981

Research on Personal, Educational, and Social Influences on Math and Science, cont'd.

Study	Perceptions and Attitudes			Performance			Participation			Professional Knowledge and Awareness		
	Student	School	Society	Student	School	Society	Student	School	Society	Student	School	Society
Khoury and Voss, 1985				✓			✓					
Kimball, 1989											✓	
Klein and Bailey, 1975												✓
Lantz and Smith, 1981	✓									✓		
Laurenz, 1987								✓				
Lee, 1984		✓			✓	✓	✓	✓				✓
Levine, 1976				✓								
Licht and Dweck, 1983				✓	✓							
Licht and Shapiro, 1982				✓	✓							
Lockheed and others, 1985				✓	✓							
Luchins, 1976				✓		✓	✓	✓	✓	✓		✓
Luchins, 1979					✓	✓		✓	✓	✓	✓	✓
McBay, 1978	✓			✓							✓	
MacCorquodale, 1980, 1984	✓			✓	✓			✓			✓	
Malcom and others, 1984				✓	✓✓		✓✓	✓				
Marrett, 1986				✓	✓✓		✓	✓				
Matthews, 1981, 1984	✓✓	✓		✓✓	✓	✓✓	✓			✓✓		
Matyas and Kahle, 1986	✓			✓	✓		✓	✓		✓		
Mullis and Jenkins, 1988				✓	✓	✓	✓	✓	✓			
Oakes, 1990				✓	✓	✓	✓	✓				
Olstad, Juarez, Davenport, and Haury, 1981				✓	✓		✓					
Orr, 1987												
Parsons, 1983												
Parsons, Adler, and Kaczala, 1982			✓	✓			✓				✓	✓

Payne, Smith, and Payne, 1983

Powell and Garcia, 1985

Prillwritz, 1983

Rendon, 1983

Reyes, 1984

Riggs, 1988

Rossi, 1965a, 1965b

Rowe, 1974a, 1974b

Schreiber, 1984

Sells, 1978

Smith and Erb, 1986

Stage, Kreinberg, Eccles, and Becker, 1985

Steel, 1978

Thomas, 1986

Tibord, 1973

Tobias, 1978

Treagust, 1980

Turner, 1983

U.S. Congress, Office of Technology Assessment, 1988a, 1988b

Valverde, 1984

Weiss, 1978

Wilkinson and Marrett, 1985

Willig, Harnisch, Hill, and Maehr, 1978

Young, 1981

Young, 1983

References

Aiken, L. R. "Attitudes Towards Mathematics." *Review of Educational Research,* 1970, *40,* 551–596.

Allen, V. L. *Children as Teachers: Theory and Research on Tutoring.* San Diego, Calif.: Academic Press, 1976.

American Council on Education. *Minorities in Higher Education.* Washington, D.C.: American Council on Education, 1988.

Anderson, B. T. "Black Participation and Performance in High School." In W. Pearson, Jr., and H. K. Bechtel (eds.), *Blacks, Science, and American Education.* New Brunswick, N.J.: Rutgers University Press, 1989.

Andrews, J. V. "Attitudes and Beliefs About Mathematics: Do Parents, Students, Teachers, Counselors and Principals Agree?" Paper presented at the annual meeting of the American Educational Research Association, San Francisco, Apr. 1989.

Arizona State University. *Minorities in Engineering Report, 1984 Summer Institutes.* Tempe: College of Engineering and Applied Sciences, Arizona State University, 1984.

Armstrong, J. M. *Achievement and Participation of Women in Mathematics: An Overview Report of a Two-Year Study.* Report no. 10-MA-00. Washington, D.C.: National Institute of Education, 1980.

Armstrong, J. M., and Kahl, S. *A National Assessment of Performance and Participation of Women in Mathematics.* Grant no. NIE-G-77-0061. Washington, D.C.: National Institute of Education, 1981.

Ashby, M. S., and Wittmaier, B. C. "Attitude Changes in Children After Exposure to Stories About Women in Traditional or Nontraditional Occupations." *Journal of Educational Psychology,* 1978, *70*(6), 945–949.

Astin, H. S. "Sex Differences in Mathematical and Scientific Precocity." In J. C. Stanley, D. P. Keeting, and L. H. Fox (eds.), *Mathematical Talent: Discovery, Description and Development.* Baltimore, Md.: Johns Hopkins University Press, 1974.

Atkinson, J. W. *An Introduction to Motivation.* New York: Van Nostrand Reinhold, 1964.

Bandura, A. "Self-Efficacy: Toward a Unifying Theory of Behavioral Change." *Psychological Review,* 1977, *84,* 191–215.

Bean, J. "What's Happening in Mathematics and Science Classrooms: Student-Teacher Interactions." Paper presented at the annual meeting of the American Educational Research Association, San Francisco, Apr. 1976.

Beane, D. B. *Mathematics and Science: Critical Filters for the Future of Minority Students.* Washington, D.C.: Mid-Atlantic Center for Race Equity, American University, 1985.

Beane, D. B. "Say YES to a Youngster's Future: A Model for Home, School, and Community Partnership." *Journal of Negro Education,* 1990, *59*(3), 360–374.

Beane, D. B. *Opening Up the Mathematics and Science Filters: Our Schools Did It, So Can Yours!* Washington, D.C.: Mid-Atlantic Equity Center, American University, 1992.

Becker, J. R. "Differential Treatment of Females and Males in Mathematics Classes." *Journal for Research in Mathematics Education,* 1981, *12,* 40–53.

Belenky, M. F., Clinchy, B. M., Goldberger, N. R., and Tarule, J. M. *Women's Ways of Knowing: The Development of Self, Voice, and Mind.* New York: Basic Books, 1986.

Benson, J., Urman, H., and Hocevar, D. "Effects of Test-Wiseness Training and Ethnicity on Achievement of Third- and Fifth-Grade Students." *Measurement and Evaluation in Counseling and Development,* 1986, *18,* 154–162.

Berger, J., Rosenholtz, S. J., and Zelditch, M., Jr. "Status-Organizing Processes." *Annual Review of Sociology,* 1980, *6,* 479–508.

Berman, P., and McLaughlin, M. W. "Implementation of Educational Innovation." *Educational Forum,* 1976, *40*(3), 345–370.

Berryman, S. F. *Who Will Do Science? Trends and Their Causes in Minority and Female Representation Among Holders of Advanced Degrees in Science and Mathematics.* New York: Rockefeller Foundation, 1983.

Biehler, R. *Psychology Applied to Teaching.* Boston: Houghton Mifflin, 1971.

Bloom, B. S. "Affective Consequences of School Achievement." In G. H. Block (ed.), *Mastery of Learning.* Troy, Mo.: Holt, Rinehart & Winston, 1971.

Bookman, A. B., and Iwanicki, E. F. "The Effects of Method of Test Preparation on Standardized Mathematics Achievement Test Performance." *Journal of Research and Development in Education,* 1983, *16*(4), 46–51.

Borow, H. "Career Development." In J. F. Adames (ed.), *Understanding Adolescence.* Boston: Allyn & Bacon, 1976.

Bossert, S. T. "Understanding Sex Differences in Children's Classroom Experiences." *Elementary School Journal,* 1981, *81*, 254–266.

Bowers, D. *Using Peer Tutoring as a Form of Individualized Instruction for the At-Risk Students in a Regular Classroom.* Fort Lauderdale, Fla.: Nova University, 1991.

Brophy, J. E., and Good, T. *Teacher-Student Relationships: Causes and Consequences.* Troy, Mo.: Holt, Rinehart & Winston, 1974.

Brown, G. H., and Campione, J. C. "Memory Strategies in Learning: Training Children to Study Strategically." In H. Pick and others (eds.), *Application of Basic Research in Psychology.* New York: Plenum Press, 1978.

Bruner, J. *The Process of Education.* New York: Vintage Books, 1963.

Brush, L. *Encouraging Girls in Mathematics: The Problem and the Solution.* Cambridge, Mass.: Abt Books, 1980.

Campbell, P. B. "What's a Nice Girl Like You Doing in a Math Class?" *Phi Beta Kappan,* 1986, *67*(7), 516–520.

Carpenter, T. P., and others. "NAEP Note: Problem Solving." *Mathematics Teacher,* 1980, *73*, 427–433.

Casserly, P. L. "An Assessment of Factors Affecting Female Participation in Advanced Placement Programs in Mathematics, Chemistry, and Physics." Unpublished manuscript, Educational Testing Service, 1975.

Casserly, P. L. "The Advanced Placement Teacher as the Critical Factor in High School Women's Decision to Persist in the Study of Mathematics." Paper presented at the annual meeting of the American Educational Research Association, San Francisco, Apr. 1979.

Chicago Public Schools. *Mathematics Teacher Development with Peer Tutoring.* Chicago: Chicago Public Schools, 1985.

Chipman, S. F., and Thomas, V. G. "The Participation of Women and Minorities in Mathematical, Scientific and Technical Fields." Unpublished paper commissioned by the Committee on Research in Mathematics, Science, and Technology Education of the National Research Council's Commission on Behavioral and Social Sciences and Education, 1984.

Clark Atlanta University. *Saturday Science Academy Booklet.* Atlanta, Ga.: Saturday Science Academy, 1987.

Clark, J. V. "Needed—More Black Math, Science Teachers." *Houston Chronicle,* July 15, 1985, p. 11.

Clewell, B. C. "What Works and Why: Research and Theoretical Bases of Intervention Programs in Math and Science for Minority and Female Middle School Students." In A. B. Champagne and L. E. Hornig (eds.), *Students and Science Learning.* Washington, D.C.: American Association for the Advancement of Science, 1987.

Clewell, B. C. "Intervention Programs: Three Case Studies." In W. Pearson, Jr., and H. K. Bechtel (eds.), *Blacks, Science, and American Education.* New Brunswick, N.J.: Rutgers University Press, 1989.

Clewell, B. C., and Anderson, B. T. "Effective Math/Science Intervention Approaches for Middle School Minority Students: What the Literature Says." Paper presented at the annual meeting of the American Educational Research Association, Washington, D.C., Apr. 1987.

Clewell, B. C., and Anderson, B. T. *Women of Color in Mathematics, Science, and Engineering: A Review of the Literature.* Washington, D.C.: Center for Women Policy Studies, 1991.

Clewell, B. C., Anderson, B. T., and Thorpe, M. E. *Integrating Theory, Research and Practice: A Continuing Challenge for Intervention Programs.* Final report submitted to the Ford Foundation. Princeton, N.J.: Educational Testing Service, 1988.

Clewell, B. C., Thorpe, M. E., and Anderson, B. T. *Intervention Programs in Math, Science, and Computer Science for Minority and Female Students in Grades Four Through Eight.* Princeton, N.J.: Educational Testing Service, 1987.

Cocking, R. R., and Mestre, J. P. *Linguistic and Cultural Influences on Learning Mathematics.* Hillsdale, N.J.: Erlbaum, 1988.

Cohen, D. K. "Educational Technology, Policy, and Practice." *Educational Evaluation and Policy Analysis,* 1987, *9*(2), 153–170.

Cohen, E. G. "On the Sociology of the Classroom." In J. Hannaway and M. E. Lockheed (eds.), *The Contributions of the Social Sciences to Educational Policy and Practice: 1965–1985.* Berkeley, Calif.: McCutchan, 1986.

Cohen, E. G., and DeAvila, E. A. *Learning to Think in Math and Science: Improving Local Education for Minority Children.* Final report to the Walter S. Johnson Foundation. Stanford, Calif.: School of Education, Stanford University, 1983.

Cohen, E. G., Intili, J. K., and Robbins, S. H. "Task and Authority: A Sociological View of Classroom Management." In D. L. Duke (ed.), *The National Society for the Study of Education Seventy-eighth Yearbook. Part II.* Chicago: University of Chicago Press, 1979.

Cohen, E. G., Lotan, R. A., and Leechor, C. "Can Classrooms Learn?" *Sociology of Education,* 1989, *62*, 75–94.

Coles, M., and Griffen, P. *Contextual Factors in Education: Improving Science and Mathematics Education for Minorities and Mathematics Education for Minorities and Women.* Madison: Wisconsin Center for Education Research, 1987.

College Entrance Examination Board and Western Interstate Commission for Higher Education. *The Road to College: Educational Progress by Race and Ethnicity.* Boulder, Colo.: College Entrance Examination Board and Western Interstate Commission for Higher Education, 1991.

Comer, J. "Home-School Relationships as They Affect the Academic Success of Children." *Education and Urban Society,* 1984, *16*(3), 323–337.

Connor, J. M., Schachman, M. E., and Serbin, L. A. "Sex-Related Differences in Response to Practice on a Visual-Spatial Test and Generalization to a Related Test." *Child Development,* 1978, *49,* 24–29.

Contreras, A., and Lee, O. "Differential Treatment of Students by Middle School Science Teachers: Unintended Cultural Bias." *Science Education,* 1990, *74,* 433–444.

Curtis, T. E., and Bidwell, W. W. *Curriculum and Instruction for Emerging Adolescents.* Reading, Mass.: Addison-Wesley, 1977.

Davis, B. G., and Humphreys, S. *Evaluating Intervention Programs: Applications from Women's Programs in Math and Science.* New York: Teachers College Press, 1985.

Davis, J. D. *The Effect of Mathematics Course Enrollment on Racial/Ethnic Differences in Secondary School Mathematics Achievement.* NAEP report no. 86-EMC. Princeton, N.J.: Educational Testing Service, 1986.

Davis, J. D. "The Mathematics Education of Black High School Students." In W. Pearson, Jr., and H. K. Bechtel (eds.), *Blacks, Science, and American Education.* New Brunswick, N.J.: Rutgers University Press, 1989.

DeAvila, E., and Duncan, S. *Finding Out/Descubrimiento.* Corte Madera, Calif.: Linguametrics Group, 1980a.

DeAvila, E., and Duncan, S. *The Language-Minority Child: A Psychological, Linguistic, and Social Analysis.* Report no. 400-65-0051. Washington, D.C.: National Institute of Education, 1980b.

DeAvila, E., Havassy, B., and Pascual-Leone, J. *Mexican-American School Children: A Neo-Piagetian Analysis.* Washington, D.C.: Georgetown University Press, 1976.

Devaney, K. *Interviews with Nine Teachers.* Berkeley: Lawrence Hall of Science, University of California, 1986.

Dewey, J. *Democracy and Education: An Introduction to the Philosophy of Education.* Norwood, Pa.: Telegraph Books, 1986. (Originally published 1916.)

DiVesta, F. J. *Language, Learning and Cognitive Processes.* Pacific Grove, Calif.: Brooks/Cole, 1974.

Dorman, G. *Middle Grades Assessment Program.* Chapel Hill: Center for Early Adolescence, University of North Carolina, 1981.

Dornbusch, S. M., and Scott, W. R. *Evaluation and the Exercise of Authority.* San Francisco: Jossey-Bass, 1975.

Dossey, J. A., Mullis, I.V.S., Lindquist, M. M., and Chambers, D. L. *The Mathematics Report Card: Are We Measuring Up? Trends and Achievement Based on the 1986 National Assessment.* Report no. 17-M-01. Princeton, N.J.: Educational Testing Service, 1988.

Duran, R. P. "Hispanics' Precollege and Undergraduate Education: Implications for Science and Engineering Studies." In L. S. Dix (ed.), *Minorities: Their Underrepresentation and Career Differentials in Science and Engineering.* Washington, D.C.: National Academy Press, 1987.

Dweck, C. S. "Motivational Processes Affecting Learning." *American Psychologist,* 1986, *41*(10), 1040–1048.

Eccles-Parsons, J. "Sex Differences in Math Participation." In M. L. Maehr and W. Steinkamp (eds.), *Women in Science.* Greenwich, Conn.: JAI Press, 1984.

Ekstrom, R. B. *A Descriptive Study of Public High School Guidance.* Final report to the Commission on Precollegiate Guidance and Counseling. Princeton, N.J.: Educational Testing Service, 1985.

Ethington, C. A., and Wolfle, L. M. "The Selection of Quantitative Undergraduate Fields of Study: Direct and Indirect Influences." Paper presented at the annual meeting of the American Educational Research Association, Washington, D.C., Apr. 1987.

Fauth, G. C., and Jacobs, J. E. "Equity in Mathematics Education: The Educational Leader's Role." *Educational Leadership,* 1980, *37,* 485–490.

Fennema, E. *Influences of Selected Cognitive, Affective and Educational Variables on Sex-Related Differences in Mathematics Learning and Studying.* National Institute of Education grant no. P-76-0274. Madison: University of Wisconsin, 1976.

Fennema, E. "Girls, Women, and Mathematics: An Overview." In E. Fennema and J. Ayer (eds.), *Women and Education: Equity or Equality?* Berkeley, Calif.: McCutchan, 1984.

Fennema, E., and Sherman, J. "Sex-Related Differences in Mathematics Learning: Myths, Realities, and Related Factors."

Paper presented at the annual meeting of the American Association for the Advancement of Science, Boston, Feb. 1976.

Fennema, E., and Sherman, J. "Sex-Related Differences in Mathematics Achievement and Related Factors: A Further Study." *Journal for Research in Mathematics Education,* 1978, *9*(3), 189–203.

Fort, D. C., and Varney, H. L. "How Students See Scientists: Mostly Male, Mostly White, and Mostly Benevolent." *Science and Children,* 1989, *26*(8), 8–13.

Fox, L. H. *The Effects of Sex Role Socialization on Mathematics Participation and Achievement.* Contract no. FN17-400-76-0114. Washington, D.C.: National Institute of Education, 1976.

Fox, L. H., Brody, L., and Tobin, D. "The Impact of Early Intervention Programs upon Course Taking and Attitudes in High School." In S. F. Chipman, L. R. Brush, and D. M. Wilson (eds.), *Women and Mathematics.* Hillsdale, N.J.: Erlbaum, 1985.

Gagne, R. M. *The Conditions of Learning.* (3rd ed.) Troy, Mo.: Holt, Rinehart & Winston, 1977.

Garcia, J., Harrison, N. R., and Torres, J. L. "The Portrayal of Females and Minorities in Selected Elementary Mathematics Series." *School Science and Mathematics,* 1990, *90*(1), 1–12.

Gartner, A., Kohler, M. C., and Riessman, F. *Children Teach Children: Learning by Teaching.* New York: HarperCollins, 1971.

Georgia State Department of Education. *Teaching Middle School Science.* Atlanta: Office of Instructional Services, Georgia State Department of Education, 1982.

Gilligan, C. *In a Different Voice: Psychological Theory and Women's Development.* Cambridge, Mass.: Harvard University Press, 1982.

Ginsberg, E. *Occupational Choice.* New York: Columbia University Press, 1951.

Girls Incorporated. *The Power Project: Operation SMART Activity Guide.* New York: Girls Incorporated, 1990a.

Girls Incorporated. *Spinnerets and Know-How: Operation SMART Planning Guide.* New York: Girls Incorporated, 1990b.

Girls Incorporated, Operation SMART. *Seeds for Growth: Operation SMART Training Guide.* New York: Girls Incorporated, 1992.

Gore, P. L. "Courses, Books, Comments." Unpublished manuscript, Bacone College, 1980.

Granville, R. C. "The Influence of Science Role Models on the Attitudes of Middle School Students Toward Women in Science." *Dissertation Abstracts International,* 1986, *47*(01-A), 69.

Graybill, L. "Sex Differences in Problem-Solving Activity." *Journal of Research in Science Teaching,* 1975, *12*(4), 341–346.

Gross, S. *Participation and Performance of Women and Minorities in Mathematics.* Vol. 1: *Findings by Gender and Racial/Ethnic Group.* Rockville, Md.: Carver Educational Services Center, Montgomery County Public Schools, 1988.

Gross, S. "Early Mathematics Performance and Achievement: The Beginning of a Downward Spiral for Blacks and Hispanics." Paper presented at the annual meeting of the American Educational Research Association, San Francisco, Mar. 1989.

Guskey, T. R. "Staff Development and the Process of Teacher Change." *Educational Researcher,* 1986, *15,* 5–12.

Hale-Benson, J. E. *Black Children: Their Roots, Culture, and Learning Styles.* (Rev. ed.) Baltimore, Md.: Johns Hopkins University Press, 1984.

Hall, P. O. *Problems and Solutions in Education, Employment and Personal Choice of Minority Women in Science.* Washington, D.C.: American Association for the Advancement of Science, 1981.

Harden, J., and Dede, C. "Discrimination Against Women in Science Education." *Science Teacher,* 1973, *40,* 18–21.

Harding, J. "Sex Differences in Examination Performance at 16 + ." *Physics Education,* 1979, *17,* 169–174.

Hart, L. E., and Stanic, G.M.A. "Attitudes and Achievement-Related Behaviors of Middle School Mathematics Students: Views Through Four Lenses." Paper presented at the annual meeting of the American Educational Research Association, San Francisco, Mar. 1989.

Haven, E. *Factors Associated with the Selection of Advanced Mathematics Courses by Girls in High School.* Princeton, N.J.: Educational Testing Service, 1972.

Havighurst, R. "Lost Innocence: Modern Junior High School Youth." *Bulletin of the National Association of Secondary School Principals,* 1965, *49,* 1–4.

Hensel, R. A. "Mathematical Achievement: Equating the Sexes." *School Science and Mathematics,* 1989, *89*(8), 646–653.

Hilgard, B. R., and Bower, G. H. *Theories of Learning.* East Norwalk, Conn.: Appleton & Lange, 1975.

Hill, J. P. *Understanding Early Adolescence: A Framework.* Carrboro, N.C.: Center for Early Adolescence, Department of Maternal and Child Health, School of Public Health, 1980.

Hodgkinson, H. L. *All One System.* Washington, D.C.: Institute of Educational Leadership, 1985.

Holland, J. L. *Making Vocational Choices: A Theory of Vocational Personalities and Work Environments.* (2nd ed.) Englewood Cliffs, N.J.: Prentice-Hall, 1985.

Howe, A. C., and Shayer, M. "Sex-Related Differences on a Task of Volume and Density." *Journal of Research in Science Teaching,* 1981, *18*(2), 169–175.

Hurlock, E. B. *Child Development.* New York: McGraw-Hill, 1972.

Iker, S. "A Math Answer for Women." *MOSAIC,* 1980, *11*(3), 39–45.

Irvine, J. J. *Black Students and School Failure: Policies, Practices, and Prescriptions.* Westport, Conn.: Greenwood Press, 1990.

Jacobowitz, T. J. "Relationship of Sex, Achievement, and Science Self-Concept to the Science Career Preferences of Black Students." *Journal of Research in Science Teaching,* 1983, *20*(7), 621–628.

Jacobs, J., and Eccles, J. "Gender Differences in Math Ability: The Impact of the Media Reports on Parents." *Educational Researcher,* 1985, *14*(3), 20–25.

James, R. K., and Smith, S. "Alienation of Students from Science in Grades 4–12." *Science Education,* 1985, *69*(1), 39–45.

Johnson, R. C. *Psychosocial Influences on the Math Attitudes and Interests of Black Junior High School Students.* St. Louis, Mo.: Institute of Black Studies, 1981.

Johnson, R. T., and Johnson, D. W. "Cooperative Learning and the Achievement and Socialization Crises in Science and Mathematics Classrooms." In A. B. Champagne and L. E. Hornig (eds.), *Students and Science Learning.* Washington, D.C.: American Association for the Advancement of Science, 1987.

Johnson, S. T. "Career Choices in Science and Mathematics Among Talented Minority Graduates." Paper presented at the 12th annual Conference on Research on Women in Education, Washington, D.C., Nov. 1986.

Johnson, S. T., and Prom-Jackson, S. *Factors Related to Science and Mathematics Career Choice in a Minority Population: A Survey of Alumni of a Better Chance, Inc.* Final report submitted to the Ford Foundation. New York: Ford Foundation, 1983.

Jones, L. R., and others. *The 1990 Science Report Card: NAEP's Assessment of Fourth, Eighth, and Twelfth Graders.* Princeton, N.J.: Educational Testing Service, 1992.

Jones, L. V. "White-Black Achievement Differences: The Narrowing Gap." *American Psychologist,* 1984, *39,* 1207–1213.

Jones, M. G., and Wheatley, J. "Factors Influencing the Entry of Women into Science and Related Fields." *Science Education,* 1988, *72,* 127–142.

Kahle, J. B. "Can Positive Minority Attitudes Lead to Achievement Gains in Science? Analysis of the 1977 National Assessment of Educational Progress, Attitudes Toward Science." *Science Education,* 1982, *66*(4), 539–546.

Kahle, J. B., and Lakes, M. K. "The Myth of Equality in Science Classrooms." *Journal of Research in Science Teaching,* 1983, *20*(2), 131–140.

Keeves, J. P. "The Home, the School, and Achievement in Mathematics and Science." *Science Education,* 1975, *59,* 439–460.

Kelly, A. (ed.). *The Missing Half: Girls and Science Education.* Manchester, England: Manchester University Press, 1981.

Kelly, A., and Smail, B. "Sex Stereotypes and Attitudes to Science Among Eleven-Year-Old Children." *British Journal of Educational Psychology,* 1986, *56,* 158–168.

Kenschaft, P. "Black Women in Mathematics." *American Mathematical Monthly,* 1981, *88,* 592–604.

Khoury, G. A., and Voss, B. E. "Factors Influencing High School Students' Science Enrollment Patterns: Academic Abilities, Parental Influences, and Attitudes Toward Science." Paper presented at the annual meeting of the National Association for Research in Science Teaching, French Lick Spring, Ind., Apr. 1985. (ED 254 408)

Kimball, M. M. "A New Perspective on Women's Math Achievement." *Psychological Bulletin,* 1989, *105*(2), 198–214.

Klein, A. H., and Bailey, M. N. "The Socialization of Achievement Orientation in Females." *Psychological Bulletin,* 1975, *80,* 345–366.

Kovacs, R., and Goldman, J. (eds.). *The Foundation Grants Index.* (18th ed.) New York: The Foundation Center, 1989.

Lantz, A. E., and Smith, G. P. "Factors Influencing the Choice of Nonrequired Mathematics Courses." *Journal of Educational Psychology,* 1981, *73,* 825–837.

Laosa, L. *Social Policies Toward Children of Diverse Ethnic, Racial, and Language Groups in the United States.* Princeton, N.J.: Educational Testing Service, 1983.

Lapointe, A. E., Askew, J. M., and Mead, N. A. *Learning Science: The International Assessment of Educational Progress.* Report no. 22-CAEP-02. Washington, D.C.: National Center for Education Statistics, U.S. Department of Education, and National Science Foundation, 1992.

Lapointe, A. E., Mead, N. A., and Askew, J. M. *Learning Mathematics: The International Assessment of Educational Progress.* Report no. 22-CAEP-01. Washington, D.C.: National Center for Education Statistics, U.S. Department of Education, and National Science Foundation, 1992.

Lawrenz, F. "Gender Effects for Student Perception of the Classroom Psychosocial Environment." *Journal of Research in Science Teaching,* 1987, *24,* 689–697.

Lawson, A. E., and Wollman, W. T. "Encouraging the Transition from Concrete to Formal Cognitive Functioning: An Experiment." *Journal of Research in Science Teaching,* 1976, *13,* 413–430.

Lazarsfeld, P. F., and Mendel, H. "On the Relation Between Individual and Collective Properties." In A. Etzioni (ed.), *Complex Organizations: A Sociological Reader.* Troy, Mo.: Holt, Rinehart & Winston, 1961.

Lee, M. K. "Debunking the Cinderella Myth." *Educational Forum,* 1984, *48*(3), 334.

Lee, V. E. *Identifying Potential Scientists and Engineers: An Analysis of the High School–College Transition.* Washington, D.C.: Office of Technology Assessment, U.S. Congress, 1987.

Levine, M. "Identification of Reasons Why Qualified Women Do Not Pursue Mathematical Careers." Report to the National Science Foundation, 1976. (ED 171 982)

Lewin, K. *A Dynamic Theory of Personality.* New York: McGraw-Hill, 1959. (Originally published 1935.)

Licht, B., and Dweck, C. "Sex Differences in Achievement Orientations: Consequences for Academic Choices and Attainments." In M. Marland (ed.), *Sex Differentiation and Schooling.* London: Heinemann, 1983.

Licht, B., and Shapiro, S. "Sex Differences in Attributions Among High Achievers." Paper presented at the annual meeting of the American Psychological Association, Washington, D.C., Aug. 1982.

Linn, M. C., and Thier, H. D. "The Effect of Experiential Science on Development of Logical Thinking in Children." *Journal of Research in Science Teaching,* 1975, *12*(1), 49–62.

Lipsitz, J. *Growing Up Forgotten: A Review of Research and Programs Concerning Early Adolescence.* Lexington, Mass.: Heath, 1977.

Lockheed, M. E., and others. *Sex and Ethnic Differences in Middle School Mathematics, Science, and Computer Science: What Do We Know?* Princeton, N.J.: Educational Testing Service, 1985.

Lotan, R. A., and Benton, J. "Finding Out About Complex Instruction: Teaching Math and Science in Heterogeneous Classrooms." In N. Davidson (ed.), *Cooperative Learning in Mathematics: A Handbook for Teachers.* Reading, Mass.: Addison-Wesley, 1990.

Luchins, E. H. "Women Mathematicians: A Contemporary Appraisal." Paper presented at the annual meeting of the American Association for the Advancement of Science, Boston, Feb. 1976.

Luchins, E. H. "Sex Differences in Mathematics: How Not to Deal with Them." *American Mathematical Monthly,* 1979, *86*(3), 161–168.

McBay, S. M. "Black Students in the Sciences: A Look at Spelman College." In C. V. Willie and R. R. Edmonds (eds.), *Black Colleges in America.* New York: Teachers College Press, 1978.

MacCorquodale, P. "Psycho-Social Influences on the Accomplishments of Mexican-American Students." Paper presented at the annual meeting of the American Association of School Administrators, Chicago, July 1980.

MacCorquodale, P. "Self-Image Science and Math: Does the Image of the 'Scientist' Keep Girls and Minorities from Pursuing Science and Math?" Paper presented at the annual meeting of the American Sociological Association, San Antonio, Tex., Aug. 1984.

McLaughlin, M. W. "Learning from Experience: Lessons from Policy Implementation." *Educational Evaluation and Policy Analysis*, 1987, *9*(2), 171–178.

Malcom, S. M. "Reclaiming Our Past." *Journal of Negro Education*, 1990, *59*(3), 246–259.

Malcom, S. M., and others. *Equity and Excellence: Compatible Goals*. AAAS publication no. 84–14. Washington, D.C: Office of Opportunities in Science, American Association for the Advancement of Science, 1984.

Marrett, C. B. *Patterns of Enrollment in High School Mathematics and Science*. Final report. Madison: Wisconsin Research and Development Center, 1981.

Marrett, C. B. "Minority Females in Precollege Mathematics: Towards a Research Agenda." Paper presented at the annual meeting of the American Educational Research Association, San Francisco, Apr. 1986.

Maslow, A. H. *Motivation and Personality*. New York: Harper-Collins, 1954.

Mathematics, Engineering, Science Achievement Program. *Student Handbook*. Berkeley: Mathematics, Engineering, Science Achievement Program, Lawrence Hall of Science, University of California, 1985.

Matthews, W. "Black Females and Mathematics: Barricade or Bridge?" *Journal of Social and Behavioral Science*, 1981, *27*, 88–92.

Matthews, W. "Influences on the Learning and Participation of Minorities in Mathematics." *Journal for Research in Mathematics Education*, 1984, *15*(2), 84–95.

Matyas, M. L., and Kahle, J. B. "Equitable Precollege Science and Mathematics Education: A Discrepancy Model." Paper presented at the Workshop on Underrepresentation and Career Differentials of Women in Science and Engineering, Washington, D.C., Oct. 1986.

Matyas, M. L., and Malcom, S. M. (eds.). *Investing in Human Potential: Science and Engineering at the Crossroads.* Washington, D.C.: American Association for the Advancement of Science, 1991.

Mead, G. H. *Mind, Self, and Society.* Chicago: University of Chicago Press, 1934.

Mentor in Engineering Program. Report of the New York Alliance for the Public Schools, 1986.

Merriam, S. B. *Case Study Research in Education: A Qualitative Approach.* San Francisco: Jossey-Bass, 1988.

Miles, M. B., and Huberman, M. A. *Qualitative Data Analysis: A Sourcebook of New Methods.* Newbury Park, Calif.: Sage, 1984.

"More Than Getting By . . ." *MESA Newsletter,* March/April 1982, p. 4.

Mullis, I.V.S., Dossey, J. A., Owen, E. H., and Phillips, G. W. *The State of Mathematics Achievement: NAEP's 1990 Assessment of the Nation and the Trail Assessment of the States.* Report no. 21-ST-04. Princeton, N.J.: Educational Testing Service, 1991.

Mullis, I.V.S., and Jenkins, L. B. *The Science Report Card: Trends and Achievement Based on the 1986 National Assessment.* Report no. 17-S-01. Princeton, N.J.: Educational Testing Service, 1988.

Mussen, P. H., Conger, J. J., and Kagan, J. *Child Development and Personality.* New York: HarperCollins, 1979.

Myers, D. G. *Psychology.* New York: Worth, 1986.

National Academy of Sciences. "Nurturing Science and Engineering Talent." Discussion paper presented at the Government-University-Industry Research Roundtable, Washington, D.C., July 1987.

National Education Goals Panel. *The National Education Goals Report: Building a Nation of Learners.* Washington, D.C.: National Education Goals Panel, 1991.

National Research Council. *Everybody Counts: A Report to the Nation on the Future of Mathematics Education.* Washington, D.C.: National Academy Press, 1989.

National Reseach Council. *Women in Science and Engineering: Increasing Their Numbers in the 1990s.* Statement on Policy and Strategy from the Committee on Women in Science and Engineering, Office of Scientific and Engineering Personnel. Washington, D.C.: National Academy Press, 1991.

National Science Board. *Educating Americans for the 21st Century: A Plan of Action for Improving Mathematics, Science and Technology Education for American Elementary and Secondary Students So That Their Achievement Is the Best in the World by 1995.* Washington, D.C.: National Science Foundation, 1983.

National Science Foundation. *Women and Minorities in Science and Engineering.* Washington, D.C.: National Science Foundation, 1988.

National Science Foundation. *Women and Minorities in Science and Engineering.* Washington, D.C.: National Science Foundation, 1990.

National Science Foundation. *Blacks in Undergraduate Science and Engineering Education.* Washington, D.C.: National Science Foundation, 1992.

Oakes, J. *Lost Talent: The Underparticipation of Women, Minorities, and Disabled Persons in Science.* Santa Monica, Calif.: RAND Corporation, 1990.

O'Hara, R. P., and Tiedeman, D. V. "Vocational Self-Concept in Adolescence." *Journal of Counseling Psychology,* 1959, *6*(4), 292–301.

Olstad, R. G., Juarez, J. R., Davenport, L. J., and Haury, D. L. *Inhibitors to Achievement in Science and Mathematics by Ethnic Minorities.* Seattle: University of Washington, 1981. (ED 223 404)

Orr, E. W. *Truce as Less.* New York: W.W. Norton, 1987.

Parsons, J. E. "Attributional Processes as Mediators of Sex Differences in Achievement." *Journal of Educational Equity and Leadership,* 1983, *3*(1), 19–27.

Parsons, J. E., Adler, T. F., and Kaczala, C. M. "Socialization of Achievement Attitudes and Beliefs: Parental Influences." *Child Development,* 1982, *3*(1), 19–27.

Parsons, J. E., Heller, K., and Kaczala, C. M. "The Effects of Teachers' Expectancies and Attributions on Students' Expectancies for Success in Mathematics." Paper presented at the annual meeting of the American Educational Research Association, San Francisco, Apr. 1979. (ED 180 787)

Payne, B. D., Smith, J. E., and Payne, D. A. "Sex and Ethnic Differences in Relationships of Test Anxiety to Performance in Science Examinations by Fourth- and Eighth-Grade Students: Implications for Valid Interpretations of Achievement Test Scores." *Educational and Psychological Measurement*, 1983, *43*(1), 267–270.

Pearson, W., Jr. *Black Scientists, White Society, and Colorless Science: A Study of Universalism in American Science.* Millwood, N.Y.: Associated Faculty Press, 1985.

Pearson, W., Jr. "The Future of Blacks in Science: Summary and Recommendations." In W. Pearson, Jr., and H. K. Bechtel (eds.), *Blacks, Science, and American Education.* New Brunswick, N.J.: Rutgers University Press, 1989.

Peng, S. *Science and Mathematics Education in American High Schools: Results from the High School and Beyond Study.* Washington, D.C.: National Center for Education Statistics, 1982. (ED 249 259)

Perrow, C. B. "A Framework for the Comparative Analysis of Organizations." *American Sociological Review*, 1961, *32*, 134–208.

Persell, C. H. *Education and Inequality: The Roots and Results of Stratification in America's Schools.* New York: Free Press, 1977.

Piaget, J. *The Child's Conception of Number.* New York: Humanities, 1952.

Piaget, J. *The Origins of Intelligence in Children.* New York: International Universities Press, 1956.

Piaget, J. *The Psychology of Intelligence.* London: Routledge & Kegan Paul, 1959.

Piaget, J. *Science of Education and the Psychology of the Child.* New York: Orion Press, 1970.

Powell, R., and Garcia, J. "Portrayal of Minorities and Women in Selected Elementary Science Series." *Journal of Research in Science Teaching*, 1985, *22*, 519–533.

Prillwitz, B. "The Correlates of Success Among Women in Mathematics and Mathematics-Related Fields: Implications in Educational Program Development." *Dissertation Abstracts International*, 1983, *44*(02-A), 349.

Rendon, L. I. *Mathematics Education for Hispanic Students in the Border College Consortium.* Laredo, Tex.: Border College Consortium, 1983.

Reyes, L. H. "Affective Variables and Mathematics Education." *Elementary School Journal*, 1984, *84*, 558–581.

Riggs, I. "A Review of Factors Related to Gender and Ethnic Differences in Math/Science Achievement Levels of Students K–12." *Educational Considerations,* 1988, *15,* 18–21.

Rogers, C. R. *Freedom to Learn.* Columbus, Ohio: Merrill, 1969.

Rosenthal, R., and Jacobson, L. *Pygmalion in the Classroom: Teachers' Expectations and Pupils' Intellectual Performance.* Troy, Mo.: Holt, Rinehart & Winston, 1968.

Rossi, A. S. "Barriers to the Career Choice of Engineering, Medicine or Science Among American Women." In J. Mattfeld and C. Van Aken (eds.), *Women and the Scientific Professions.* Cambridge, Mass.: MIT Press, 1965a.

Rossi, A. S. "Women in Science: Why So Few?" *Science,* 1965b, *148,* 1196–1202.

Rowe, M. B. "Wait-Time and Rewards as Instructional Variables: Their Influence on Language, Logic, and Fate Control. Part I: Wait-Time." *Journal of Research in Science Teaching,* 1974a, *11,* 81–94.

Rowe, M. B. "Relation of Wait-Time and Rewards to the Development of Language, Logic, and Fate Control. Part II: Rewards." *Journal of Research in Science Teaching,* 1974b, *11,* 291–308.

Ryman, D. "Teaching Methods, Intelligence, and Gender Factors in Pupil Achievement on a Classification Task." *Journal of Research in Science Teaching,* 1977, *14,* 401–409.

Saturday Science Academy. *Saturday Science Academy Booklet.* Atlanta: Clark Atlanta University, 1987.

Saunders, W. L., and Shepardson, D. "A Comparison of Concrete and Formal Science Instruction upon Science Achievement and Reasoning Ability of Sixth Grade Students." *Journal of Research in Science Teaching,* 1987, *24*(1), 39–51.

Schoderbek, P. P., Schoderbek, C. G., and Kefalas, A. G. *Management Systems.* Plano, Tex.: Business Publications, 1985.

Schreiber, D. A. "Factors Affecting Females' Attitude Formation Toward Science: Specific Reference to 12–14-Year-Old Female Adolescents and Their Affective Orientation Toward Middle School Science." Unpublished master's thesis, University of Cincinnati, 1984. (ED 256 617)

Scott, K. P., and Feldman-Summers, S. "Children's Reactions to Textbook Stories in Which Females Are Portrayed in

Traditionally Male Roles." *Journal of Educational Psychology,* 1979, *71,* 396–402.

Scribner, H. B., and Stevens, L. B. *Make Your Schools Work: Practical, Imaginative and Cost-Free Plans to Turn Public Education Around.* Amherst: University of Massachusetts, 1975.

Sells, L. "Mathematics: A Critical Filter." *Science Teacher,* 1978, *45*(2), 28–29.

Shapiro, E. W. "Attitudes Toward Arithmetic Among Public School Children in the Intermediate Grades." *Dissertation Abstracts International,* 1962, *22,* 3927A.

Shields, P. M., and David, J. L. *The Implementation of FAMILY MATH in Five Community Agencies.* Berkeley: Lawrence Hall of Science, University of California, 1988.

Skinner, B. F. *Science and Human Behavior.* New York: Macmillan, 1953.

Slavin, R. E. "Team-Assisted Individualization: Combining Cooperative Learning and Individualized Instruction in Mathematics Achievement." In R. Slavin and others (eds.), *Learning to Cooperate, Cooperating to Learn.* New York: Plenum Press, 1985.

Sloane, K. *The Families of FAMILY MATH Research Project.* Berkeley: Lawrence Hall of Science, University of California, 1990.

Smail, B. *Girl-Friendly Science: Avoiding Sex Bias in Curriculum.* York, England: Longman, 1984.

Smith, W. S., and Erb, T. O. "Effect of Women Science Career Role Models on Early Adolescents' Attitudes Toward Scientists and Women in Science." *Journal of Research in Science Teaching,* 1986, *23*(8), 667–676.

Stage, E. K., Kreinberg, N., Eccles, J., and Becker, J. R. "Increasing the Participation and Achievement of Girls and Women in Mathematics, Science, and Engineering." In S. S. Klein (ed.), *Handbook for Achieving Sex Equity Through Education.* Baltimore, Md.: Johns Hopkins University Press, 1985.

Steel, L. *Origins of Sex Differences in High School Mathematics Achievement and Participation.* Palo Alto, Calif.: American Institutes for Research in the Behavioral Sciences, 1978.

Stenmark, J., Thompson, V., and Cossey, R. *Family Math.* Berkeley: University of California, 1986.

Stenmark, J., Thompson, V., and Cossey, R. *Mathemáticas para la familia* [Mathematics for the family]. (J. López, trans.) Berkeley: University of California, 1987.

Stenmark, J., Thompson, V., and Cossey, R. *Matte hemma, Matte i skolan* [Math in the home, math in the school]. (M. Josefsson, trans.) Berkeley: University of California, 1988.

Strain, P. S. (ed.). *The Utilization of Classroom Peers as Behavior Change Agents.* New York: Plenum Press, 1981.

Sullivan, H. S. *The Interpersonal Theory of Psychiatry.* New York: W.W. Norton, 1953.

Super, D. E. *The Psychology of Careers.* New York: HarperCollins, 1957.

Task Force on Women, Minorities, and the Handicapped in Science and Technology. *Changing America: The New Face of Science And Engineering.* Washington, D.C.: Task Force on Women, Minorities, and the Handicapped in Science and Technology, 1988.

"Technical Career Counseling (TC²)." *National Technical Association Newsletter, Akron (Ohio) Chapter,* 1985, *3,* 1.

Thomas, A. H., and Stewart, N. R. "Counselor Response to Female Clients with Deviate and Conforming Career Goals." *Journal of Counseling Psychology,* 1971, *18,* 352–357.

Thomas, G. E. "Cultivating the Interest of Women and Minorities in High School Mathematics and Science." *Science Education,* 1986, *70,* 31–43.

Thomas, G. E. "Black Science Majors in Colleges and Universities." In W. Pearson, Jr., and H. K. Bechtel (eds.), *Blacks, Science, and American Education.* New Brunswick, N.J.: Rutgers University Press, 1989.

Thompson, V., and Kreinberg, N. *Family Math: A Report of an Intervention Program That Involves Parents in Their Children's Mathematics Education.* Berkeley: University of California, 1986.

Tibord, M. "Toward the Development of an Instrument to Measure Attitudes Toward Science of Negro Students: A Research Paper." *School Science and Mathematics,* 1973, *73,* 367–372.

Tobias, S. *Overcoming Math Anxiety.* New York: W.W. Norton, 1978.

Treagust, D. F. "Gender-Related Differences in Spatial Representational Thought." *Journal of Research in Science Teaching,* 1980, *17* (2), 91–97.

Turner, H. M. *Factors Influencing Persistence/Achievement in the Sciences and Health Professions by Black High School and College Women.* Final report. Atlanta, Ga.: Center for Research on Women in Science, Morris Brown College; Washington, D.C.: National Institute of Education, 1983.

U.S. Congress, Office of Technology Assessment. *Educating Scientists and Engineers: Grade School to Grad School.* Report no. OTA-SET-377. Washington, D.C.: U.S. Government Printing Office, 1988a.

U.S. Congress, Office of Technology Assessment. *Elementary and Secondary Education for Science and Engineering: A Technical Memorandum.* Report no. OTA-TM-SET-41. Washington, D.C.: U.S. Government Printing Office, 1988b.

U.S. Department of Commerce. *Statistical Abstract of the United States, 1986.* Washington, D.C.: Bureau of the Census, U.S. Department of Commerce, 1986.

Valverde, L. A. "Underachievement and Underrepresentation of Hispanics in Mathematics and Mathematics-Related Careers." *Journal for Research in Mathematics Education,* 1984, *15*(2), 123–133.

Vergason, G. A., and Anderegg, M. L. "Beyond the Regular Education Initiative and the Resource Room Controversy." *Focus on Exceptional Children,* 1991, *23*(7), 1–7.

Vetter, B. M. *Recruiting Doctoral Scientists and Engineers for the Twenty-First Century.* Occasional Paper no. 90-3. Washington, D.C.: Commission on Professionals in Science and Technology, 1990.

Vygotsky, L. *Thought and Language.* Cambridge, Mass.: MIT Press, 1962.

Weiss, I. R. *Report of the 1977 National Survey of Science, Mathematics, and Social Studies Education.* Report no. SE-78-72. Washington, D.C.: U.S. Government Printing Office, 1978.

Whitner, E. "Taft Middle School." *Moving Up* (Detroit-Area Pre-College Engineering Program newsletter), 1991 Science Fair issue, p. 2.

Whorf, B. L. *Language, Thought and Reality.* Cambridge: Massachusetts Institute of Technology, 1989. (Originally published 1956.)

Wilkinson, L. C., and Marrett, C. B. (eds.). *Gender Influences in Classroom Interaction.* San Diego, Calif.: Academic Press, 1985.

Willig, A. C., Harnisch, D. L., Hill, K. T., and Maehr, M.
L. "Sociocultural and Educational Correlates of Success/
Failure Attributions and Evaluation Anxiety in the School
Setting for Black, Hispanic, and Anglo Children." *American
Educational Research Journal,* 1978, *20*(3), 385–410.
Young, H. A. "Retaining Blacks in Science: An Affective Model."
In G. E. Thomas (ed.), *Black Students in Higher Education: Con-
ditions and Experiences in the 1970s.* Westport, Conn.: Green-
wood Press, 1981.
Young, H. A. "Cultural Differences That Affect Retention of
Minorities on Predominantly White Campuses." Paper pre-
sented at the annual meeting of the American Educational
Research Association, Toronto, Apr. 1983.

Index